How We Hear: An Introduction to Auditory Perception

How We Hear: An Introduction to Auditory Perception

Emma Holmes

Adele M. Goman

Great Clarendon Street, Oxford, OX2 6DP,
United Kingdom

Oxford University Press is a department of the University of Oxford.
It furthers the University's objective of excellence in research, scholarship,
and education by publishing worldwide. Oxford is a registered trade mark of
Oxford University Press in the UK and in certain other countries

© Emma Holmes and Adele M. Goman 2025

The moral rights of the authors have been asserted.

All rights reserved. No part of this publication may be reproduced, stored in a retrieval system, transmitted, used for text and data mining, or used for training artificial intelligence, in any form or by any means, without the prior permission in writing of Oxford University Press, or as expressly permitted by law, by licence or under terms agreed with the appropriate reprographics rights organization. Enquiries concerning reproduction outside the scope of the above should be sent to the Rights Department, Oxford University Press, at the address above.

You must not circulate this work in any other form
and you must impose this same condition on any acquirer.

Published in the United States of America by Oxford University Press
198 Madison Avenue, New York, NY 10016, United States of America

British Library Cataloguing in Publication Data

Data available

Library of Congress Control Number: 2025936005

ISBN 9780192844705

The manufacturer's authorised representative in the EU for product safety is
Oxford University Press España S.A., Parque Empresarial San Fernando de Henares,
Avenida de Castilla, 2 – 28830 Madrid (www.oup.es/en).

Links to third party websites are provided by Oxford in good faith and
for information only. Oxford disclaims any responsibility for the materials
contained in any third party website referenced in this work.

Preface

Hearing is fundamental in daily life. It's frequently used for communication; it underlies the appreciation of music; and it is a sense that people often rely on to ensure their safety, as when crossing the road. For most people, these functions seem automatic and effortless, yet they involve a variety of intricate processes that take place along the pathway from the ears to the brain. The sound that reaches the ears includes a variety of overlapping pressure waves. It is therefore quite astounding that what people typically perceive is not simply unintelligible noise, but a complex scene that may contain spoken words, the hum of an air conditioning unit, and the sounds of nearby traffic. Intriguingly, what people hear sometimes bears little resemblance to the sound pressure waves that entered their ears, showing the variety of ways in which auditory perception can be 'fooled'.

In addition to its inherent scientific value, understanding the typical functions of the human auditory system, how these give rise to the perceptual experience of sounds, and the multitude of ways in which these can go awry is relevant to a number of current societal trends. For example, the world's population is getting older, on average, and as a result age-related hearing loss is becoming more prevalent. Research that characterises the effects of hearing loss and possible interventions is, therefore, of growing importance. Alongside this, there is increasing awareness that some people who seek professional help with their hearing report struggling to hear in noisy places but don't meet the clinical criteria for a hearing loss diagnosis; understanding the reasons for this difficulty is an active area of research that draws on measurements of various stages of the auditory pathway and various types of auditory perception tests. More generally, there is a drive to characterise the large variety of differences in auditory perception that are relatively common among the population.

Another societal trend is an increasing interest in speech technology—such as speech-to-text (also called 'automatic speech recognition' or 'transcription') and text-to-speech (also called 'speech synthesis' or 'voice generation'). As these technologies become more integrated into our everyday lives, this raises relevant questions about how speech-to-text technologies can extract the wide variety of information that people perceive in speech, and how text-to-speech technologies might emulate people's perception of natural voices. The combination of visual and auditory information is also relevant, given an increasing societal preference for video (i.e. audio-visual) calls over more traditional phone (i.e. audio only) calls. The continued development of virtual reality also involves considerations about how people hear, how best to convey sounds through virtual reality, and how auditory and visual information interact. Another consideration is that the number of sources of auditory information in the environment is expanding, given the growing number of devices that emit sounds, which all compete for the listener's attention. An understanding of auditory perception will be critical for helping people to navigate these noisy environments; for example, headphones with active noise cancellation already utilise knowledge of sound waves and how they are perceived. We could imagine even more sophisticated technologies being developed in the future to help people navigate noisy places.

We have written this volume as an introductory resource for readers who are new to auditory perception. Many other introductions to auditory perception begin from a physics or engineering perspective. In contrast, this text is targeted at readers who are seeking a gentle introduction to auditory perception without needing to familiarise themselves with mathematical equations. We hope that the reader will find this an accessible introduction to auditory perception, and that it appeals to readers from a variety of backgrounds—including those studying psychology and related disciplines.

This volume covers a variety of topics relevant to auditory perception. Part 1, comprising Chapters 1–3, covers what we term the 'Fundamentals of hearing'. These chapters introduce core concepts of auditory perception. Chapter 1 describes various types of sounds and defines several important acoustic attributes of sounds. It also outlines key stages of processing along the auditory pathway, from ear to brain. Chapter 2 builds upon this foundational knowledge by focusing on three aspects of auditory perception: loudness, location, and pitch. Chapter 3 moves on to consider how people perceive multiple sounds that are either close together or overlap in time.

Part 2—'Hearing in action'—applies the concepts introduced in the first part to everyday settings. Chapter 4 describes the acoustic properties of speech and explains how people work out what's being said, who's speaking, and how they're saying it. Chapter 5 then combines topics from Chapters 3 and 4 to explain how people understand speech when other sounds are present in their environment. Chapter 6 considers how people perceive music. Chapter 7 explains how visual information affects auditory perception and vice versa; it introduces the conditions under which visual and auditory information are integrated and explores how integration can 'trick' people into seeing or hearing things that aren't really there. Finally, Chapter 8 describes various ways of measuring someone's hearing and explains how hearing loss can impact auditory perception.

Ultimately, we hope that this volume will equip readers with foundational knowledge of a wide range of topics in hearing research, insights into how scientific evidence has led to current thinking in these areas, and an understanding of some of the key debates that have motivated researchers. The text has been written as an interactive ebook, so readers will find relevant audio demonstrations and interactive activities embedded within the online version of the book. We have also provided analogies and everyday examples throughout, which we hope will facilitate understanding and make reading more enjoyable.

For those interested in additional reading that builds upon the material introduced here, the following resources provide more detailed and advanced information, which would be suitable for postgraduate or advanced undergraduate students who already have some familiarity with auditory perception.

Plack, C. J. (2018). *The Sense of Hearing*. Abingdon and New York: Routledge.
Moore, B. C. (2012). *An Introduction to the Psychology of Hearing*. Leiden: Brill.

About the authors

Dr Emma Holmes is an Associate Professor at University College London (UCL), and Principal Investigator of the Cognitive Hearing Lab in the Department of Speech Hearing and Phonetic Sciences at UCL. Emma first became interested in auditory perception when learning to play the piano as a child, and she also became fascinated by attention—specifically, the great extent to which it can affect perceptual experience. She went on to complete a BA in Experimental Psychology at the University of Oxford and a PhD in Psychology at the University of York. During her PhD, Emma examined brain responses when people direct attention to speech when competing speech is present, and compared these responses between people with and without hearing loss. Over her career, Emma has conducted research at universities in the UK, Australia, and Canada, and the impact of her research has been recognised by a 'Young Investigator Award' from the Association for Research in Otolaryngology and a 'Rising Star' award from the Association for Psychological Science. Emma's current research interests include how cognitive factors, such as attention and prior knowledge, affect speech perception in people with and without hearing loss, and the impacts of hearing loss on social participation. Alongside her research, Emma teaches Perception, Attention, and Learning to first-year undergraduate students, and teaches an advanced course on Auditory Cognitive Neuroscience.

Dr Adele Goman is a Lecturer at Edinburgh Napier University and Associate Faculty of the Johns Hopkins Cochlear Center for Hearing and Public Health. Adele first became interested in hearing science when she was studying for her undergraduate degree in Psychology at the University of York. During her undergraduate degree, she undertook advanced modules in hearing science and completed research projects in the auditory perception laboratories, which led her to pursue a PhD. She received her PhD in Psychology from the University of York, in which she investigated the clinical and cost effectiveness of interventions for adults with severe to profound hearing loss. She then completed postdoctoral training with a focus on hearing loss epidemiology, public health, and clinical trials at Johns Hopkins University in Baltimore, USA. The impact of her research has been recognised by a 'Rising Star' award from the American Geriatrics Society and National Institute on Aging Sensory Impairment and Cognitive Decline workshop, and results from some of her previous work on hearing loss prevalence provided foundational evidence towards legislative changes in the United States to improve access to hearing technology. Her current research interests include the individual and societal impact of hearing loss and hearing loss interventions on health and wellbeing, and addressing barriers and inequalities in hearing care and hearing technology utilisation.

The authors contributed equally to this work.

Author ORCID iDs: 0000-0002-0314-6588; 0000-0002-5084-0185

Acknowledgements

We are grateful to the following people for their support. Martin Corley for proposing the idea for the volume, for supporting us throughout the process, and for providing initial feedback on some of the chapters; Edward Silson for reviewing an early draft of some of the chapters and for providing assistance with Figure 7.6; Mark Hymers for reviewing early drafts of Chapters 1 and 6, providing assistance with Figure 6.2, and assistance with the signal-to-noise interactive activity in Chapter 5; Carolyn McGettigan for playing 'Happy Birthday to You' on the violin for an audio demonstration in Chapter 6; Colin Goman for permitting his photograph to be taken and used for Figure 8.9; and anonymous external reviewers who provided feedback on the chapters. Finally, we would like to thank the editors at OUP who supported us at various stages of the process—including Emma Sheffield, Katherine Jones, and Martha Bailes.

Outline Contents

Preface ... v
About the authors ... vii
Acknowledgements ... viii

PART 1 Fundamentals of Hearing

1. How Do We Hear Sounds? ... 3
2. Perceptual Characteristics of Sound ... 29
3. Perceiving Multiple Sounds ... 55

PART 2 Hearing in Action

4. Perceiving Speech ... 73
5. Perceiving Speech in Noisy Places ... 99
6. Perceiving Music ... 121
7. Hearing and Vision ... 149
8. Hearing Difficulties ... 173

Glossary ... 193

Detailed Contents

PART 1 Fundamentals of Hearing

1 How Do We Hear Sounds? — 3
- 1.1 What is sound? — 3
  - 1.1.1 Sounds as pressure waves — 3
  - 1.1.2 Visualising sounds — 3
    - 1.1.2.1 Visualising sounds over time — 3
    - 1.1.2.2 Visualising sounds over frequency — 7
    - 1.1.2.3 Visualising sounds over time and frequency — 8
  - 1.1.3 Types of sounds — 9
    - 1.1.3.1 Tones — 9
    - 1.1.3.2 Noise — 10
    - 1.1.3.3 Natural sounds — 12
- 1.2 How do we hear? — 13
  - 1.2.1 Outer ear — 13
  - 1.2.2 Middle ear — 14
  - 1.2.3 Inner ear — 15
  - 1.2.4 Auditory nerve — 19
  - 1.2.5 Brainstem and thalamus — 20
  - 1.2.6 Primary auditory cortex — 23
  - 1.2.7 Secondary auditory cortex and beyond — 25
  - 1.2.8 Descending pathways — 25
- Summary — 26

2 Perceptual Characteristics of Sound — 29
- 2.1 Loudness — 29
  - 2.1.1 Loudness and intensity — 29
  - 2.1.2 Loudness and duration — 32
  - 2.1.3 Loudness and frequency — 32
  - 2.1.4 Loudness and the auditory system — 34
- 2.2 Location — 35
  - 2.2.1 Detecting differences in location — 35
  - 2.2.2 Locating sounds horizontally — 36
  - 2.2.3 Locating sounds vertically — 38
  - 2.2.4 How close is a sound? — 40
  - 2.2.5 Locating sounds in reverberant places — 40
  - 2.2.6 Coding location — 41
- 2.3 Pitch — 43
  - 2.3.1 What is pitch? — 43
  - 2.3.2 The relationship between pitch and sound attributes — 44

		2.3.3 Coding pitch	47
		2.3.4 Pitch and the brain	49
	Summary		51

3 Perceiving Multiple Sounds — 55

- 3.1 The challenge of overlapping sounds — 55
  - 3.1.1 Assigning sounds to sources — 55
  - 3.1.2 Dealing with ambiguity — 56
  - 3.1.3 Focusing on one sound — 57
- 3.2 Perceptual organisation — 57
  - 3.2.1 Simultaneous grouping — 58
  - 3.2.2 Sequential grouping — 60
  - 3.2.3 Prior knowledge — 64
- 3.3 Multiple sounds in the brain — 65
  - 3.3.1 How are sounds 'bound' together? — 65
  - 3.3.2 Where does segregation occur? — 66
  - 3.3.3 Neural indicators of perceptual organisation — 67
- Summary — 69

PART 2 Hearing in Action

4 Perceiving Speech — 73

- 4.1 What is speech? — 73
  - 4.1.1 Speech as a sound pressure wave — 73
  - 4.1.2 Variations within the speech signal — 74
- 4.2 How do people recognise words? — 77
  - 4.2.1 Speech segmentation — 78
  - 4.2.2 The building blocks of speech — 79
  - 4.2.3 Categorical perception — 81
  - 4.2.4 Lack of invariance — 82
- 4.3 Voices — 84
  - 4.3.1 Size — 84
  - 4.3.2 Voice gender — 84
  - 4.3.3 Age — 85
  - 4.3.4 Identity — 85
- 4.4 Prosody — 86
  - 4.4.1 Conveying meaning — 86
  - 4.4.2 Conveying emotion — 87
- 4.5 Speech processing in the brain — 89
  - 4.5.1 Decoding speech from brain activity — 89
  - 4.5.2 Are brain responses to speech special? — 89
  - 4.5.3 Speech intelligibility in the brain — 90
  - 4.5.4 Lateralisation of brain responses — 92

		4.5.5	Involvement of motor cortex	93
		4.5.6	Brain processing of non-linguistic aspects of speech	95
	Summary			95

5 Perceiving Speech in Noisy Places — 99

5.1	Types of noise		99
	5.1.1	Steady-state noise	99
	5.1.2	Amplitude-modulated noise	101
	5.1.3	Competing speech	102
5.2	Factors affecting intelligibility in noise		106
	5.2.1	Spatial separation	106
	5.2.2	Level differences	107
	5.2.3	Timing differences	108
	5.2.4	Context	109
	5.2.5	Prior knowledge	111
	5.2.6	Familiarity	111
5.3	Directing attention in noisy places		112
	5.3.1	Selective attention	112
	5.3.2	Switching attention	116
	5.3.3	Divided attention	116
Summary			117

6 Perceiving Music — 121

6.1	Making sense of music		121
	6.1.1	Pitch in music	121
	6.1.2	Timing in music	123
	6.1.3	Timbre in music	125
	6.1.4	Perceptual organisation of music	125
	6.1.5	Music and emotion	129
6.2	Music and the brain		130
	6.2.1	Brain responses to musical structure	131
	6.2.2	Comparing brain responses to music and speech	132
6.3	Individual differences in music perception		134
	6.3.1	Effects of musical training	135
	6.3.2	Absolute pitch	137
	6.3.3	Amusia	139
	6.3.4	Effects of language experience and culture	143
Summary			145

7 Hearing and Vision — 149

7.1	Sensory dominance		149
	7.1.1	Visual dominance	150
	7.1.2	Auditory dominance	150
	7.1.3	Which sense dominates?	152

	7.2	Audio-visual integration	154
		7.2.1 Integration of audio-visual speech	154
		7.2.2 Neural integration	157
		7.2.3 Conditions for integration	159
	7.3	Cross-modal plasticity	161
		7.3.1 Cross-modal plasticity and neuronal responses	161
		7.3.2 Cross-modal plasticity and perception	162
		7.3.3 The purpose of cross-modal plasticity	163
	7.4	Correspondences between the senses	164
		7.4.1 Common correspondences	164
		7.4.2 Synaesthesia	165
	Summary		167
8	**Hearing Difficulties**		**173**
	8.1	Measuring hearing	173
		8.1.1 Audiometry	173
		8.1.2 Self-reported hearing	177
		8.1.3 Speech measures	178
	8.2	Hearing loss	178
		8.2.1 Types of hearing loss	178
		8.2.2 Hearing loss severity	181
		8.2.3 Hearing loss across the lifespan	182
		8.2.4 Consequences of hearing loss	183
	8.3	Interventions for hearing loss	186
		8.3.1 Hearing aids	186
		8.3.2 Cochlear implants	187
		8.3.3 Bimodal aiding	190
	8.4	Other hearing differences	190
		8.4.1 Tinnitus	190
		8.4.2 Hyperacusis	190
	Summary		191
Glossary			193

Part 1
Fundamentals of Hearing

How Do We Hear Sounds?

Imagine you're at a party. What might you hear? You might notice people around you talking, music blaring from a loudspeaker, and someone's phone vibrating. These sounds are all different. In our everyday lives, sounds are all around us, and come in a variety of 'shapes' and 'sizes'. This chapter introduces various types of sounds and explains how we hear them.

1.1 What is sound?

This section explains how sounds differ, and why the sound made by a phone vibrating differs from the sound of people talking around you.

1.1.1 Sounds as pressure waves

When a phone vibrates on a table, people can often see it vibrating and hear it making a sound. The origin of sound is always an object that vibrates. When objects vibrate, they create pressure waves, which can reach the ears through the air. When a phone vibrates, it causes molecules in the surrounding air to vibrate, and these vibrations are transmitted to neighbouring molecules, like a domino effect. Eventually, the molecules next to the ears vibrate, and most people hear these vibrations as sound.

Just as the eyes are sensitive to light, the ears are sensitive to pressure. People can perceive very small changes in pressure—even from vibrations that they can't see with their eyes—which makes hearing all the more impressive.

1.1.2 Visualising sounds

To understand properties of sounds, it can be helpful to draw them. We can draw them in different ways, as we'll describe in this section.

1.1.2.1 Visualising sounds over time

Perhaps the most intuitive way of visualising sounds is by looking at the effect of their vibrations over *time*—in other words, the changes in sound pressure that occur as the object vibrates. Figure 1.1 visualises a simple sound by plotting the changes in sound pressure over time (which is called a **time series**): notice how the sound looks like a wave. The sound pressure at a specific moment in time is referred to as a sound's **amplitude** and that's what's plotted on the vertical axis of Figure 1.1. From Figure 1.1, notice that the amplitude of the sound changes over time, increasing and decreasing rapidly. A sound's maximum amplitude is known as its **peak amplitude**. Most people perceive sounds that have greater peak amplitudes as being louder.

> You can learn more about loudness in **Chapter 2**.

Just like reaching the top of a hill, the peak amplitude of a sound wave is where it has the highest amplitude (Figure 1.1). Pressure waves travel in three dimensions but, when we visualise a sound, we can imagine that we've taken one point in space (e.g. next to the vibrating object)—and plotted the sound at that location.

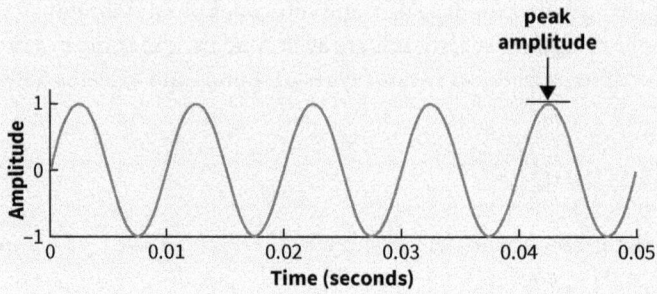

Figure 1.1 Sound wave with peak amplitude labelled.

Notice that the sound wave in Figure 1.2(a) repeats: we call each repeat one **cycle**. An important property of sounds is the number of cycles per second, which we call a sound's **frequency**. In everyday life, we often use frequency as a way of referring to how often something occurs in a given time period, for example the number of trains per hour or the number of times that a washing machine spins per minute. In hearing science, we use frequency to refer to the number of cycles in a sound per second. In general, objects that vibrate faster have higher frequencies. Have you ever noticed that a washing machine's sound changes while it spins? As the washing machine spins faster, it vibrates faster, and most people perceive the sound changing. When the washing machine spins faster, the sound it produces contains more cycles per second and, therefore, it has a higher frequency. The sound in Figure 1.2(a) contains five cycles, but look at the horizontal axis—it's only showing 0.05 seconds (1/20th of a second). In 1 second, this sound wave would repeat 100 times and, therefore, its frequency is 100 Hz.

Figure 1.2(b) shows a sound that repeats twice as quickly as the sound shown in Figure 1.2(a): its frequency is 200 Hz. Figure 1.2(c) shows a sound that repeats even faster—three times as quickly as the sound shown in Figure 1.2(a): its frequency is 300 Hz. Most people can hear sounds with very low frequencies and very high frequencies: people with normal hearing can typically hear frequencies as low as 20 Hz and as high as 20,000 Hz (Robles & Ruggero, 2001). If a sound contains 1,000 cycles per second (in other words, it repeats 10 times as quickly as the sound in Figure 1.2(a)), its frequency is 1,000 Hz, also known as 1 **kilohertz** (kHz).

WHAT IS SOUND?   5

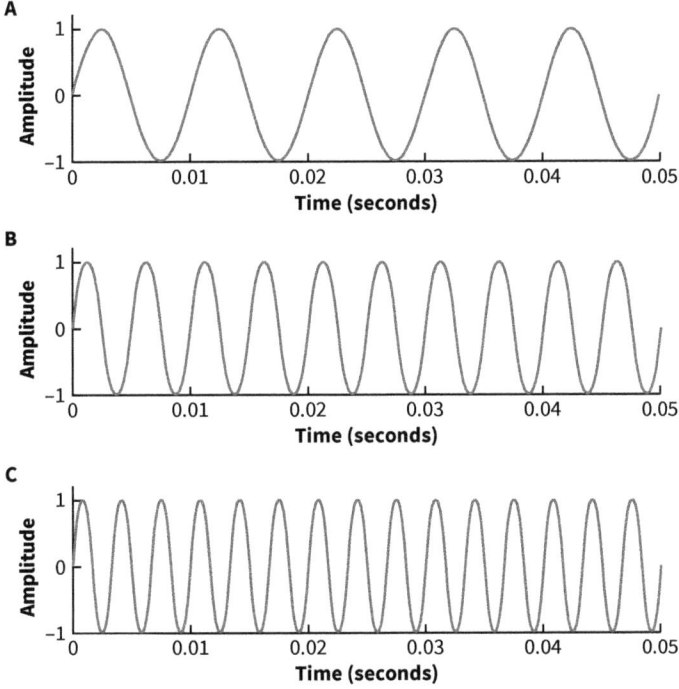

Figure 1.2 Graphs (time series) showing three sounds at frequencies of 100 Hz (panel a), 200 Hz (panel b), and 300 Hz (panel c). These graphs show the amplitude of each sound over time, which you can think of as the sound pressure, normalised between −1 and 1. Notice how the sound in panel c contains more cycles than the sounds in the other two panels; that's because it has a higher frequency.

A cycle is one repeat of a sound wave (Figure 1.3).

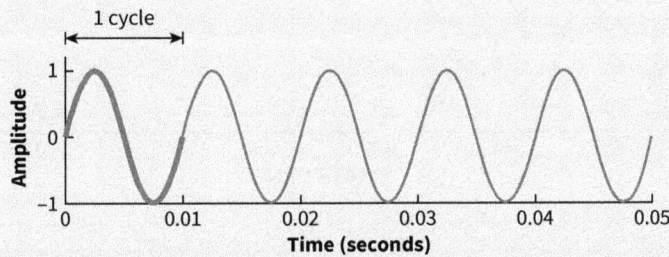

Figure 1.3 The first cycle of this sound is shown in bold.

A different way of talking about the number of cycles is to consider how long it takes for one cycle: the duration of one cycle is called the **wavelength** (Figure 1.4). A sound's wavelength is intimately coupled to its frequency: the wavelength of a sound, in seconds, is always equal to 1 second divided by its frequency in Hertz.

Recall how a sound's wavelength is related to its frequency. A sound with a frequency of 200 Hz has a wavelength of 1/200 seconds—in other words, 0.005 seconds.

(continued...)

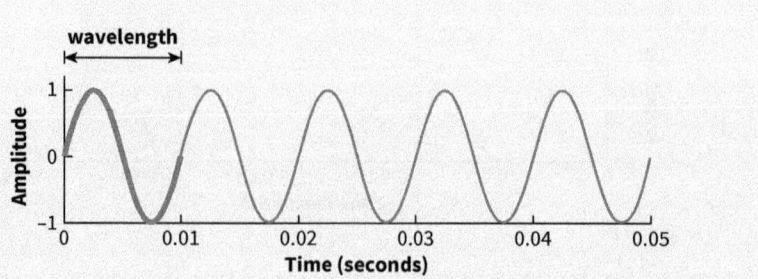

Figure 1.4 Wavelength is defined as the duration of one cycle. The first cycle of this sound is shown in bold. Look at the horizontal axis: the sound's wavelength is 0.01 seconds.

Another important property of a sound is its **phase**, which tells us what part of its cycle it's in. At the moment, you're reading **Chapter 1** of this book. You may be further ahead than your classmate who has only just opened the cover, but behind another classmate who's already reading **Chapter 6**. In this example, each person's position within this book corresponds to their phase. In hearing science, phase describes the position within a cycle (rather than your position within this book).

Phase is measured in degrees. There are 360 degrees in one cycle so a phase of 180° means the sound is half-way through a cycle (Figure 1.5).

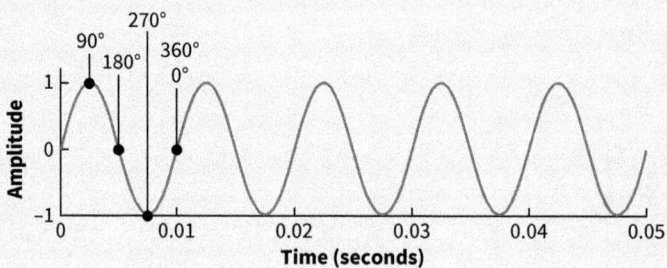

Figure 1.5 Sound wave showing the phases at four places in the cycle. Notice how we can consider the end of the first cycle as 360° relative to the beginning of the first cycle, which is equivalent to 0° for the second cycle.

Figure 1.6(a) shows three sounds that have the same frequency and amplitude, but notice that they differ in phase. If you were to place a ruler vertically at any time on the plot, you would see that the sounds are at different positions (i.e. different phases) in their cycle. For example, if you look at the time point corresponding to 0.05 seconds on the graph, notice that the three sounds differ in phase.

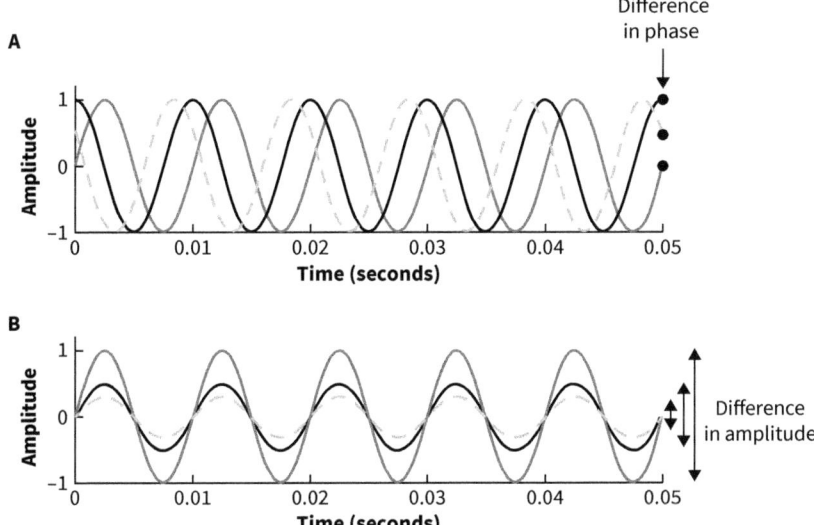

Figure 1.6 Graphs showing the time series representations of tones that differ in phase (panel a) or amplitude (panel b). In both panels, the darkest line shows the same 100-Hz sound that's displayed in Figure 1.2(a), with the same amplitude and phase. In panel a, the lighter lines show sounds that have the same amplitude and frequency but different phases. In panel b, the lighter lines show sounds that have the same frequency and phase but different peak amplitudes (0.5 and 0.3).

Sounds have the same phase if, at a given point in time, they're at the same position in their cycle (e.g. both half-way through), even if they have different amplitudes or frequencies. If you were to place a ruler vertically on Figure 1.6(b), you should notice that all three sounds are at the same position in their cycle, even though their amplitude differs.

1.1.2.2 Visualising sounds over frequency

It's difficult to work out a sound's frequency when we plot it as a function of time: in Section 1.1.2.1, we needed to count the number of cycles in Figure 1.2(a) to calculate the sound's frequency. There are many more exciting things to do in life than count cycles in a sound wave, so—rather than putting time on the horizontal axis—we can put frequency on the horizontal axis, which allows us to quickly visualise the frequency of a sound. Some examples of this type of graph—which is called a **spectrum**, or **spectra** for plural—are shown in Figure 1.7, which shows the same three sounds that are in Figure 1.2. From these new plots in Figure 1.7, we can easily deduce that the frequencies of the three sounds are 100 Hz, 200 Hz, and 300 Hz. This way of visualising sounds becomes particularly useful later in this chapter, in which we plot sounds that contain more than one frequency.

One disadvantage of the plots in Figure 1.7 is that they don't tell us about the duration of the sounds, because time is collapsed. In our simple examples here, it doesn't matter that time is collapsed, because the sounds stay the same (i.e. they repeat) over time. However, sometimes we may wish to visualise a sound's duration—and time becomes particularly important if a sound *changes* over time. We can convert back and forth between putting

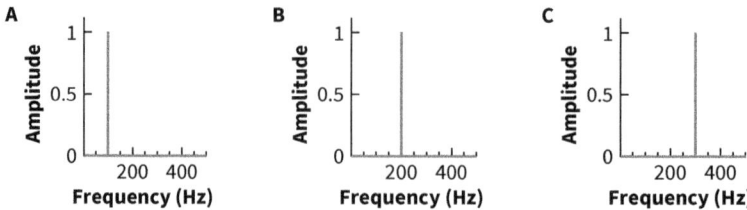

Figure 1.7 Graphs (spectra) of the same sounds that are shown in Figure 1.2. Panel a shows a 100-Hz sound, panel b shows a 200-Hz sound, and panel c shows a 300-Hz sound. Notice that frequency is plotted on the horizontal axis.

time or frequency on the horizontal axis, depending on which property we want to convey. To convert between time and frequency representations of a sound, we use a mathematical transformation called the 'Fourier transform'.

1.1.2.3 Visualising sounds over time and frequency

If we want to visualise both time and frequency together, we need a different type of plot. It's difficult on a two-dimensional graph, because we're trying to represent three dimensions: time, frequency, and amplitude. Instead, we use a three-dimensional graph, like the ones in Figure 1.8. A three-dimensional graph of time, frequency, and amplitude can be called a **'spectrogram'** or, alternatively, a 'time–frequency representation'.

Figure 1.8 shows the same three sounds that are illustrated in Figures 1.2 and 1.7, but this time, all three properties (time, frequency, and amplitude) are displayed together. Notice how the horizontal axis shows time, the vertical axis shows frequency, and a grey scale indicates the peak amplitude of the sound. Parts of the sound with greater peak amplitudes are displayed in black, and parts displayed in white indicate that there's zero amplitude (i.e. no sound) at that time and frequency. From Figure 1.8, we can easily see that the frequency of each of these sounds remains the same over time.

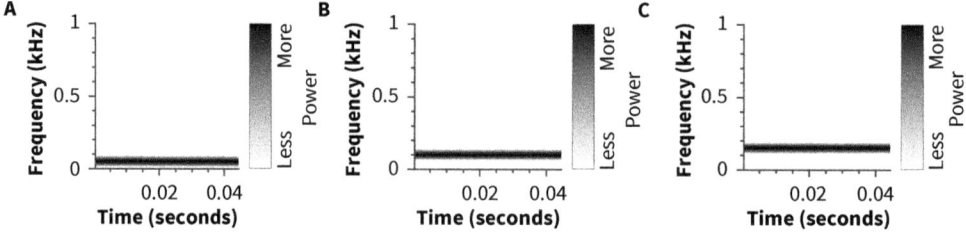

Figure 1.8 Graphs (spectrograms) of the same sounds that are shown in Figures 1.2 and 1.7. The areas of the plots that are associated with more power indicate times and frequencies where the sound has the greatest peak amplitude. Notice that panel a has the most power at 100 Hz, panel b has the most power at 200 Hz, and panel c has the most power at 300 Hz. In addition, the area containing the greatest power remains at the same frequency over time; this is because these are pure tones and the frequencies of the sounds don't change.

1.1.3 Types of sounds

When someone is at a party, they will typically hear many different types of sounds, such as conversations going on around them, music blaring from a loudspeaker, or a person's phone ringing. This section introduces some common—but more basic—types of sounds and describes how they differ from each other.

1.1.3.1 Tones

In hearing science, researchers often use simple artificial sounds to study how people hear. All of the sounds we've visualised so far are **pure tones**. Pure tones are the most basic type of sound and are quite boring because they only contain one frequency (e.g. 100 Hz, like the sound displayed in Figures 1.2(a), 1.7(a), and 1.8(a)). People don't usually encounter pure tones in everyday life, because no natural sounds are pure tones; the closest is the sound made by a tuning fork, which is used to tune musical instruments. Nevertheless, pure tones are simple and are useful for probing properties of the auditory system, so they're often used in hearing science.

Many of the sounds that people encounter in everyday life are **complex tones**; for example, the sounds produced by musical instruments. Complex tones sound richer than pure tones, because they contain more than one frequency. One way that we can generate a complex tone is by adding together two or more pure tones. Figure 1.9 shows an example, in which the pure tones shown in Figure 1.2 (i.e. 100, 200, and 300 Hz) have been added together. Notice how the frequencies contained within the sound are easier to see when frequency is displayed on the horizontal axis (in Figure 1.9(b)) than when time is displayed on the horizontal axis (in Figure 1.9(a)). Nevertheless, this sound still remains the same (i.e. it repeats) over time and is, therefore, much simpler than many of the sounds that people encounter in everyday life.

> You can learn more about music sounds in **Chapter 6**.

The amplitude of natural sounds often changes over time; for example, have you ever noticed that a lion's roar begins quiet, gets gradually stronger, and then fades out? A tone that changes amplitude, like the one shown in Figure 1.10(c) and (d), is called an

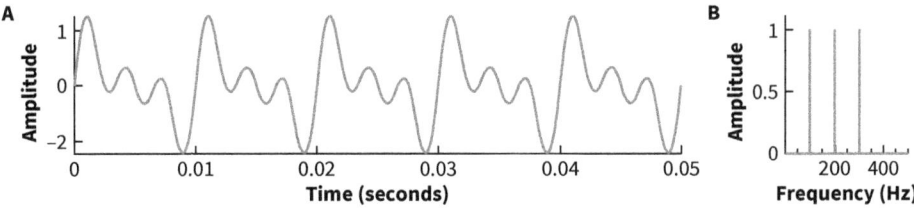

Figure 1.9 Complex tone, constructed by summing pure tones at frequencies of 100 Hz, 200 Hz, and 300 Hz (i.e. those from Figures 1.2, 1.7, and 1.8). The complex tone can be visualised as a time series representation (panel a) or a spectrum (panel b): the two are interchangeable.

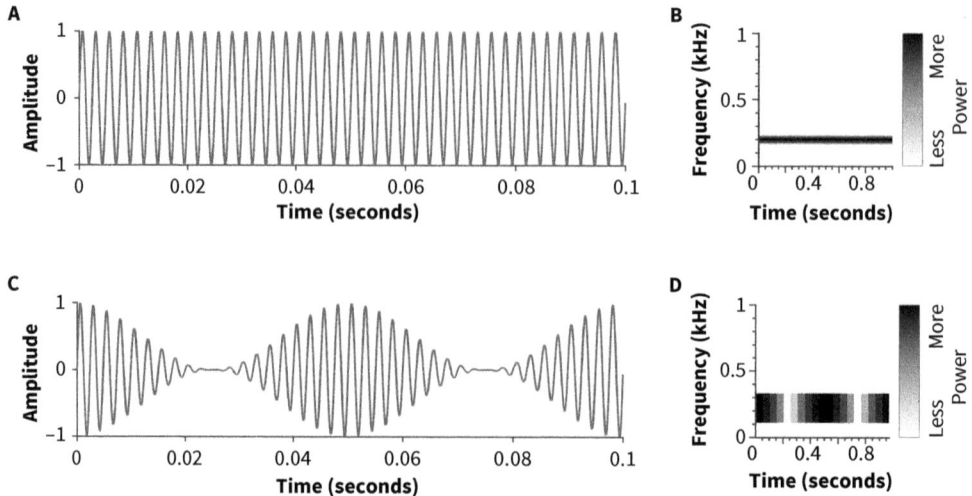

Figure 1.10 A pure tone compared to an amplitude-modulated tone. A pure tone at 400 Hz is shown as a time series representation (panel a) and a spectrogram (panel b). The same pure tone is shown in panels c and d, but it is modulated in amplitude and is, therefore, an amplitude-modulated tone. Notice that the rapid changes are the same in panels a and c, but the peak amplitude in panel c varies over time.

amplitude-modulated tone. Compare this to the pure tone shown in Figure 1.10(a) and (b), which has a constant peak amplitude. You can create a similar amplitude-modulated tone yourself by playing a pure tone through your computer speakers, and rapidly turning the volume of the speaker up and down.

Sounds can also vary in frequency over time: we call them **frequency-modulated tones** (see Figure 1.11). An everyday example of a frequency-modulated sound is the sound made by a washing machine as it changes during its spin cycle.

1.1.3.2 Noise

An entirely different type of sound is noise. We sometimes think of noise as being undesirable: the environment frequently contains some sort of noise that obscures what someone is trying to listen to. For example, if someone is at a noisy party, the sound of a large fan might make it difficult for them to hear what their friend's saying. However, in auditory science, 'noise' typically refers to a specific type of sound that's different to those we've considered so far.

Unlike tones, noise doesn't contain neatly repeating cycles: for this reason, noise sounds more chaotic and random than a tone. Nevertheless, we can still describe the frequencies it contains: different types of noise contain different frequencies. We can describe the frequencies in noise by naming it with different colours. For example, **white noise** has the same amplitude across all frequencies (Figure 1.12(a)), whereas **pink noise** (Figure 1.12(b)) has greater amplitude at lower frequencies than at higher frequencies: it contains similar frequencies to speech. There are various other 'colours' of noise that have different frequency distributions. It can be useful to use specific types of noise in auditory science, although everyday examples of noise—such as that generated by an air-conditioning unit—don't have such idealised frequency distributions.

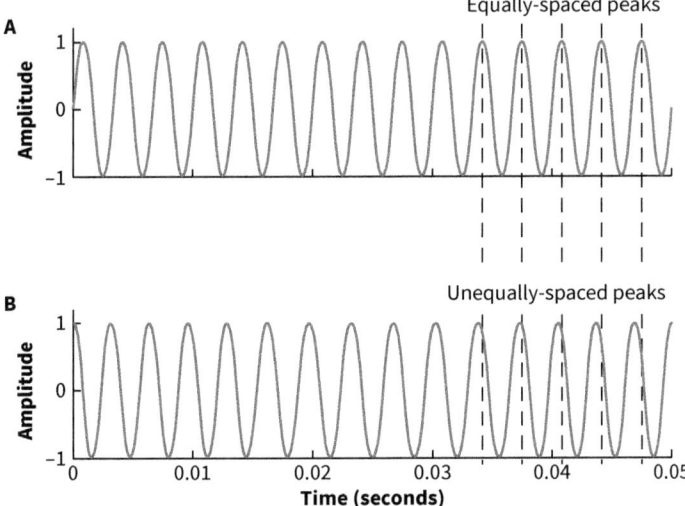

Figure 1.11 Illustration (time series) of a frequency-modulated tone. Panel a shows the same 300-Hz pure tone that is shown in Figure 1.2(c), which has no frequency modulation. Panel b shows a similar tone that is modulated in frequency. Notice that in panel a, the peaks are spaced equally, showing that the frequency remains the same over time. In contrast, the peaks in panel b are not equally spaced (i.e. if you look closely, the difference in time between the peak and the dashed vertical line increases on each cycle within the figure), which is characteristic of a tone that is modulated in frequency. In other words, its frequency and wavelength change over time.

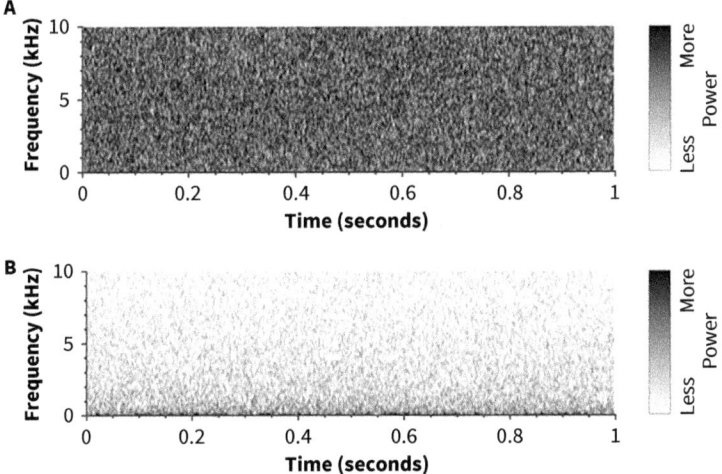

Figure 1.12 Graphs (spectrograms) of white noise (panel a), and pink noise (panel b). Notice that panel a contains power across all of the frequencies displayed on the plot, whereas panel b contains less power as frequency increases (i.e. towards the top of the graph).

1.1.3.3 Natural sounds

The properties of natural sounds depend on the size, shape, and material of the object that produced it (Further Insights 1.1). Figure 1.13(b) and (c) shows examples of speech and music excerpts: notice how they differ from the pure tone displayed in Figure 1.13(a), because they're modulated in both amplitude and frequency. Even though these natural sounds are more complex than the tones and noises we've discussed so far, we can describe them using the same terms: for example, we can describe their amplitudes, frequencies, and modulations.

> You can learn more about the features of speech and music sounds in **Chapters 4** and **6**.

> **Further insights 1.1** Resonance
>
> Have you ever tapped on a wall to work out if it's solid or what material it's made from? Different materials sound distinct, because they vibrate at different frequencies. The natural vibrating frequency of an object is known as its **resonant frequency**. The sound an object makes provides clues about its physical properties, such as its size, shape, volume, or stiffness. If you tap a glass, it makes a sound at its resonant frequency. Interestingly, if you sing at that same frequency (or play a sound at that same frequency) the glass will vibrate, which in some cases can cause the glass to break!

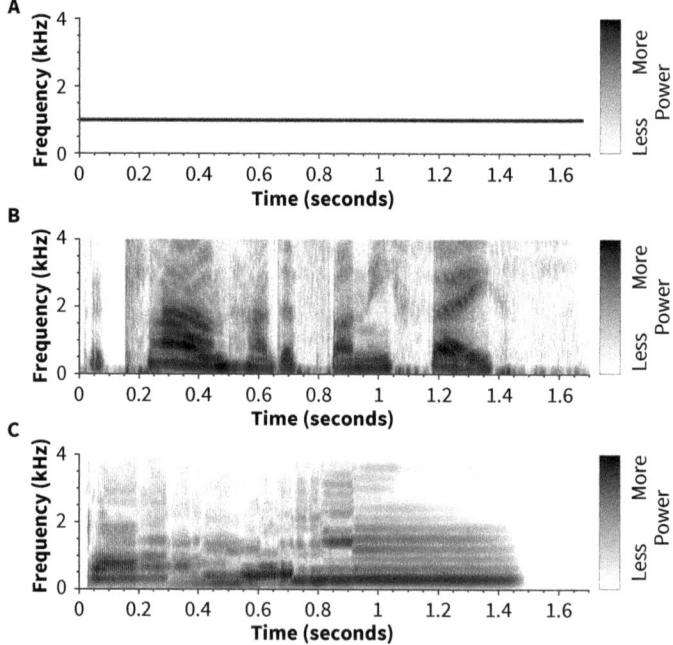

Figure 1.13 Graphs (spectrograms) of a pure tone at 1 kHz (i.e. 1,000 Hz; panel a), speech (a spoken sentence: 'The clown had a funny face'; panel b), and music (a saxophone sliding from a lower to a higher musical note; panel c).

1.2 How do we hear?

When most people think of hearing, they think about the ears. However, the auditory pathway contains multiple stages between the ears and brain (Figure 1.14), each of which plays a crucial role in hearing. Together, the stages in the auditory pathway allow people to make sense of their acoustic environments.

We can think of a sound's journey through the auditory system like a crowd of people taking a train journey across a country: there are lots of key stops along the way. This section highlights the key 'destinations' along the auditory pathway.

1.2.1 Outer ear

To go on a train journey, we need to start at a train station—and, on the auditory pathway, the first station is the ear. When most people talk about their ears, they're actually referring only to the visible part of the ear (Figure 1.15), which protrudes from the side of the head and is known as the outer ear. The purpose of the outer ear is to collect and focus sound waves towards the middle ear.

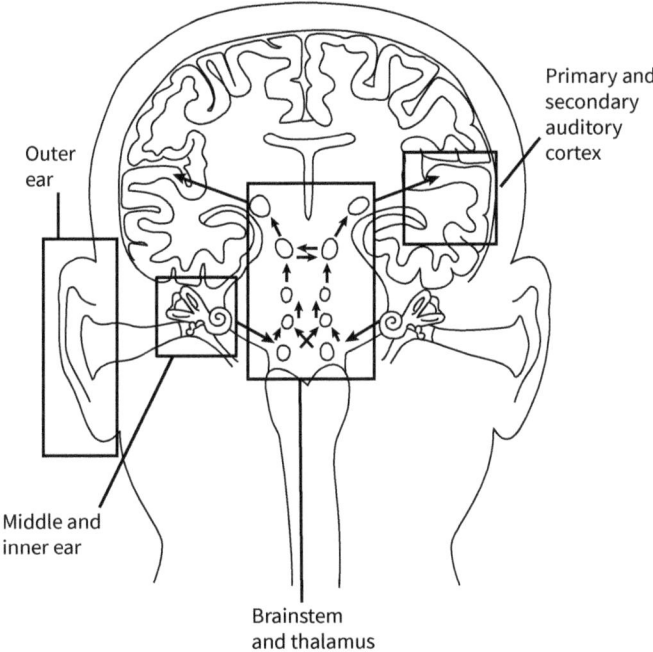

Figure 1.14 Summary of the auditory pathway. When a sound reaches the ears, it is usually conveyed through the outer ear, middle ear, inner ear, auditory nerve (not shown), brainstem, thalamus, primary auditory cortex, and secondary auditory cortex. Notice that all of the structures are present bilaterally (i.e. on both the left and right sides), even though only one side may be labelled in the figure.

Source: adapted from McDermott, J. H. (2014). 'Audition.' In K. Ochsner & S. M. Kosslyn (eds), *The Oxford Handbook of Cognitive Neuroscience, Volume 1: Core Topics*. New York: Oxford University Press.

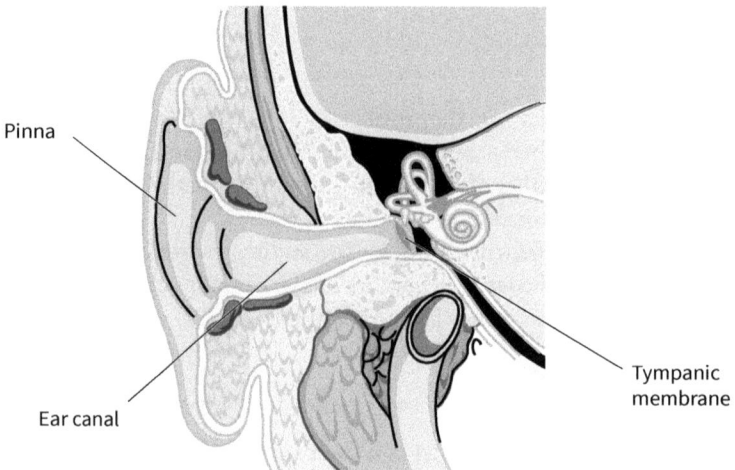

Figure 1.15 The outer ear. After passing through the ear canal, sounds reach the tympanic membrane, which marks the boundary of the outer ear and middle ear.

Source: adapted from Wolfe et al. (eds) (2009), *Sensation & Perception* (second edition). Sunderland, MA: Sinauer Associates Inc.

The external part of the ear is called the **pinna**. Have you ever noticed that the pinna has curves and folds? Their shape means that sounds are altered differently depending on where they come from, which helps us to locate sounds.

> You can learn about how most people locate sounds in **Chapter 2**.

Sound waves can enter the **ear canal** directly, or indirectly by reflecting off the pinna. Just as a ticket barrier at a train station separates the concourse from the platforms, the **tympanic membrane** separates the outer and middle ears. The tympanic membrane is a very thin structure, more commonly known as the eardrum, because it vibrates a bit like a drum when sounds reach it.

1.2.2 Middle ear

On our journey through the auditory pathway, the middle ear can be considered as the station platform. Just as a station platform serves to get people from the station onto a train, the purpose of the middle ear (Figure 1.16) is to convey sound from the outer ear to the inner ear. This is an important task, because sound travels through air in the outer ear, but—as you will read in Section 1.2.3—it travels through fluid in the inner ear. The middle ear helps to bridge this gap.

When a sound wave reaches the tympanic membrane, the membrane vibrates. This vibration travels through the middle ear by three bones that are collectively known as the **ossicles**. The ossicles are the smallest bones in the human body: you could easily fit all three bones on your fingernail. The three bones that make up the ossicles are the malleus, incus, and stapes. The stapes has a flat part called the stapes footplate and that is what pushes onto an opening to the inner ear called the **oval window**. The vibrations from the tympanic

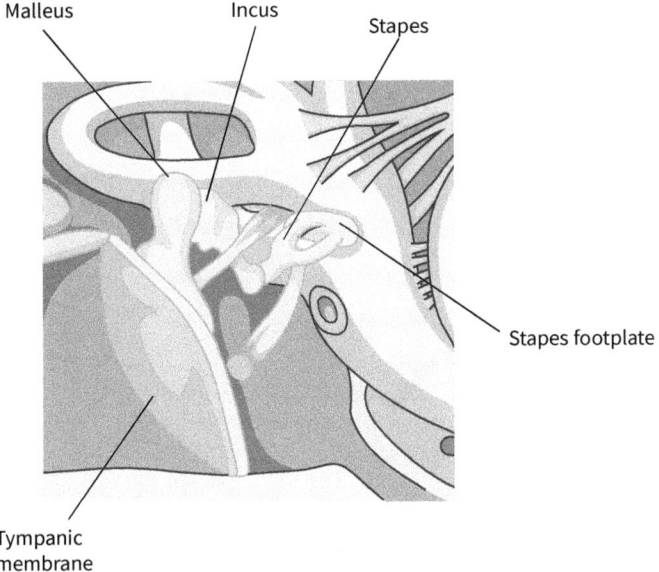

Figure 1.16 The middle ear. Notice how the ossicles include three bones that bridge the gap between the tympanic membrane and the inner ear.

Source: adapted from Wolfe et al. (eds) (2009), *Sensation & Perception.*

membrane pass through each ossicle in turn. When the final ossicle vibrates, it pushes onto the oval window—and this completes the pathway from the outer ear to the inner ear.

As well as bridging the gap between the outer ear and inner ear, the middle ear amplifies the vibrations. This is important because the fluid in the inner ear is harder to move than the air in the outer ear and—without help from the middle ear—the vibrations from the tympanic membrane wouldn't be strong enough to move the inner ear fluid and pass the sound onwards. Notice in Figure 1.16 that the part of the ossicles that pushes on the oval window (the **stapes footplate**) is much smaller than the tympanic membrane, which means that the sound pressure is concentrated on a smaller area. Additionally, the ossicles act a bit like a lever, strengthening vibrations from the tympanic membrane. These two features help the vibrations from the outer ear to be detected at the inner ear.

> The way the middle ear is structured means sounds from the outer ear can be amplified. This is a necessary step to ensure there is sufficient force to move the fluid in the inner ear. The stapes footplate is about 20 times smaller than the tympanic membrane which, together with the ossicles strengthening vibrations, helps to provide greater force for the sound to pass to the inner ear.

1.2.3 Inner ear

The inner ear (Figure 1.17) includes the spiral-shaped **cochlea**. If you could unwind the cochlea, it would be about the length of a pen lid (Koch et al., 2017) and—similar to a snail's shell—it would be wider at one end (the base) and gradually taper towards the other end (the apex). If you could cut a slice out of the cochlea, it would reveal three fluid-filled sections (Figure 1.17(b) and (c)).

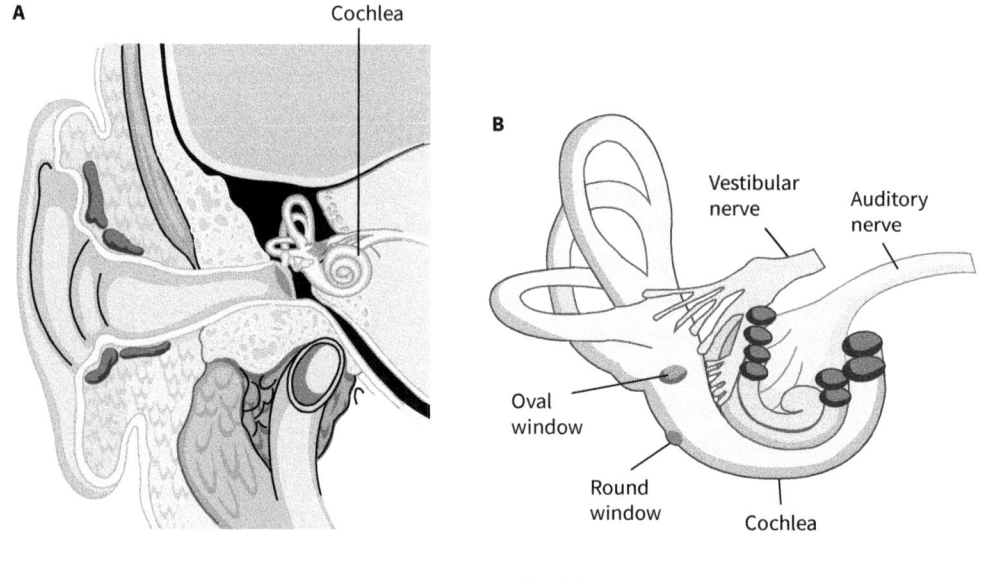
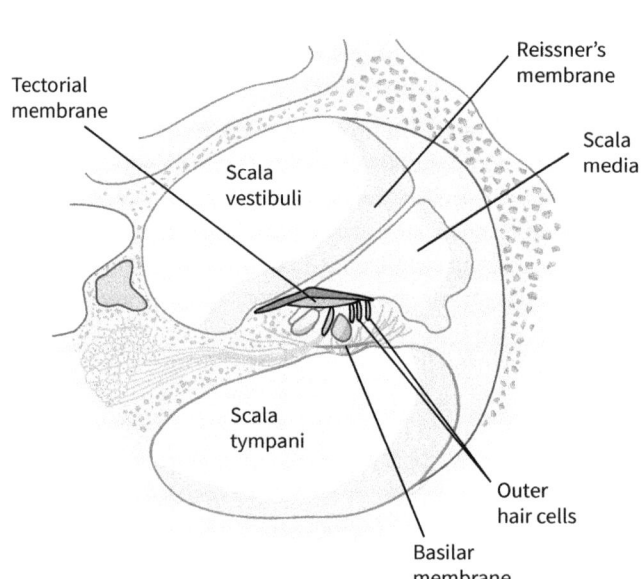

Figure 1.17 Parts of the ear, at different scales. Panel a shows the position of the inner ear relative to the outer ear and middle ear. Panel b contains a close-up of the cochlea, showing the position of the oval window. In this illustration, part of the cochlea has been removed to visualise the sections inside. Notice how the cochlea has a spiral shape. Panel c shows a cross-section of the cochlea. Notice that the basilar membrane is directly underneath the organ of Corti, within the scala media.

Source: adapted from Wolfe et al. (eds) (2009), *Sensation & Perception* (second edition). Sunderland, MA: Sinauer Associates Inc.

Running along the length of the cochlea is the **basilar membrane**, which plays a key role in hearing. When the oval window is pushed by the stapes footplate, it causes the basilar membrane to vibrate. However, the way that the basilar membrane vibrates depends upon the frequencies in the sound, as we go on to explain.

To understand how the basilar membrane is sensitive to the frequencies in a sound, we first need to understand its physical properties. Opposite to the overall diameter of the cochlea, the basilar membrane is *narrower* at the base of the cochlea and *wider* at the apex (Figure 1.18). The flexibility of the basilar membrane reflects how someone might feel if they try out a yoga class for the first time—near the base, the basilar membrane is stiff and difficult to move, but, similar to becoming more flexible towards the end of a yoga class, the basilar membrane gradually becomes more flexible and easier to move towards the apex.

Higher-frequency sounds vibrate the basilar membrane the most nearer the base of the cochlea, whereas lower-frequency sounds vibrate the basilar membrane the most nearer the apex (Figure 1.18). Ultimately, each part of the basilar membrane is most sensitive (i.e. vibrates the most) to a particular frequency, which is known as the **characteristic frequency**. The characteristic frequency doesn't decrease linearly across the basilar membrane: if it did, we would either run out of space or need a much longer cochlea, because the ears are sensitive to such a wide range of frequencies! Instead, it decreases quickly at the base and much more slowly towards the apex (Figure 1.18).

Although each part of the basilar membrane vibrates most to its characteristic frequency, it also vibrates—to a lesser extent—to neighbouring frequencies. The extent to which a part of the basilar membrane vibrates to other frequencies depends on how 'tuned' it is: if it's broadly tuned, it vibrates to a wide range of frequencies, whereas if it's narrowly tuned, it

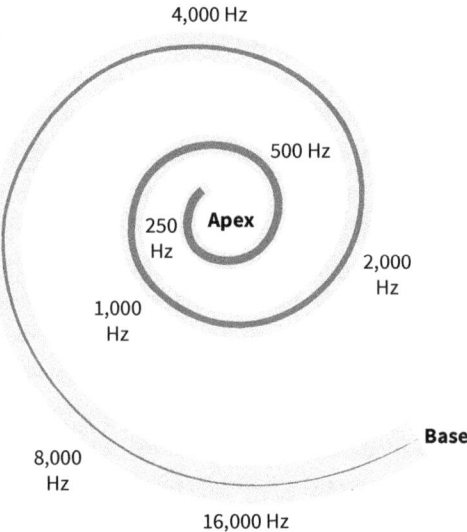

Figure 1.18 The basilar membrane inside the cochlea, indicating the approximate locations of characteristic frequencies (Spoendlin & Schrott, 1989). The characteristic frequency is high at the base and decreases towards the apex. Notice how the basilar membrane extends almost to the apex of the cochlea but not quite: there is a small gap at the apex where the scala tympani and scala vestibuli connect.

only vibrates to a small range of frequencies. The basilar membrane is broadly tuned at the base (i.e. for higher frequencies) and gets progressively more narrowly tuned towards the apex (i.e. for lower frequencies).

Most of the time, sounds contain more than one frequency. Sounds that contain more than one frequency make multiple parts of the basilar membrane vibrate strongly. Let's consider a complex tone containing frequencies of 100 Hz, 1,000 Hz, and 10,000 Hz. This sound will produce peak vibrations at three different positions along the basilar membrane. Recall that different parts of the basilar membrane are most sensitive to particular frequencies. This means that the locations of these peak vibrations along the basilar membrane aren't random (Figure 1.18). A key goal for the cochlea is to work out which frequencies are in a sound, and the sensitivity of different parts of the basilar membrane to different frequencies allows the cochlea to do that.

The next stop on our journey along the auditory pathway is the **organ of Corti**, which is attached to—and runs along the length of—the basilar membrane. The organ of Corti (Figure 1.19) contains a carpet of hair cells, and the hair cells move when the basilar

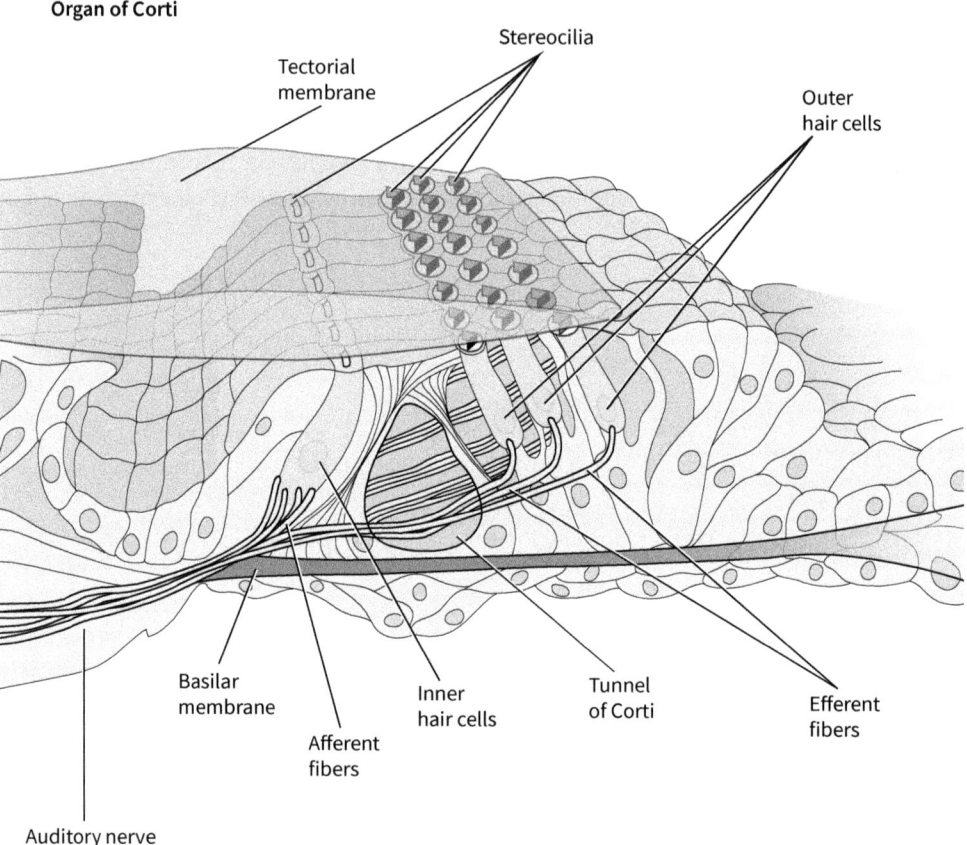

Figure 1.19 The organ of Corti. Notice how the hair cells are directly underneath the tectorial membrane.
Source: adapted from Wolfe et al. (eds) (2009), *Sensation & Perception* (second edition). Sunderland, MA: Sinauer Associates Inc.

membrane underneath them vibrates. There are two types of hair cell: a single row of **inner hair cells** and three to four rows of **outer hair cells** (Ashmore, 2008; see Further Insights 1.2).

Hair cells get their name because they have small 'hairs' at the top of them, called **stereocilia**. The role of inner hair cells is to convert vibrations of the basilar membrane into electrical activity, and the 'hairs' play a key role in this process. When the basilar membrane vibrates, the stereocilia move, and they convert the vibrations into electrical signals. Importantly, the inner hair cells only transmit vibrations into electrical signals when the stereocilia move in one direction, which means that electrical signals are only generated at a specific phase of the sound. The alignment of electrical signals with the phase of a sound is called 'phase locking'.

Stereocilia are positioned at the top of inner hair cells (Figure 1.20) and are linked together near their tips by the aptly named '**tip links**' (Pickles et al., 1987).

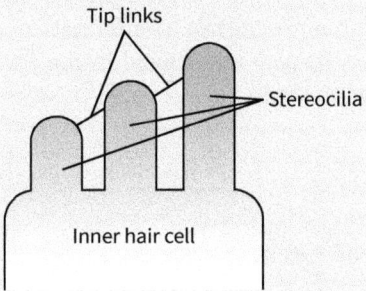

Figure 1.20 The top of an inner hair cell.

Further insights 1.2   Outer hair cells

The inner ear contains approximately 3,500 inner hair cells, but approximately 11,000 outer hair cells! Outer hair cells help to amplify the vibrations of the basilar membrane by shortening and stretching. Auditory science doesn't often feature in mainstream media, but in the late 1980s, a video of a 'dancing' outer hair cell showing this effect was broadcast on British television. The video showed an outer hair cell from a guinea pig, but the effect has also been shown in humans (Ashmore, 2008).

1.2.4 Auditory nerve

Sometimes, when you're on a long journey, you need to transfer from one train to another. In our journey along the auditory pathway, we've done just that: at the hair cells, we transferred from a 'vibration train' onto an electric train. The **auditory nerve** contains over 30,000 auditory nerve fibres which receive information from the inner hair cells. Importantly, the information about frequency, amplitude, and phase that was extracted at the cochlea is passed onwards to the auditory nerve, similar to how each passenger on a train brings their luggage with them when they change trains.

1.2.5 Brainstem and thalamus

On a long journey, a train often passes through several different regions, each containing key stations. In the auditory pathway, the regions in the middle of our journey are the **brainstem** and **thalamus** (Figure 1.14).

The brainstem and thalamus contain different types of **neurons**, which are sensitive to different parts of sounds: some respond only at the beginning or end of a sound, whereas others respond continuously from when the sound starts until it stops. Different neurons are also sensitive to different frequencies. Just as different parts of the basilar membrane have different characteristic frequencies, we call a neuron's preferred frequency (i.e. the frequency to which it responds most) its characteristic frequency. Neurons also differ in the *range* of frequencies they're sensitive to (i.e. their tuning): some respond to a variety of frequencies, whereas others show a strong preference for a particular frequency and don't respond to other frequencies. As we describe below, the properties of neurons—and how they're connected—vary in different parts of the brainstem and thalamus.

After passing through the auditory nerve, the next stop in our journey is the **cochlear nucleus** (Figure 1.21) in the brainstem. Just as information about a sound's frequency is present in the auditory nerve, it's also maintained in the cochlear nucleus, and is passed forwards along the auditory pathway.

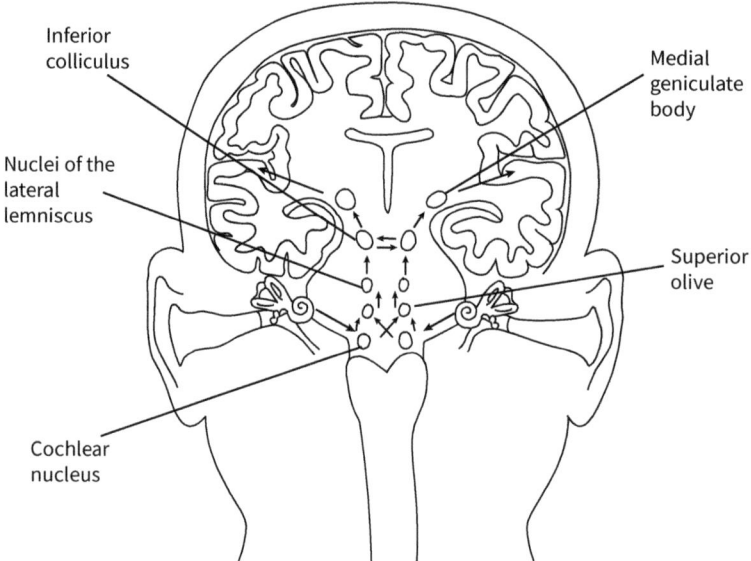

Figure 1.21 Illustration of the auditory pathway, with labels highlighting key stages of the pathway in the brainstem and thalamus. Sounds are processed in the cochlear nucleus, superior olive, nuclei of the lateral lemniscus, inferior colliculus, and medial geniculate body. *Notice that all of the structures are present bilaterally, even though only one side is labelled in the figure.*

Source: adapted from McDermott (2014), 'Audition.' In Ochsner & Kosslyn (eds). *The Oxford Handbook of Cognitive Neuroscience, Volume 1*.

The next station is the **superior olive** (Further Insights 1.3), which is the first structure where signals from the two ears are combined. Notice in Figure 1.21 that the two superior olives both receive input from the left and the right cochlear nuclei. Just as different platforms in a train station receive trains from different places, different parts of the superior olive receive different inputs. Ultimately, this means that different parts of the superior olive combine information from the two ears differently. Neurons in the medial superior olive (i.e. the part of the superior olive that's closest to the midline) respond most when a sound reaches both ears at the same time (Figure 1.22(a)). Contrastingly, most neurons in the lateral superior olive (i.e. the part of the superior olive that's furthest away from the midline) respond most when a sound reaches one ear but not the other. Neurons in the lateral superior olive are most sensitive to sounds on the **ipsilateral** side: the right lateral superior olive is most sensitive to sounds on our right (Figure 1.22(b)) and less sensitive to sounds on our left (Figure 1.22(c)). Similarly, the left lateral superior olive is most sensitive to sounds on our left and less sensitive to sounds on our right.

Neurons are connected to one another, but they can be connected in different ways. Sometimes, a neuron gets excitatory input from another neuron. This means that the neuron is more likely to fire if the other neuron fired. Other times, a neuron gets inhibitory input from another neuron. This means it is *less* likely to fire when the other neuron fires. Generally speaking, a neuron's pattern of connections to other neurons makes it sensitive to particular attributes of sounds, as shown in Figure 1.22.

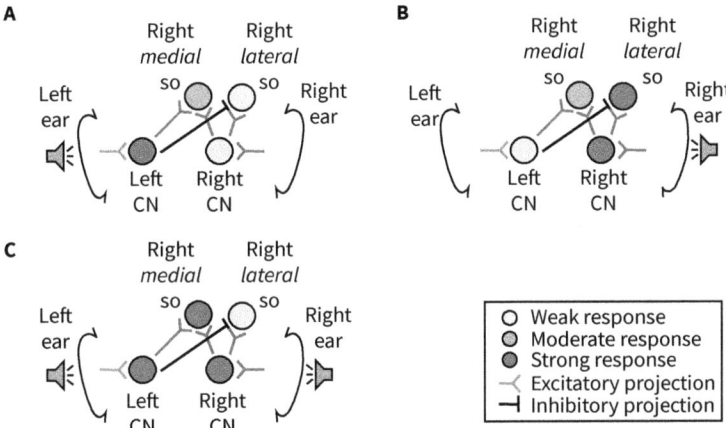

Figure 1.22 Illustration of lateral and medial superior olive (SO) responses to sounds presented to both ears (panel a), the right ear (panel b), or the left ear (panel c). Notice how the lateral and medial SO respond to sounds differently, because of their different balance of excitatory and inhibitory connections from the cochlear nucleus (CN). The right medial SO responds most when sounds are presented simultaneously to both ears, whereas the right lateral SO responds most when sounds are presented only to the right (i.e. ipsilateral) ear. The left SO (not displayed) could be imagined as a mirror image of the right SO, with the left medial SO responding most to simultaneously presented sounds and the left lateral SO responding most when sounds are presented only to the left ear.

> **Further insights 1.3   Brain anatomy terminology**
>
> Human cortex contains bumps and folds: the ridges are called **gyri** and the grooves are called **sulci**.
> Many parts of the brain are labelled according to their location, as shown in Figure 1.23. When areas are described as superior or inferior, it doesn't mean that one area is better than another; rather, **superior** means closer to the top of the brain, and **inferior** means closer to the bottom. Not shown in the figure, **lateral** and **medial** mean closer to the outside and middle, respectively. All the terms are relative: while the entire temporal lobe is inferior to the frontal lobe, the superior, middle, and inferior temporal gyri indicate their positions relative to one another.
>
>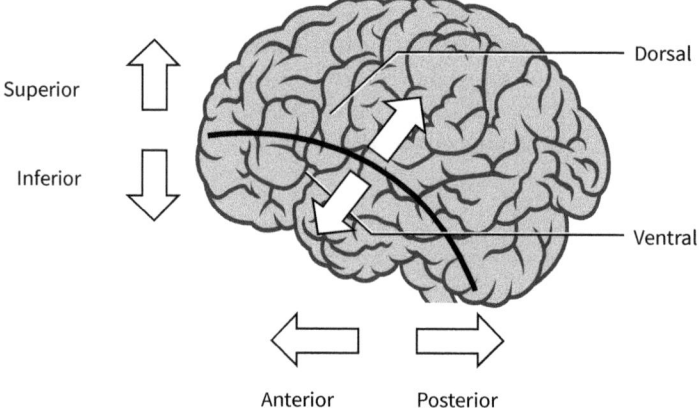
>
> **Figure 1.23** Terminology for describing brain anatomy. Dorsal and ventral are relative to the axis indicated by the black line, which goes from the spinal cord to the front of the brain.

After the superior olive, our journey continues to the **nuclei of the lateral lemniscus**. The nuclei of the lateral lemniscus can be considered as a 'hub' station that contains lots of platforms. They receive input from the superior olive, but they also receive direct input from the cochlear nuclei. In other words, returning to our analogy, some trains from the cochlear nuclei travel directly to the nuclei of the lateral lemniscus without stopping at the superior olive. Different nuclei of the lateral lemniscus are connected differently to these previous structures. Ultimately, this means that some nuclei of the lateral lemniscus receive inputs that originate from both ears, whereas others receive inputs that mainly originate from one ear.

The **inferior colliculus** (Figure 1.21) is further along the auditory pathway: it is located higher up in the brainstem. Part of the inferior colliculus contains neurons that respond best to different frequencies: these neurons are arranged like a map (which is known as a **tonotopic** map), with neurons that respond to high frequencies on one side and neurons that respond to low frequencies on the other. This spatial arrangement by frequency is known as tonotopic organisation. Tonotopic organisation is prevalent throughout the auditory pathway: recall that the basilar membrane in the cochlea is arranged by frequency.

> Inferior colliculi is the plural for inferior colliculus. There is one inferior colliculus on the left and one on the right (Figure 1.21).

In contrast, neurons in other parts of the inferior colliculus don't have a strong preference for particular frequencies. The inferior colliculus has been ascribed several functions—such as detecting a sound's amplitude modulation, working out where a sound is coming from, and perceiving the pitch of a sound (Felix et al., 2018). Interestingly, the inferior colliculi also receive input from senses other than audition (Liu et al., 2022).

> You can learn about pitch in **Chapter 2**.

After leaving the inferior colliculus in the brainstem, our journey passes into the thalamus, where it reaches a structure called the **medial geniculate body**. The medial geniculate body was traditionally thought to forward inputs from the inferior colliculus to auditory cortex, like you might forward an email without editing it. However, we now know that it's actively involved in processing sounds—for example, selectively conveying aspects of sounds that are relevant to the task at hand (Bartlett, 2013). The medial geniculate body also sends information to other areas of the brain outside of auditory cortex.

1.2.6 Primary auditory cortex

The next step in our journey along the auditory pathway is the cortex. **Primary auditory cortex** can be found in the left and right **hemispheres** of the **temporal lobes** (see Figure 1.24(a)): it is buried within the deep horizontal **fissure** (i.e. gap) that separates the temporal lobe from the frontal lobe (shown as the orange line in Figure 1.24(a)). When we look inside this fissure (Figure 1.24(b)), we can see auditory cortex more clearly. The fissure that separates the temporal lobe from the frontal lobe is called the 'lateral sulcus'.

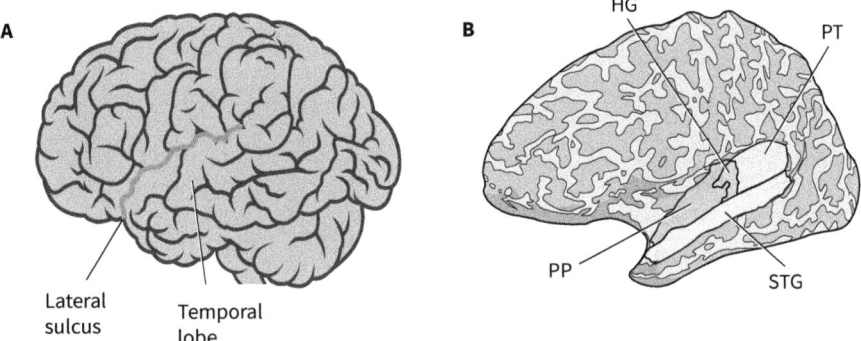

Figure 1.24 Panel a highlights the lateral sulcus, which separates the temporal lobe from the frontal and parietal lobes. The superior temporal gyrus (STG) is visible directly below the lateral sulcus, but Heschl's gyrus (HG) is buried deep within the lateral sulcus. HG can be seen more clearly in panel b, when we open out the lateral sulcus by inflating the cortex—as if we were blowing up a balloon; regions in light grey are gyri and regions in dark grey are sulci. This allows us to visualise HG and surrounding areas planum polare (PP) and planum temporale (PT).

Source: panel b adapted from Berlot et al. (2018), 'Mapping frequency specific tone predictions in the human auditory cortex at high spatial resolution.' *Journal of Neuroscience.* 38, 2205–2217.

Primary auditory cortex is located on **Heschl's gyrus**, and is surrounded by secondary auditory areas. The shape and location of primary auditory cortex vary among people—and it is not uncommon to have *two* Heschl's gyri on the left and/or right **hemisphere** of the brain. The exact location of primary auditory cortex is still debated (Baumann et al., 2013), but it is thought to lie in the medial portion of Heschl's gyrus (Figure 1.24(b); Further Insights 1.4).

> **Further insights 1.4** Auditory cortex in non-human animals
>
> The distinction between primary and secondary auditory cortex has been largely informed by research on monkeys and other animals (Sweet et al., 2005). Although—to complicate matters—how auditory cortex is organised and divided into sub-regions differs among species (see Figure 2 in Malmierca & Hackett, 2012). There is no direct mapping of areas across species, and the terminology for different regions of auditory cortex differs across species. Nevertheless, several parallels have been drawn between auditory areas in humans and non-human animals.

Like the rest of human cortex, auditory cortex is made up of six layers (which are labelled I to VI, from **superficial** to deep) (Figure 1.25). Primary auditory cortex can be distinguished from other areas of cortex because it has a high density of neurons (i.e. the neurons are tightly

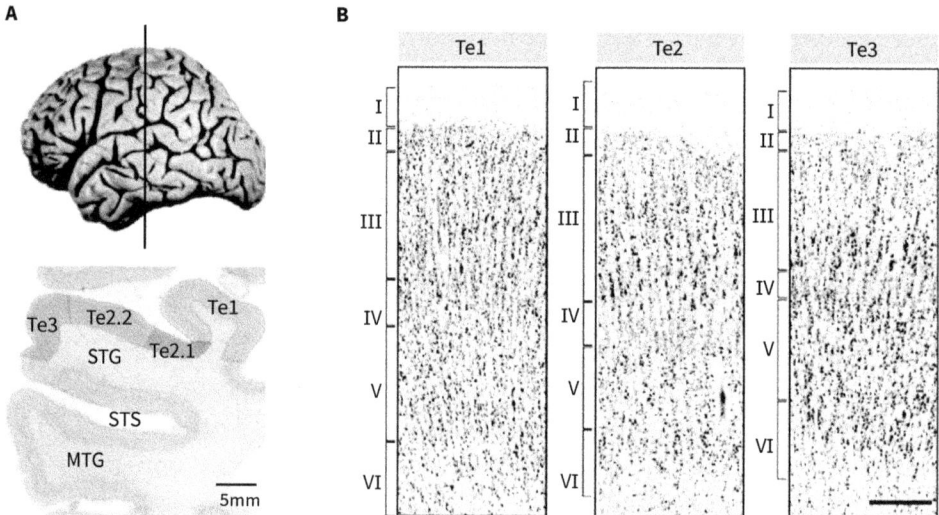

Figure 1.25 Structure of auditory cortex. Panel a displays a section through the brain, showing the relative positions of four temporal areas (Te1, Te2.1, Te2.2, Te3) relative to the superior temporal gyrus (STG), superior temporal sulcus (STS), and middle temporal gyrus (MTG). Te1 is on Heschl's gyrus and is thought to correspond to primary auditory cortex, whereas Te2 (which includes Te2.1 and Te2.2) and Te3 are thought to be higher (e.g. secondary) auditory areas. Panel b shows neurons in three different cortical areas (revealed using cell staining), which reveal a layered structure. The six layers are labelled I–VI and are characterised by differences in the size, form, and density of neurons. Notice that the positions of the six layers (shown by the labels I–VI on the left side) differ among the three areas. Also, if you look very closely at the stains, you might notice that Te1 has high density (i.e. tightly packed neurons) in layer IV.

Source: panel a is an excerpt of a figure in Zachlod et al. (2020) 'Four new cytoarchitectonic areas surrounding the primary and early auditory cortex in human brains.' *Cortex* 128, 1–21; panel b is from Amunts et al. (2012) 'Auditory system'. In Mai & Paxinos (eds), *The Human Nervous System* (pp. 1270–1300). London; Waltham, MA and San Diego, CA: Academic Press.

packed) in layer IV. Layer IV is mainly where inputs from other areas—predominantly the medial geniculate body—enter primary auditory cortex. Its other layers contain neurons that connect locally within primary auditory cortex, and which send information to higher areas of cortex.

Like other parts of the auditory pathway, neurons in primary auditory cortex are organised like a map by their preferred frequency, from low to high (Formisano et al., 2003). Most of its neurons also respond best to sounds that come from a particular location (e.g. a sound on the left). However, unlike for frequency, for location these neurons don't seem to be organised in a systematic map. Instead, they appear to be interspersed in no discernible pattern.

Primary auditory cortex was traditionally thought to encode sounds exactly as they occur in the world, but it's now known to have a more flexible representation. Its responses depend on attention and the context in which sounds are heard. Generally speaking, primary cortex responds best to stimuli that are relevant to the task at hand.

1.2.7 Secondary auditory cortex and beyond

Secondary auditory cortex lies next to primary auditory cortex (Figures 1.24(b) and 1.25(a)). Yet, it is physiologically distinct: it has a lower cell density, a different distribution of neurons across its layers (Figure 1.25(b)), and a different chemical composition (Jones, 2003). Just as a cross-country train can take different routes to reach its destination, inputs to secondary auditory cortex arrive from different parts of the auditory pathway: some inputs to secondary auditory cortex arrive from primary auditory cortex, whereas others travel directly from the medial geniculate body, skipping primary auditory cortex.

Generally, neurons within secondary auditory cortex respond to a broader range of frequencies than neurons in primary auditory cortex, and are most sensitive to combinations of features. For example, some neurons respond best to sounds that contain particular combinations of frequencies, such as sounds produced by the voice. These findings are consistent with the idea that the transfer of information from primary to secondary auditory cortex involves a transformation from simple to more complex acoustic features (Khalighinejad et al., 2021).

Secondary auditory cortex sends information to other areas of the brain more widely than primary auditory cortex does. A variety of brain areas—such as those responsible for attention, memory, and emotion—are involved in aspects of sound processing, even though their functions are not restricted to audition. Ultimately, people's experience of sound is not confined to basic sound processing.

> You can learn about speech sounds, which are one type of sound produced by the voice, in **Chapter 4**. Other sounds produced by the voice include laughter and animal vocalisations.

1.2.8 Descending pathways

It is also worth mentioning the numerous descending connections throughout the auditory system, which extend from the *cortex* to the *cochlea*. In other words, some of the journeys through the auditory pathway *begin* with neurons responding in higher areas, such as cortex, which are conveyed to lower levels of the auditory pathway (King, 2020). Rather than a single pathway, these descending pathways are often conceptualised as local circuits that travel through particular areas. A well-studied example is the **medial olivocochlear reflex**—a circuit that connects the cochlear nucleus, superior olive, and cochlea. This reflex may protect the cochlea from high sound levels by controlling the motion of the basilar membrane (Rajan, 2000), or suppress ongoing noise to enhance responses to short sounds that occur among the noise (May & McQuone, 1995). Other descending connections have been studied in less detail, and their functional significance remains to be determined (Lesicko & Geffen, 2022).

Summary

In everyday life, people encounter a variety of sounds with different acoustic properties. Variations in these properties help to explain why the sound made by a phone vibrating differs from the sound of a person's voice. The ear converts sound pressure waves into electrical signals, and these signals are sent to the brainstem and cortex to interpret the sounds in the environment. Ultimately, someone's perceptual experience reflects the combination of processes occurring at all levels of their auditory pathway.

Further your understanding

Schnupp, J., Nelken, I., & King, A. (2011). *Auditory Neuroscience: Making Sense of Sound.* Cambridge, MA: MIT Press. ISBN 9780262113182 (Chapter 2: 'The Ear').

Malmierca, M. S. & Hackett, T. A. (2012). 'Structural organization of the ascending auditory pathway.' In A. R. Palmer & A. Rees (eds) *The Oxford Handbook of Auditory Science: The Auditory Brain* (pp. 9–42). New York: Oxford University Press. doi:10.1093/oxfordhb/9780199233281.001.0001

References

Amunts Morosan, P., Hilbig, H., & Zilles, K. (2012) 'Auditory system'. In J. K. Mai & G. Paxinos (eds) *The Human Nervous System* (pp. 1270–1300). London; Waltham, MA and San Diego, CA: Academic Press.

Ashmore, J. (2008). 'Cochlear outer hair cell motility.' *Physiological Reviews*, Vol. 88, 173–210. https://doi.org/10.1152/physrev.00044.2006

Bartlett, E. L. (2013). 'The organization and physiology of the auditory thalamus and its role in processing acoustic features important for speech perception.' *Brain and Language*, 126(1), 29–48. https://doi.org/10.1016/j.bandl.2013.03.003

Baumann, S., Petkov, C. I., & Griffiths, T. D. (2013). 'A unified framework for the organization of the primate auditory cortex.' *Frontiers in Systems Neuroscience*, 7, 1–19. https://doi.org/10.3389/fnsys.2013.00011

Berlot, E., Formisano, E., & De Martino, F. (2018). 'Mapping frequency specific tone predictions in the human auditory cortex at high spatial resolution.' *Journal of Neuroscience*, 38, 2205–2217.

Felix, R. A., Gourévitch, B., & Portfors, C. V. (2018). 'Subcortical pathways: Towards a better understanding of auditory disorders.' *Hearing Research*, 362, 48–60. https://doi.org/10.1016/j.heares.2018.01.008

Formisano, E., Kim, D. S., Di Salle, F., Van De Moortele, P. F., Ugurbil, K., & Goebel, R. (2003). 'Mirror-symmetric tonotopic maps in human primary auditory cortex.' *Neuron*, 40(4), 859–869. https://doi.org/10.1016/S0896-6273(03)00669-X

Jones, E. G. (2003). 'Chemically defined parallel pathways in the monkey auditory system.' *Annals of the New York Academy of Sciences*, 999, 218–233. https://doi.org/10.1196/annals.1284.033

Khalighinejad, B., Patel, P., Herrero, J. L., Bickel, S., Mehta, A. D., & Mesgarani, N. (2021). 'Functional characterization of human Heschl's gyrus in response to natural speech.' *Neuroimage*, 235, 118003. https://doi.org/10.1016/j.neuroimage.2021.118003

King, A. J. (2020). 'Feedback systems: Descending pathways and adaptive coding in the auditory system.' In B. Fritzsch (ed.) *The Senses: A Comprehensive Reference* (pp. 732–748). Elsevier. https://doi.org/10.1016/B978-0-12-809324-5.24188-6

Koch, R. W., Ladak, H. M., Elfarnawany, M., & Agrawal, S. K. (2017). 'Measuring cochlear duct length—A historical analysis of methods and results.' *Journal of Otolaryngology—Head and Neck Surgery*, 46(19), 1–11. https://doi.org/10.1186/s40463-017-0194-2

Lesicko, A. M. H., & Geffen, M. N. (2022). 'Diverse functions of the auditory cortico-collicular pathway.' *Hearing Research*, Vol. 425. https://doi.org/10.1016/j.heares.2022.108488

Liu, M., Dai, J., Zhou, M., Liu, J., Ge, X., Wang, N., & Zhang, J. (2022). 'Mini-review: The neural circuits of the non-lemniscal inferior colliculus.' *Neuroscience Letters*, Vol. 776. https://doi.org/10.1016/j.neulet.2022.136567

Malmierca, M. S., & Hackett, T. A. (2012). 'Structural organization of the ascending auditory pathway.' In A. R. Palmer & A. Rees (eds) *The Oxford Handbook of Auditory Science: The Auditory Brain* (pp. 9–42). Oxford University Press. doi:10.1093/oxfordhb/9780199233281.001.0001

May, B. J., & McQuone, S. J. (1995). 'Effects of bilateral olivocochlear lesions on pure-tone intensity discrimination in cats.' *Auditory Neuroscience*, 1(4), 385–400.

McDermott, J. H. (2014). 'Audition.' In K. Ochsner & S. M. Kosslyn (eds) *The Oxford Handbook of Cognitive Neuroscience, Volume 1: Core Topics*. New York: Oxford University Press.

Pickles, J. O., Osborne, M. P., & Comis, S. D. (1987). 'Vulnerability of tip links between stereocilia to acoustic trauma in the guinea pig.' *Hearing Research*, 25(2–3), 173–183. https://doi.org/10.1016/0378-5955(87)90089-X

Rajan, R. (2000). 'Centrifugal pathways protect hearing sensitivity at the cochlea in noisy environments that exacerbate the damage induced by loud sound.' *Journal of Neuroscience*, 20(17), 6684–6693. https://doi.org/10.1523/jneurosci.20-17-06684.2000

Robles, L., & Ruggero, M. A. (2001). 'Mechanics of the mammalian cochlea.' *Physiological Reviews*, 81(3), 1305–1352.

Spoendlin, H., & Schrott, A. (1989). 'Analysis of the human auditory nerve.' *Hearing Research*, 43(1), 25–38. https://doi.org/10.1016/0378-5955(89)90056-7

Sweet, R. A., Dorph-Petersen, K. A., & Lewis, D. A. (2005). 'Mapping auditory core, lateral belt, and parabelt cortices in the human superior temporal gyrus.' *The Journal of Comparative Neurology*, 491(3), 270–289. https://doi.org/10.1002/CNE.20702

Zachlod, D., Rüttgers, B., Bludau, S., Mohlberg, H., Langner, R., Zilles, K., & Amunts, K. (2020) 'Four new cytoarchitectonic areas surrounding the primary and early auditory cortex in human brains.' *Cortex*, 128, 1–21.

2 Perceptual Characteristics of Sound

While you're reading this book, you might be able to hear some sounds around you. Some might be quiet, like birds chirping. Others might be loud, like a car horn beeping. Perhaps you can hear some people chatting on your left, a train passing in the distance, or some music that contains high and low notes. In daily life, most people perceive a wide variety of sounds, and this chapter focuses on three aspects of auditory perception: loudness, location, and pitch.

2.1 Loudness

Have you ever been to a party or nightclub and noticed that the music was really loud? Contrast this with a time you've been somewhere—such as an empty café—where you could hear very quiet background music, and you've needed to listen very carefully to identify what song's playing. **Loudness** is a term that describes how people perceive sound, and it ranges from very quiet to very loud. Loudness isn't an attribute of sound; rather, it's a *perception* of sound. Most people experience variations in loudness all the time. This section outlines how attributes of sound influence the perception of loudness, and how loudness relates to responses in the auditory pathway.

2.1.1 Loudness and intensity

Imagine someone playing their favourite song and gradually turning up the volume. As they increase the volume, they're increasing the amount of sound energy, and most people would perceive the music as getting louder. Conversely, if someone reduces the volume, the amount of sound energy decreases, and most people would perceive the music as getting quieter.

When someone changes the volume, they're changing the sound's **intensity**, which is a physical attribute of sound—although loudness is closely related to intensity. Intensity defines how much acoustical energy per second is passing through a given area. Often, when describing sounds, we use a measure of relative intensity that's called **sound level** and is measured in **decibels** (dB) (see Further insights 2.1). There are different notations for decibels depending upon what the sound level is relative to. Decibels sound pressure level (dB SPL) uses the quietest sound humans can typically hear as a reference.

> Intensity is related to amplitude (a property of sound introduced in **Chapter 1**). As the amplitude of a sound increases, its intensity increases; similarly, when its amplitude decreases, its intensity decreases.

> **Chapter 8** introduces another notation for decibels: decibels hearing level (dB HL).

> **Further insights 2.1** Intensity and sound level
>
> Intensity is typically measured in watts per square metre (W/m^2) but, because people can hear such a wide range of sound intensities (from around 0.000000000001 W/m^2 up to 20 W/m^2), this unit can be awkward to use. To overcome this issue, we can use decibels, which are on a logarithmic scale. Unlike a ruler, on which the numbers increase linearly, a logarithmic scale makes it easier to describe (and visualise) a large range of sound intensities. Using a logarithmic scale means the range of numbers is much smaller. When using the decibel scale, we're describing a ratio between two intensities—which we refer to as sound level.

Figure 2.1 shows some everyday sounds on the decibel scale. Notice how the scale can extend below zero: 0 dB SPL doesn't mean there's no sound at all, but instead means the sound is similar to the quietest sound that humans can hear, on average. Sounds above 100 dB SPL can be uncomfortable and sounds above 120 dB SPL can be intolerable (and even painful) for many people. If someone is exposed to high sound levels, it can damage their hearing. For example, people can experience noise-induced hearing loss from a brief but very loud sound (such as a gunshot or an explosion nearby) or from prolonged exposure to loud sounds (such as loud machinery) (Natarajan et al., 2023). Loud sounds can harm the cochlea—for instance by damaging the hair cells.

> You can learn more about hair cells in **Chapter 1** and hearing loss in **Chapter 8**.

From Figure 2.1, notice that a quiet conversation is around 50 dB SPL and a phone ringing is around 80 dB SPL. However, if someone is having a quiet conversation with a friend when their phone rings, it wouldn't be as loud as an aeroplane taking off (130 dB SPL)! Similarly, if two phones (80 dB SPL and 80 dB SPL) start ringing in a quiet room, they wouldn't be louder than fireworks (140 dB SPL)! This is because sounds don't simply add together on the decibel scale (because decibels are on a logarithmic scale; see Further insights 2.1). Instead, a doubling in intensity is equivalent to an increase of approximately 3 dB SPL. Therefore, two phones ringing in a quiet room would be about 83 dB SPL, rather than 160 dB SPL.

Have you ever been told that you're playing music too loud, and been surprised because you thought the level was perfectly acceptable? While loudness is related to sound level,

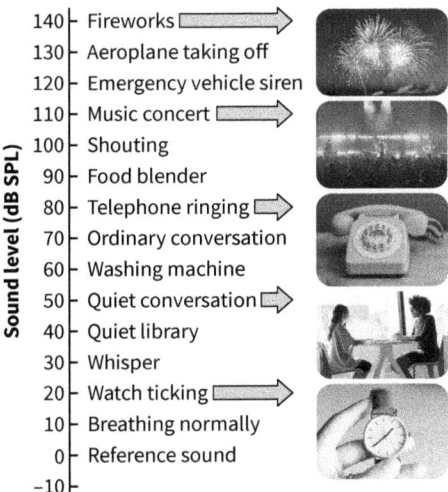

Figure 2.1 The decibel sound pressure level (dB SPL) scale can be used to describe the sound level of everyday sounds, such as the examples displayed in this figure. The reference sound at 0 dB SPL is the quietest level at which most people can hear a 1-kHz pure tone. Other sounds on the dB SPL scale are compared against this reference sound level. Therefore, the decibel scale extends below 0 dB SPL.

not everyone experiences the same change in intensity as an equal increase in loudness. We can't describe loudness using decibels, because loudness is subjective, which begs the question, how do we measure it? It feels intuitive to most people to say that the sound of an aeroplane taking off is louder than the sound of a kettle boiling—but can you say *how much* louder? If your friend says that the traffic outside their window is twice as loud as the traffic outside your window, what do they mean, and would you come to the same conclusion? Ultimately, because loudness is a subjective percept, it can't be measured directly. Nevertheless, researchers have developed several methods to gain understanding of how people experience loudness (Further insights 2.2).

> **Further insights 2.2 How can we measure loudness?**
>
> One way to assess loudness is to use 'magnitude estimation', in which listeners are presented with a sound and are asked to rate its loudness by assigning it a number. They're asked to assign bigger numbers to louder sounds, but they can choose any numbers. Magnitude estimation can tell us which, out of several sounds, listeners perceive to be louder. For example, most people would give a bigger number to an aeroplane taking off than to a kettle boiling. However, because each person can choose any number, this method doesn't allow researchers to compare responses across people. For example, if someone decides to rate the sound of an aeroplane taking off as 8 and another person rates it as 16, that doesn't necessarily mean that one person thinks the sound is twice as loud as the other person; instead, they're each using different scales.
>
> *(continued...)*

> Another way to assess loudness is to use 'loudness matching', in which people are asked to judge when two sounds are equally loud. Someone is presented with two sounds and is asked to adjust the level of one of the sounds until they perceive it as matching the loudness of the other sound. Loudness matching is useful for finding sounds that are equally loud, but it can't describe differences in loudness *between* sounds—for example, *how much* louder one sound is compared to another (e.g. the traffic outside your window compared to the traffic outside your friend's window).
>
> Despite their limitations, both of these methods have allowed researchers to discern how various attributes of sounds (e.g. a sound's level or duration, or the frequencies in a sound) affect someone's perception of loudness.

2.1.2 Loudness and duration

The most obvious attribute of a sound that influences loudness is sound level, but a sound's duration can also influence people's judgements about how loud it is. When people listen to two pure tones that are the same—except that they have different durations—they generally perceive the longer sound as being louder. In other words, at equal sound levels, people usually perceive longer tones to be louder than shorter tones. This effect has been established using magnitude-estimation and loudness-matching tasks (see Further insights 2.2) (Epstein & Florentine, 2006).

Duration has a greater effect on loudness for some sounds than for others. For example, duration only affects loudness for sounds that are relatively short (i.e. a few hundred milliseconds). Also, the impact of duration depends on the sound level. Duration has the greatest effect on loudness when the sound level is in the middle of the range of sounds that people typically hear—at about the level of an ordinary conversation or a phone ringing (Figure 2.2). Whereas, if the stimuli have very low or very high sound levels (like the sound of someone breathing or of people shouting), changing the duration of the stimuli has a much smaller effect on loudness.

2.1.3 Loudness and frequency

Frequency is another physical property of sound that impacts loudness: at a given sound level, some frequencies will be perceived as being louder than others. Helpfully, researchers have come up with 'units' for loudness, which we can use to illustrate how a sound's frequency and level impact loudness. The 'units' that have been ascribed to loudness are **phons**. Unlike other units we've used in this book (such as decibels and Hertz), phons are the units for a *subjective* percept rather than for an objective property of the physical stimulus. The idea is that sounds that are usually perceived as equally loud will have the same value in phons. We can visualise the variation in loudness (using phons) by frequency and sound level using **equal-loudness curves**, which are shown in Figure 2.3.

For example, find the curve for 40 phons in Figure 2.3. This curve crosses 60 dB SPL for a 125-Hz tone, 50 dB SPL for a 250-Hz tone, and 40 dB SPL for a 1000-Hz tone. This means that these three tones should be perceived as being equally loud, even though they have

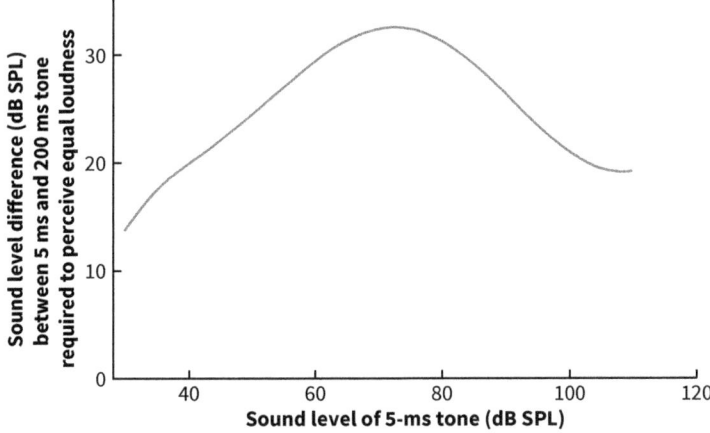

Figure 2.2 Results of an experiment that studied how duration affects loudness judgements (Epstein & Florentine, 2005). In this experiment, participants changed the sound level of a 5-ms pure tone to match a 200-ms pure tone. The 5-ms tone always needed to be increased in level to be perceived as equally loud to the 200-ms tone—although notice that the difference in loudness between the short tone and the longer tone is greatest for medium sound levels, and is smaller for lower and higher sound levels. dB SPL: decibels sound pressure level.

Source: data from Epstein, M., & Florentine, M. (2005). 'A test of the equal-loudness-ratio hypothesis using cross-modality matching functions.' *Journal of the Acoustical Society of America*, 118(2), 907–913. https://doi.org/10.1121/1.1954547

different sound levels. For any combination of frequency and sound level, you could use the equal-loudness curves to work out the sound level at which you would need to present a tone for it to be perceived as being equally loud to a tone of a different frequency.

To understand why most people perceive pure tones as louder as the frequency increases, look back at Figure 2.3. Notice that for a given sound level, the perceived loudness of a tone increases as its frequency increases, up to about 1000 Hz. For example, find 50 dB SPL on the vertical axis of Figure 2.3, then follow the horizontal line. At a sound level of 50 dB SPL, a 125-Hz tone would have a phons value of about 26, a 250-Hz tone would have a phons value of about 40, a 500-Hz tone would have a phons value of about 48, and a 1000-Hz tone would be 50 phons. This increase in phons indicates an increase in perceived loudness for most people.

From Figure 2.3, you might notice that 1000 Hz has a unique place on the phons scale. Find 1000 Hz on the horizontal axis of Figure 2.3, then follow the red vertical line that crosses through each curve. Notice that the phons label for each curve is the same number as the decibel value at which the curve crosses the 1000-Hz line. That's because 1000 Hz is used as the reference for the phons scale. A 1000-Hz tone at 20 dB SPL is 20 phons, a 1000-Hz tone at 30 dB SPL is 30 phons, and so on.

Visualising phons on equal-loudness curves is useful for finding sounds that are (as the name suggests) equally loud. However, phons can't describe differences in loudness *between* sounds—for example by *how much louder* one sound is compared to another (e.g. the traffic outside your window compared to the traffic outside your friend's window). That's because phons are an ordinal scale. This means that, although larger phons values indicate louder

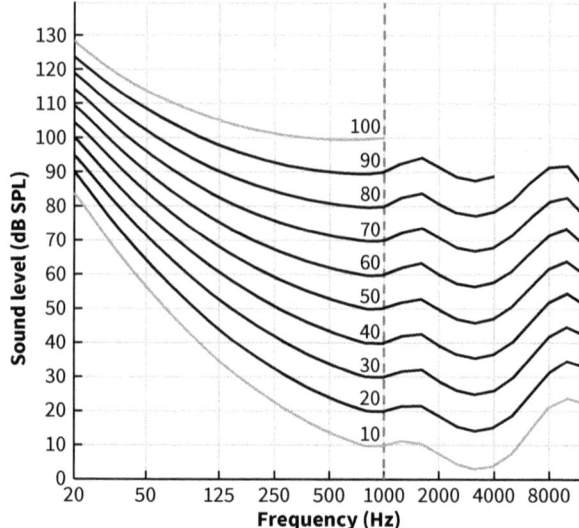

Figure 2.3 Equal-loudness curves for pure tones. 1000 Hz is used as a reference. Notice that, if you follow the dashed line at 1000 Hz, the number of phons (which indicate loudness and are labelled towards the middle of the figure) matches the sound level in decibels sound pressure level (dB SPL). Researchers have sufficient data to be confident in the curves for 20–90 phons, but less data exists for the curves at 10 phons and 100 phons. Notice how loudness varies across frequencies—for example, a 125-Hz tone at 60 dB SPL sounds as loud as a 1000-Hz tone at 40 dB SPL.

Source: data for this figure are from BS ISO 226:2023: Acoustics. Normal equal-loudness-level contours. (2023). British Standards Institute.

sounds, the units don't scale linearly. The person who comes first in a running race hasn't necessarily run twice as fast as the person who comes second—and, likewise, a doubling in phons doesn't necessarily indicate a doubling in loudness.

> 'Sones' are another way of quantifying the perception of loudness. The sone scale uses a 1000 Hz tone at 40 dB as a reference (1 sone). 2 sones are considered to be twice as loud as 1 sone, and 4 sones are considered to be four times as loud as 1 sone. Above 40 dB, an increase of 10 dB is about a doubling in sones (50 dB = 2 sones, 60 dB = 4 sones). Whereas, below 40 dB, the relationship between sones and sound level isn't as straightforward.

2.1.4 Loudness and the auditory system

Given that the perception of loudness doesn't depend exclusively on any individual attribute of a sound, can we locate a part of the auditory pathway where responses reflect the perception of loudness? Auditory nerve fibres respond at higher rates as the intensity of a sound increases, which results in greater responses in the brainstem, thalamus, and auditory cortex (Behler & Uppenkamp, 2016)—but remember, intensity isn't the same as loudness

(Section 2.1.1). Responses in the auditory nerve seem to be more closely aligned with intensity, rather than with someone's perception of loudness. Most auditory nerve fibres are already at their maximum response rate by 50 dB SPL (Auerbach & Gritton, 2022)—whereas, the perception of loudness can continue to increase above this level. For example, an ordinary conversation is about 70 dB SPL (see Figure 2.1), but people usually perceive fireworks—which are approximately 140 dB SPL—as being much louder! Therefore, the perception of loudness can't be based on the rate of auditory nerve firing alone.

Neuroimaging studies have helped to distinguish parts of the auditory pathway that respond to physical properties of sounds (such as intensity) from those that relate to someone's perception of loudness. In general, like auditory nerve fibres, brainstem responses seem to be more closely related to physical properties of sound (e.g. intensity, duration, and frequency), rather than someone's overall perception of loudness—whereas responses in auditory cortex have been found to scale with the perception of loudness (Uppenkamp & Röhl, 2014). These results imply that physical properties of sound are represented at early stages of the auditory pathway, and these physical properties are somehow converted in auditory cortex, so that they more closely reflect the perception of loudness (Behler & Uppenkamp, 2016)—although, precisely how this conversion happens remains to be discovered.

2.2 Location

When someone is at a party, they might be able to find one of their friends based on where their friend's voice is coming from. The ability to localise sounds (i.e. to work out where they're coming from) can be important for someone's safety too: when crossing the road, many people rely on their hearing to work out whether it's safe to cross if they can't see around the corner. Working out whether a sound is coming from our left or right side is more complex than you might think! This section examines how the auditory system interprets the signals that reach the ears to work out where sounds are coming from.

2.2.1 Detecting differences in location

In general, people are remarkably good at telling where sounds are coming from. If two pure tones are coming from in front of us, but one is slightly to the left of the other, most people can detect a difference in their location if the sounds are separated by only 1 degree—which is approximately the width of your finger when it's held out at arm's length. However, if both sounds are coming from the side, it's more difficult for people to detect differences in location: the minimum angle that most people can differentiate gets larger as sounds travel from directly in front of them to their left or right side (Figure 2.4). It's also more difficult to detect differences in vertical location (i.e. if one sound originates from a higher location than the other) than horizontal location: the smallest difference in vertical location that most people can detect is just under 4 degrees (Perrott & Saberi, 1990). So, if a bee is buzzing around someone's head, they'll probably be better determining where it is horizontally than where it is vertically.

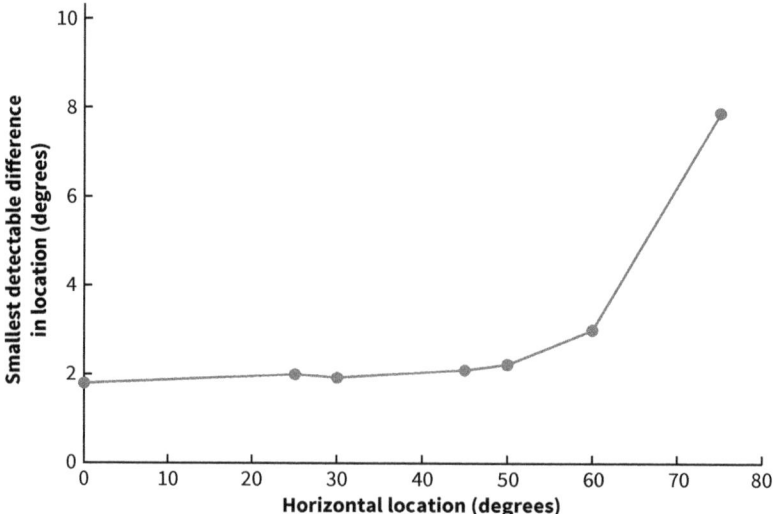

Figure 2.4 The smallest difference in location that most people can detect varies across horizonal locations. The difference is small for a location directly in front of the listener (0 degrees) but gradually increases towards the periphery.

Source: data replotted from Litovsky & Macmillan (1994) and Grantham (1995) as cited in Briley, Kitterick, & Summerfield (2013). 'Evidence for opponent process analysis of sound source location in humans.' *Journal of the Association for Research in Otolaryngology*, 14(1), 83–101.

> The smallest difference in location that a person can detect is typically referred to as the 'minimum audible angle'.

2.2.2 Locating sounds horizontally

If someone is trying to find their friend at a party, it's usually not very useful to just know that their friend is in a *different* location to the loudspeaker that's playing music. Instead, they probably want to know *where* in the room their friend is—in other words, whether the listener needs to turn to their left or right to find their friend. One advantage of having two ears, one placed on each side of the head, is that it can help people to work out where sounds are coming from.

Imagine you're sitting between two loudspeakers. When a sound is presented from the right loudspeaker, it'll reach your right ear slightly before it reaches your left ear (Figure 2.5). Sound travels incredibly fast—about 345 metres per second (which means it travels a greater distance than the length of three football pitches or 14 tennis courts in 1 second!)—so a sound from the loudspeaker on your right will only reach your right ear about 0.0007 seconds before it reaches your left ear. Yet, even though that's an extremely small difference in time, the auditory system is very good at detecting the difference. Incredibly, the auditory system can detect differences in time between the two ears of 10 microseconds (i.e. 0.00001 seconds)! The difference in arrival time between the two ears is called the **interaural time difference** or **ITD** (interaural means 'between the ears'). The ITD is largest when a sound comes from the side, straight to your left or right, because the sound has to travel the furthest possible distance (i.e. the full width of your head) to reach the other ear.

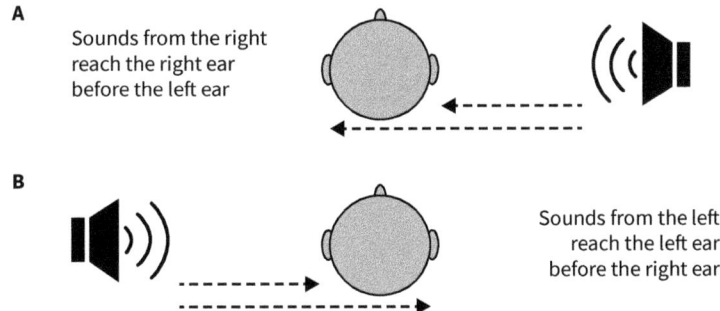

Figure 2.5 The separation of the ears on either side of the head produces interaural time and level differences. In panel a, sounds from the right side of a listener reach the right ear first and must travel a bit further to reach the left ear. Similarly, in panel b, sounds from the left side of a listener reach the left ear first and must travel a bit further to reach the right ear.

Also, when a sound is presented from the loudspeaker on your right, it'll probably be slightly louder at your right ear than at your left ear, because it's closer to your right ear. The sound needs to travel a little further to reach your left ear (Figure 2.5) and the head acts as an acoustic barrier, often called the 'head shadow', which means that less sound energy will reach the left ear. The difference in level between the two ears is called the **interaural level difference (ILD)**. The human auditory system can detect ILDs as small as about 0.5 dB.

The head provides a more effective acoustic barrier for high-frequency sounds than low-frequency sounds. Recall from **Chapter 1** that high-frequency tones have a short wavelength, whereas low-frequency tones have a longer wavelength; for this reason, high-frequency tones can't bend around the head as easily as low-frequency tones. Therefore, less energy from a high-frequency tone reaches the opposite ear compared to a low-frequency tone. As a result, ILDs tend to be larger for sounds with higher frequencies.

Given that ILDs are most obvious for high-frequency sounds, one theory (put forward in the early 1900s) proposed that people rely more on ILDs for locating high-frequency sounds, and more on ITDs for locating low-frequency sounds (Rayleigh, 1907). This distinction seems to hold for pure tones, but it doesn't always apply to complex sounds (e.g. Moore, 2003). Given that people rarely encounter pure tones in everyday life, it's likely that people usually rely on *both* ITDs and ILDs to determine where sounds are coming from.

> The theory that asserts people rely on ITDs for low-frequency sounds and ILDs for high-frequency sounds is called 'duplex theory'.

When a sound is coming from either directly in front of you or directly behind you, it'll reach your left and right ears at the same time (i.e. with an ITD of zero) and with the same level (i.e. with an ILD of zero) (Figure 2.6(a) and (c)). Therefore, without other contextual cues (such as seeing the object that's making the sound), it can be difficult to work out whether a sound is in front of or behind you. In these instances, moving your head can help. If you turn your head to the right and the sound is behind you, it'll arrive a little sooner and

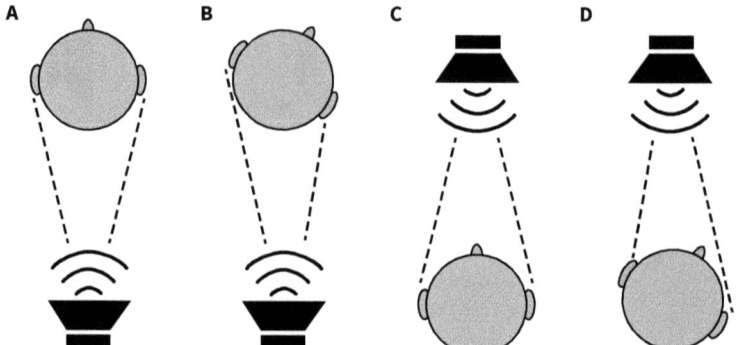

Figure 2.6 Sounds from directly behind or directly in front of a listener reach both ears at the same time, as shown in panels a and c. Therefore, the interaural time difference and interaural level difference are both zero. Turning the head to the side enables the listener to use interaural time and level differences because the sound will arrive a little sooner and will have a higher sound level at one ear than at the other. If you turn your head to the right and the sound is behind you, as shown in panel b, it will reach your right ear first and will have a higher sound level at your right ear. If you turn your head to the right and the sound is in front of you, as shown in panel d, it will reach your left ear first and will have a higher sound level at your left ear.

will have a higher sound level at your right ear than your left ear (Figure 2.6(b)); whereas if you turn your head to the right and the sound is in front of you, then it'll arrive a little sooner and will have a higher sound level at your left ear (Figure 2.6(d)).

2.2.3 Locating sounds vertically

The previous section considered how people locate sounds horizontally, but how do people work out whether a sound is coming from above or below ear level? ITDs and ILDs aren't useful for locating sounds vertically, because two sounds coming from the same direction (e.g. 30 degrees to your left) will have the same ITD and ILD as each other, even if one is above your head and the other is at ground level.

For any ITD, there are several places where the sound could be coming from. These together are known as the 'cone of confusion' (Figure 2.7). The cone of confusion typically describes ambiguities in location arising from the same ITD, although the cone of confusion probably applies to ILDs too. There are two ways people can resolve these types of ambiguities. First—like resolving the front–back ambiguities described above—head movements can help. If you tilt your head so that your right ear moves closer to the ground, the sound will arrive a little sooner and will have a higher sound level at your right than your left ear if the sound is below you, whereas the opposite will happen if the sound is above you. Second, the shape of the pinnae (the plural of pinna) changes the spectrum of sounds, which provides clues about a sound's location when ITDs and ILDs are ambiguous, even without moving the head.

You can review parts of the ear in **Chapter 1**.

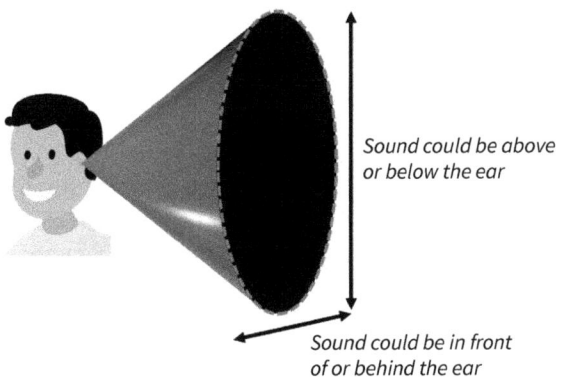

Figure 2.7 Cone of confusion. For a given interaural time difference, there are many possible locations where the sound could be coming from, which are indicated by the dashed line in the image.

You've probably noticed that the pinnae have curves and folds, but you might not have realised that this alters the spectra of sounds. In this way, the pinna acts like a filter—amplifying some frequencies and attenuating others. If you look at someone's ear, notice that the curves and folds of the pinna aren't symmetrical from top to bottom: for this reason, the pinna will filter a sound differently depending on whether the sound approaches the ear from below or from above (Figure 2.8). Previous experiments have shown that people rely on pinna filtering for locating sounds. For example, when people wear moulds that alter the curves and folds of their pinna (but still allow sounds through their ear canal), they find it difficult to tell whether a sound is coming from above or below; although, remarkably, if people continue to wear the moulds for a few weeks, their ability to locate sounds with the ear moulds gradually returns, as they adapt to the curves and folds in the mould (Hofman et al., 1998).

The size and shape of the head and body also contribute to the filtering of sounds.

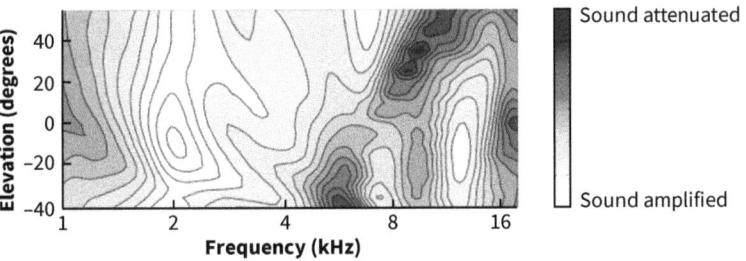

Figure 2.8 The pinna alters the spectra of sounds differently depending on the elevation of a sound. Notice, for example, how sounds between 8 and 16 kHz are attenuated when they are above the ear (i.e. positive elevations) but tend to be amplified for locations below the ear (i.e. negative elevations).

Source: adapted from Hofman, Van Riswick, & Van Opstal, (1998). 'Relearning sound localization with new ears.' *Nature Neuroscience*, 1(5), 417–421.

2.2.4 How close is a sound?

In everyday life, sounds aren't always stationary, so being able to tell whether a sound is close to you or far away can be helpful. For example, if a car is moving towards you, you might need to move out of the way! The level of a sound can help people to determine whether an object is close or far away, and if it's moving towards or away from them. When someone hears a car engine, they can probably tell whether it's far away or close to them, depending on how loud it sounds. If it's getting louder, the car is probably moving towards the person and they might need to move out of its way, whereas if it's getting quieter, then it's probably moving away from them and they can relax.

2.2.5 Locating sounds in reverberant places

If someone plays a sound from a loudspeaker in their kitchen, it'll reach their ears directly from the loudspeaker, but also indirectly by reflecting off the ceiling, walls, floor, and other items in the room (Figure 2.9). This creates a challenge for locating the sound—each reflection comes from a different direction, so how can people work out where the sound source is?

The auditory system utilises the fact that reflections are essentially repeats of the same sound, and the direct sound reaches the ear first, before the reflections. Researchers have examined how people integrate reflections by playing two identical short sounds, each from a different location and separated by a short delay. When the second sound is played up to 0.005 seconds after the first, people typically perceive a single sound coming from the location of the first sound. In other words, listeners consider the second sound to be a reflection of the first (Litovsky et al., 1999). This phenomenon is known as the **precedence effect**. If the delay is longer than 0.005 seconds, people are more likely to perceive two separate sounds,

Figure 2.9 Sounds reflect off surfaces within a room, so a sound can reach a listener's ear from multiple directions. The first sound to reach the ear is from the most direct route (solid line), whereas reflections of a sound (dashed lines) take longer to reach the ear. The auditory system works out that the later inputs to the ear are reflections of the first input, which allows people to perceive a single sound—such as one person playing a saxophone.

rather than a single sound with a reflection. Therefore, identical sounds are judged to be from the same source if the timing is plausible as a reflection, but are considered to be a repeating sound otherwise.

2.2.6 Coding location

So, how does the location of a sound affect brain responses? One influential theory is that the auditory system uses neuronal 'coincidence detectors' to determine a sound's location (Jeffress, 1948) (see Figure 2.10). Under this theory, neurons receive input from both ears and respond maximally when the inputs from both ears reach the neuron at the same time (i.e. when the inputs are coincident). Crucially, this theory proposes that different neurons receive inputs from the two ears with different delays. This means that different neurons respond maximally to different ITDs and are, therefore, tuned to different locations.

To get a sense of how this could work, imagine you're going to meet a friend for coffee along a street that has lots of cafés. Imagine you're travelling from the east end of the street and your friend is travelling from the west end of the street, and you decide to walk towards each other until you reach each other then go to the nearest café. If you set off at the same time from opposite ends of the street, you'll reach each other next to a café that's in the middle of the street. However, if your friend is delayed in setting off, then you would instead reach each other at a café that's closer to the west end of the street. In this analogy, you and your friend are the two signals travelling from the left and right ears, and the cafés are different neurons that are each sensitive to particular ITDs. Under the coincidence detector theory, the neurons that respond maximally depend on the ITD. Research in barn owls seems to be consistent with the idea that neurons receive input from the two ears with different delays, although this idea hasn't been supported by studies in humans (McAlpine & Grothe, 2003).

An alternative theory, known as 'opponent process theory', seems to be supported by studies that have measured brain activity in humans (Briley et al., 2013). Under opponent process theory, horizontal space is represented in the auditory system by two 'channels' made up of neurons that are sensitive to different ranges of ITDs (Figure 2.10(a) and (b)). One 'channel' responds more to sounds on the left and the other responds more to sounds on the right. As an analogy, imagine being at a football stadium when a goal is scored. If someone knew nothing about football, they might be able to work out which team had just scored a goal by comparing the responses of the fans in the stadium supporting the two teams. Similarly, under opponent process theory, the auditory system compares the responses of the two 'channels' of neurons to work out whether a sound is located towards the left or right. Yet, opponent process theory goes further than our football analogy because it assumes the auditory system compares the responses from the two channels to work out by *how much* to the left or right the sound is located.

A modification to opponent process theory introduces a third channel that responds more to sounds towards the midline (i.e. directly in front of the listener) (Figure 2.10(a) and (c)). To test this theory, researchers have examined how brain responses adapt to sounds presented from various directions, because neurons that respond strongly to a sound when it's first presented are known to respond less strongly if the same sound is repeated multiple times. Therefore, the patterns of brain responses that researchers observe to repeated sounds can shed light on the underlying neural processes. The two- and three-channel theories predict the

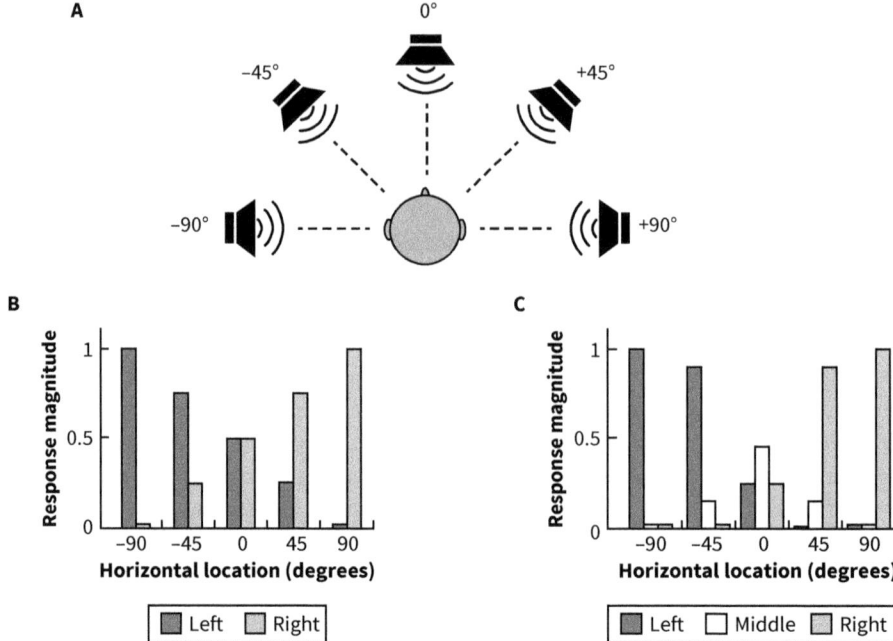

Figure 2.10 Opponent process theory for human sound localisation. Panel a shows a schematic of a listener surrounded by five loudspeakers from left (−90 degrees) to right (90 degrees). Panel b is an illustration of neuronal responses predicted by the two-channel opponent process theory, in response to sounds originating from the five locations shown in panel a: one channel responds more to sounds on the left and the other channel responds more to sounds on the right. Notice that the left channel responds more to sounds that are further to the left (i.e. −90 degrees) than those that are only slightly to the left (i.e. −45 degrees). In contrast, the right channel responds more to sounds that are further to the right. When the sound is directly in front of the listener (0 degrees) the responses of the two channels are equal. Panel c is an illustration of neuronal responses predicted by the three-channel opponent process theory, in which one channel responds more to sounds on the left, another channel responds more to sounds on the right, and a third channel responds more to sounds in the middle.

Source: data for panel B inferred from Briley, P. M., Kitterick, P. T., & Summerfield, A. Q. (2013). 'Evidence for opponent process analysis of sound source location in humans'. *JARO*, 14, 83–101. https://doi.org/10.1007/s10162-012-0356-x
data used in panel C inferred from Briley, P. M., Goman, A. M., & Summerfield, A. Q. (2016). 'Physiological evidence for a midline spatial channel in human auditory cortex'. *Journal of the Association for Research in Otolaryngology*, 17, 331–340. https://doi.org/10.1007/s10162-016-0571-y

same patterns of adaptation when sounds are presented repeatedly to the left and right sides: after sounds are presented repeatedly to the sides, responses to subsequent sounds on the sides should be reduced (because the left and right channels are stimulated by these sounds under both theories and adapt to reduce their responses). Yet, the theories make different predictions for brain responses to a sound directly in front of the listener depending on whether the previous sounds came from directly in front or to the sides. The three-channel model predicts that brain responses to the sound in front will be lowest when the previous sounds also came from in front, because the midline channel should adapt most for sounds in front; whereas the two-channel theory predicts that brain responses to the sound in front will be lowest when the previous sounds came from the sides, because the two-channel theory only has channels that are sensitive to the left or right sides—and these should adapt the most when previous sounds come from the sides (rather than from in front). The predictions of the three-channel theory are supported by findings in humans (Briley et al., 2016), although precisely how information from three channels is combined to determine sound location remains unclear.

> The adaptation of neuronal responses described here is known as 'stimulus-specific adaptation' and has been used to study many different characteristics of sounds (Song et al., 2023), and neural responses in other sensory modalities, such as vision.

Opponent process theories have been criticised for being too simplistic and not accounting for some findings that demonstrate varied neuronal responses depending on the task and stimuli. For example, neural recordings in monkeys have shown that individual neurons exhibit different responses when there are multiple sounds, compared to when a sound is presented alone (Caruso et al., 2018). In addition, recordings in cats have shown that a single neuron that responds indiscriminately to sounds from any location when the cat isn't engaged in a task can respond more selectively when the cat's task is to localise the sound (Middlebrooks, 2021). A study in humans also demonstrates that location tuning is affected by attention: different responses were observed when the listener was passively listening to sounds compared to when they were selectively attending to one location (Ozmeral et al., 2021). As a result, there is still lively debate about how humans localise sounds, particularly in complex listening situations.

2.3 Pitch

Pitch is perhaps one of the most intriguing aspects of sound. Most people intuitively know what pitch is when they hear it, but it can be difficult to describe in words. Despite this, the ability to perceive pitch underlies the perception of melodies in music (e.g. working out if someone is singing 'Happy Birthday' or 'Twinkle, Twinkle, Little Star') and it conveys a wealth of information about the nature of a sound source—for example, large adult lions make a deeper, lower-pitched roar than small young lions. Despite its fundamental nature, the perception of pitch is quite complex. This section describes which properties of sounds influence the perception of pitch and provides an overview of how pitch might be represented in the auditory pathway.

2.3.1 What is pitch?

Pitch is a sensation by which we describe sounds as being on a scale from low to high: compare rumbling thunder to a squeaky whistle, a man's deep voice to a child's cry, and a double bass to a violin. Like loudness, pitch is an aspect of perception rather than a physical attribute of sound.

2.3.2 The relationship between pitch and sound attributes

The sensation of pitch is closely related to the physical attribute of frequency. Recall from **Chapter 1** that pure tones only contain one frequency. For pure tones, pitch is intimately related to frequency—when the frequency of a pure tone is higher, most people perceive its pitch to be higher.

For example, most people would perceive a 300-Hz tone as sounding the highest, and a 200-Hz tone as sounding higher than a 100-Hz tone.

What happens if a sound contains more than one frequency, like a complex tone? When people listen to a complex tone that contains three frequencies, they don't tend to hear three separate pitches: instead, they usually get a sensation of a single pitch.

> Recall from **Chapter 1** that many sounds are complex tones, like the sounds played by musical instruments.

To understand why this is, you first need to understand a bit more about complex tones. A type of complex tone is a **harmonic complex tone**. For a complex tone to be *harmonic*, all of its frequencies must be integer multiples of a single **fundamental frequency** (which is the number of times its entire waveform repeats in 1 second). When frequencies are integer multiples of a common frequency, we say they're harmonically related. We can assign numbers to the frequencies, based on their position in the harmonic series. Suppose that a harmonic complex tone contains frequencies of 100, 200, and 300 Hz (see Figure 1.9). The fundamental frequency is the first harmonic (100 Hz), two times the fundamental frequency is the second harmonic (200 Hz), three times the fundamental frequency is the third harmonic (300 Hz), and so on. The pitch of a harmonic complex tone is closely related to its fundamental frequency, and that's why the pitch of the example complex tone above sounds most similar to the pitch of the 100-Hz pure tone.

To complicate matters, not all the harmonics need to be present—not even the first one (i.e. the fundamental frequency)—for a sound to be a harmonic complex tone. For example, a harmonic complex tone with a fundamental frequency of 400 Hz could contain 400, 800, 2000, 2400, and 2800 Hz (Figure 2.11(a)); or, it could contain 1200, 2000, 2400, and 2800 Hz (Figure 2.11(b)). Both examples have a fundamental frequency of 400 Hz, but the first example contains harmonics 1, 2, 5, 6, and 7, whereas the second example contains harmonics 3, 5, 6, and 7.

> The sounds in Figure 2.11(a) and (b) have different spectra, so we can say they have different timbres: even though they are usually perceived as having the same pitch, the two sounds are usually perceived as having different qualities.

We can work out a sound's fundamental frequency by calculating the greatest common factor of its frequencies. The greatest common factor is the largest number by which all the frequencies are exactly divisible (i.e. with no remainder or decimal places). The greatest common factor of 400, 800, 2000, 2400, and 2800 Hz (Figure 2.11(a)) is 400 Hz, and the greatest common factor of 1200, 2000, 2400, and 2800 Hz (Figure 2.11(b)) is also 400 Hz.

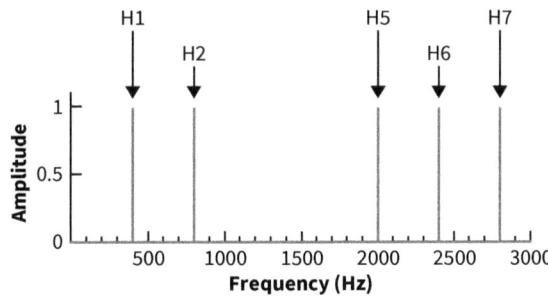

Figure 2.11(a) Spectrum of a harmonic complex tone. The harmonic complex tone in panel a contains the first harmonic (H1)—which is the same as the fundamental frequency (400 Hz)—and the second (H2), fifth (H5), sixth (H6), and seventh (H7) harmonics.

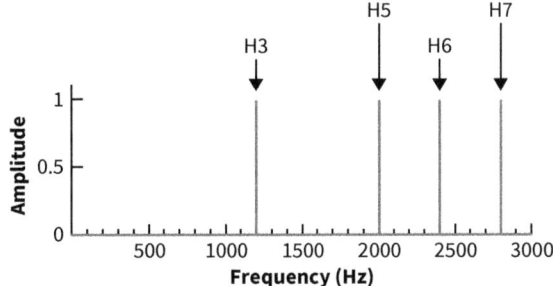

Figure 2.11(b) Spectrum of a harmonic complex tone. The two tones in panels a and b both have a fundamental frequency of 400 Hz but differ in which harmonics are present. Panel b doesn't contain the first harmonic (the fundamental frequency); it contains the third (H3), fifth (H5), sixth (H6), and seventh (H7) harmonics. The harmonic complex tone in panel c has a fundamental frequency of 500 Hz and contains the second (H2), third (H3), fifth (H5), and sixth (H6) harmonics.

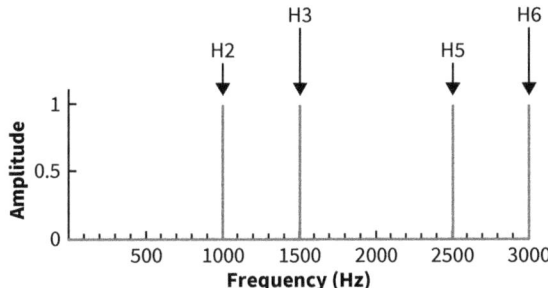

Figure 2.11(c) Spectrum of a harmonic complex tone. This harmonic complex tone has a fundamental frequency of 500 Hz and contains the second (H2), third (H3), fifth (H5), and sixth (H6) harmonics. Due to its higher fundamental frequency, the pitch of the harmonic complex tone that's shown in panel c is usually perceived as being higher than the pitch of the tone that's shown in panels a and b.

Even when the first harmonic (i.e. the fundamental frequency) is missing from the sound, it's still possible to hear its pitch. Therefore, the perception of pitch doesn't require the first harmonic to be present.

The 'pitch of the missing fundamental' is a phenomenon that refers to the pitch of a sound being the same when the fundamental frequency is removed.

If we increase the greatest common factor of the harmonic frequencies, people usually perceive the pitch of the sound as increasing—such as a musical scale that progresses from low to high notes. Crucially, the pitch increases if we increase the greatest common factor of the harmonics *even if the lowest harmonic that's present in the tone goes down*. For example, the lowest harmonic in Figure 2.11(b) is 1200 Hz and the lowest harmonic in Figure 2.11(c) is 1000 Hz, yet the pitch of the tone in Figure 2.11(c) is *higher* than the tone in Figure 2.11(b), because the greatest common factor is 500 Hz (rather than 400 Hz).

If the frequencies within a complex tone don't follow a harmonic series (i.e. they're not all integer multiples of a fundamental frequency), we say the tone is **inharmonic**. A common example is when all the harmonics within a harmonic complex tone have been shifted by a small amount. Returning to the example in Figure 2.11(a), shifting all of the components by 5 Hz would result in components at 405 Hz, 805 Hz, and so on. We can describe the extent of a tone's **inharmonicity** by the amount that the frequencies differ from integer multiples of a fundamental frequency: in this example, they differ by 5 Hz. Studies have also investigated the role of inharmonicity in pitch perception by shifting a single frequency in a harmonic complex tone by different amounts. If an individual harmonic is shifted by more than 3%, people typically perceive the shifted harmonic as a separate tone, and also perceive two pitches rather than one. Thus, inharmonicity can influence pitch perception.

> For more detail about perceiving multiple sounds, see **Chapter 3**.

In addition to changing inharmonicity, researchers have examined how changing other aspects of sounds affects pitch perception (Further insights 2.3).

Further insights 2.3   How do temporal fine structure and envelope affect pitch perception?

Imagine pouring beads into a container: their appearance is influenced by both the size of the beads and the size and shape of the container. In a similar way, sounds depend on two different aspects. Comparable to the size of the beads in a container, a sound contains rapid changes in amplitude, which is determined by the frequencies in the sound. These rapid changes in amplitude are called the **temporal fine structure** (the solid line in Figure 2.12). **Chapter 1** describes different types of temporal fine structure, which depend on the frequencies in a pure tone or a harmonic complex tone. The temporal fine structure is so rapid that people don't perceive these changes in amplitude. However,

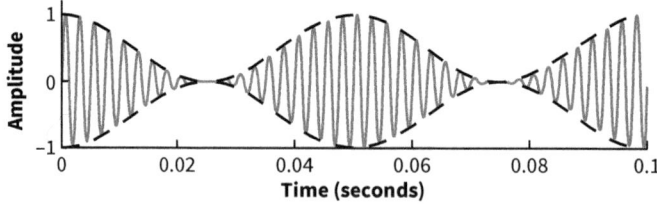

Figure 2.12 Time series representation of an amplitude-modulated tone (solid line) with the amplitude envelope overlaid as a dashed line. The rapid change in the amplitude of the sound (the solid line) is known as the temporal fine structure.

the amplitude is also affected by the **envelope** of the sound (dashed line in Figure 2.12), which is comparable to the size and shape of the container into which you imagined pouring beads. Most of the sounds described in **Chapter 1** have a flat envelope—in other words, the amplitude of the envelope is constant. However, an amplitude-modulated tone—like that illustrated in Figure 2.12—has an envelope that isn't flat. Like the beads and the container, the envelope and temporal fine structure of a sound are separable. Researchers have used this idea to ask: How do the temporal fine structure and envelope of a sound contribute to the perception of its pitch?

Researchers have examined how a sound's envelope and temporal fine structure contribute to people's perception of pitch by artificially manipulating sounds, so that the envelope of one sound is combined with the temporal fine structure of a different sound. When the temporal fine structure of one melody is paired with the envelope of another melody, people predominantly identify the melody as being that which the temporal fine structure came from (Smith et al., 2002). This result suggests that temporal fine structure provides important information for pitch perception, whereas the envelope has little effect on a sound's pitch.

2.3.3 Coding pitch

Humans can typically hear sounds that have frequencies between 20 and 20,000 Hz, but usually only perceive pitch between 30 and 5,000 Hz (Oxenham, 2013). Section 2.3.2 described how people can estimate the pitch of a complex tone by working out the greatest common factor of its harmonics—but, given that the auditory system doesn't have access to a spectrum plot like those in Figure 2.11, how do people perceive pitch? For many years, researchers have studied how the auditory system represents the pitch of sounds—and, even today, there's lively debate on this topic. This section introduces two key theories: 'place' theory and 'temporal' theory. Each theory makes different predictions. This section describes how researchers have tested these two theories by pitting them against each other.

Recall from **Chapter 1** that different places along the basilar membrane respond most strongly to different characteristic frequencies. Place theory suggests that pitch is determined by the 'places' along the basilar membrane that vibrate the most in response to the harmonics of a sound (which then pass on to specific 'places' in the auditory nerve).

When the fundamental frequency is present in the sound, the fundamental frequency would be easily accessible under place theory, because the place on the basilar membrane that responds best to that frequency will respond strongly. Place coding would be a straightforward way to perceive pitch. But what if the fundamental frequency isn't present in a sound? Recall from Section 2.3.2 that people can still perceive pitch for sounds that don't contain the first harmonic, so how would place theory account for this finding? Place theory assumes that people must be able to use the 'places' of other harmonics within the sound to perceive pitch. So, we can test this theory by asking: What happens when researchers reduce the availability of place information for other harmonics?

We can reduce place information by removing most of the lower harmonics within a sound. Frequency selectivity in the cochlea is often conceptualised with a series of auditory filters that detect harmonics within a certain range of frequencies—and the range of frequencies within each filter gets broader at higher frequencies (Figure 2.13(a)). Imagine going to watch a weight-lifting competition that includes competitors of a wide variety of ages. There will probably be different categories for different age groups: the age

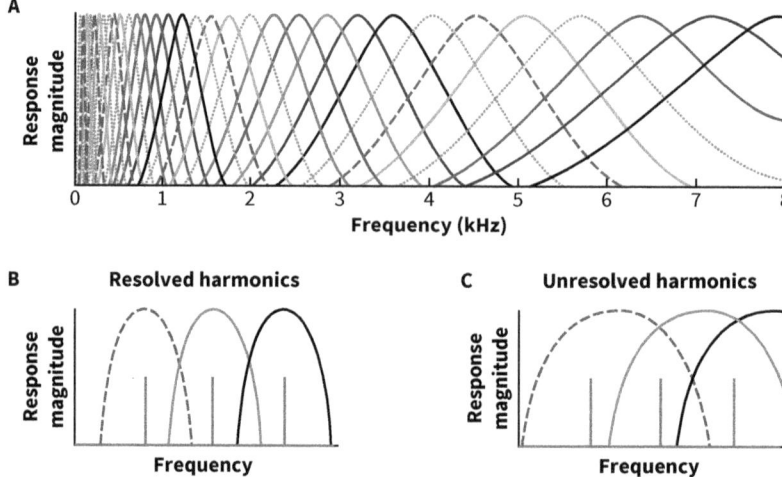

Figure 2.13 Panel a illustrates auditory filters across frequency: each curve represents one filter. Notice how the filters become wider with increasing frequency. Panels b and c illustrate zoomed-in versions of auditory filters at lower and higher frequencies, respectively. Notice that, in panel b, each harmonic (solid vertical lines) is detected by a different filter (curves), and they are, therefore, resolved—whereas in panel c, each filter contains multiple harmonics and, therefore, the harmonics are unresolved.

brackets might be quite narrow for the youngest competitors (e.g. ages 8–10 and 11–13), but wider for older competitors (e.g. ages 18–25, 26–30, and 31–45). Therefore, for any competitor in the younger group, you could guess their age quite precisely, whereas you might have a harder time determining the precise age of a competitor in one of the older groups (e.g. in the 31–45 group). In a similar vein, lower harmonics are each 'detected' by separate auditory filters and are therefore represented quite precisely by place information—these are known as *resolved* harmonics (Figure 2.13(b)). In contrast, because the filters are broader at higher frequencies, several higher harmonics are detected by the same auditory filter; therefore, the place representations of higher harmonics are not as precise and these are known as *unresolved* harmonics (Figure 2.13(c)). In other words, for resolved harmonics place cues are available, whereas for unresolved harmonics place cues aren't available. So, we can test whether place information is essential for pitch perception by presenting sounds that only contain higher, unresolved harmonics. Interestingly, people can still hear differences in pitch between two tones that are closer in frequency than could possibly be resolved through a place representation alone (Plack et al., 2014), which contradicts place theory.

In contrast to place theory, temporal theory proposes that the *timing* of auditory nerve responses gives rise to pitch. Recall from **Chapter 1** that the vibrations of the basilar membrane are converted to electrical signals by the movement of stereocilia. Importantly, the electrical signals are only generated at a specific time (or **phase**) of the sound wave. Temporal theory proposes that this timing information gives rise to pitch.

Generally, listeners perceive pitch up to around 5 kHz, which seems to support temporal theory, because this corresponds to the supposed upper limit of phase locking. To get a sense for why phase locking would be limited, try clapping your hands once per second; then, increase the rate of clapping, so that you're clapping your hands twice a second, then four times a second ... What's the fastest rate that you can clap at? At some point, the rate will be too fast for you to continue. Similarly, there's a limit to how fast electrical signals can be generated from phase locking.

> Recall from **Chapter 1** that electrical signals are only generated at a specific phase of the sound—a concept known as phase locking.

We can measure phase locking by recording directly from neurons, although this is too invasive to measure in humans. Research in animals has shown that phase locking has an upper limit, and the limit is believed to be around 4–5 kHz in humans (Oxenham et al., 2011). While this seems to correspond to humans perceiving pitch up to around 5 kHz, some research has shown that it is still possible for humans to perceive pitch for sounds that only contain harmonics above 5 kHz (see e.g. Oxenham et al., 2011). This result suggests that either temporal information isn't needed to perceive pitch, or that the upper limit of phase locking in humans is higher than currently believed, which still remains to be resolved.

Ultimately, neither the place theory nor the temporal theory of pitch perception can fully explain the perception of pitch. Possibly, the auditory system makes use of both place and timing information for pitch, and could be supplemented with other mechanisms for determining pitch that don't rely on the greatest common factor (Further insights 2.4).

> **Further Insights 2.4   Multiple methods for perceiving pitch**
>
> Research using inharmonic sounds has revealed that humans likely use different methods for perceiving pitch, depending on the task that they're carrying out (McPherson & McDermott, 2018). Working out a sound's fundamental frequency by calculating the greatest common factor of its frequencies is one method. We know this method is important, because people are better at recognising other people's voices and identifying musical intervals from harmonic sounds (in which the harmonics are all integer multiples of the sound's fundamental frequency, so the greatest common factor can be calculated), compared to inharmonic sounds (in which the harmonics do not all have a discernible common factor). Nevertheless, people might not always need to work out a sound's fundamental frequency to perceive its pitch. When listeners are asked to simply detect a *change* in pitch (like detecting whether one musical note is higher or lower in pitch than another), their performance isn't any worse for inharmonic sounds than for harmonic sounds—which suggests that they might be tracking the spectral pattern (i.e. the amplitudes of the frequencies within the sound) to infer pitch, rather than relying on calculating the sound's fundamental frequency. Furthermore, listeners can still detect pitch changes when sounds have no fundamental frequency and no consistent spectral pattern, which implies they could be using another method to infer pitch—although the specific method remains to be determined.

2.3.4 Pitch and the brain

Recall from **Chapter 1** that frequency is a major organising principle of the auditory pathway. Frequency information is present all the way from the cochlea to auditory cortex, which contains 'maps' of neurons that are organised by frequency (Humphries et al., 2010). Yet, remember that frequency and pitch are not the same: frequency is an attribute of sound whereas pitch is a *perception* of sound. So, researchers have asked: Is the sensation of pitch represented in the brain?

> This spatial arrangement of neurons by frequency is known as tonotopic organisation and it is present throughout the auditory pathway.

One of the challenges of searching for pitch responses in the auditory pathway is that researchers need to show that neurons aren't simply responding to physical stimulus attributes, such as frequency—which can be difficult to rule out, because pitch is closely related to frequency (see Section 2.3.2).

One way to approach this question is to look for evidence that's consistent with the ways in which pitch could be computed. For example, researchers have examined evidence for phase locking, as proposed by the temporal theory of pitch perception (Section 2.3.3). This research has shown that timing information from phase locking at the auditory nerve seems to be maintained as far as the brainstem, but neurons in the cortex do not seem to phase lock to frequencies above about 200 Hz (Oxenham, 2023). Thus, timing information from phase locking (at least for higher frequencies) might need to be converted into a different type of code to be processed at higher stages—although researchers don't yet know if (or how) this happens (Oxenham, 2018).

Another way to approach the question is based upon the fact that information from the two ears isn't combined until the superior olive (which is in the brainstem). Researchers have examined what percept is elicited when different sounds are presented to the left and right ears, that don't elicit a pitch percept individually, but would do when they're presented together; for example, white noise doesn't have a discernible pitch.

We can create different versions of white noise by changing the phase of some of the frequencies contained within it. Interestingly, if you present two different versions of white noise (that are identical except for a narrow range of frequencies that differ in phase) at the same time—one to the right ear and the other to the left ear—most people will hear a clear pitch, that sounds like a pure tone, within the noise. This is quite incredible, because each stimulus on its own does not elicit a clear pitch—yet, when presented together, most people hear a clear pitch percept, which is known as 'Huggins pitch' (Gockel et al., 2011). This phenomenon implies that pitch is processed in the auditory pathway after information from the right and left ears is combined, which happens at the superior olive. Therefore, pitch is probably computed at the superior olive or further along the auditory pathway. **Chapter 1** provides you an overview of the auditory pathway.

Over the years, researchers have found it difficult to identify a specific area that processes pitch (and not frequency), so one idea is that pitch may not be computed in a single brain area, but may instead be processed more broadly across brain regions (Bizley & Cohen, 2013). Yet, some neuroimaging studies provide evidence that some parts of the brain might contain pitch 'maps', in which pitch is represented in an orderly way. Lateral parts of Heschl's gyrus and planum temporale respond more to sounds that elicit a strong pitch percept than those that elicit a weaker pitch percept, which has led researchers to suggest that these areas might constitute a 'pitch centre' in the brain.

In one study, researchers compared responses to harmonic complex tones and noise in auditory cortex (Norman-Haignere et al., 2013). They found that anterior parts of auditory cortex responded more to harmonic complex tones than to noise. In addition, responses

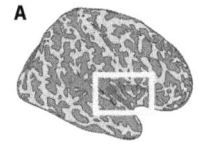 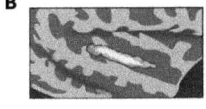 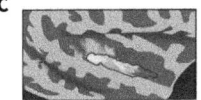

25% 50%
Percentage of participants that have a pitch response in this area

0.2 kHz 6.4 kHz
Frequency of maximum response

Figure 2.14 Cortical pitch and frequency responses. Panel a shows an outline of the area of the brain displayed in panels b and c. Panel b shows the percentage of participants with a response to pitch (i.e. a greater response to resolved harmonics than noise) in each area. In panel c, the pitch responsive area (black outline) shown in panel b is displayed in relation to the frequency preferences of areas in auditory cortex. Notice how the pitch responsive region overlaps partially with areas that respond to lower frequencies. Only the right hemisphere is displayed in the figure, but a similar pattern of results is observed in the left hemisphere.

Source: panels b and c adapted from Norman-Haignere et al. (2013). 'Cortical pitch regions in humans respond primarily to resolved harmonics and are located in specific tonotopic regions of anterior auditory cortex.' *Journal of Neuroscience*, 33(50), 19451–19469. https://doi.org/10.1523/JNEUROSCI.2880-13.2013

in these areas were much stronger when the complex tones contained resolved harmonics (which typically elicit a stronger pitch percept) compared to only unresolved harmonics (which typically elicit a weaker pitch percept) (Figure 2.14(a) and (b)). Both of these findings are consistent with the idea that these areas are sensitive to pitch. The location of these areas partially overlaps with tonotopic maps of frequency in auditory cortex (Figure 2.14(a) and (c)). Another study that carefully controlled for variations in spectra between sounds also found pitch-selective responses in auditory cortex—providing further evidence that these areas are responding to pitch rather than to frequency (Allen et al., 2022).

> Recall from **Section 2.3.3** that resolved harmonics are those that are detected by separate auditory filters and are therefore represented quite precisely by place information.

Summary

Loudness, location, and pitch are fundamental aspects of auditory perception. If you can hear someone playing a piano, you're probably aware of how loud it is, where the sound is coming from, and whether it forms a melody containing high and low notes. Interestingly, while these sensations are related to physical attributes of sounds, they don't simply reflect a single attribute. For example, loudness scales with a sound's intensity, but it's also affected by the frequency and duration of the sound. Researchers have sought to uncover the 'code' that the auditory pathway uses to determine these fundamental perceptual phenomena—and have made decent progress—although there's still a lot to discover about how the auditory pathway represents these fundamental aspects of hearing.

Further your understanding

Akeroyd, M. (2006). 'The psychoacoustics of binaural hearing.' *International Journal of Audiology*, 45 (Supplement 1), S25–S33.

Plack, C. (2018). Chapter 7, 'Pitch and Periodicity Coding.' In *The Sense of Hearing* (third edn). Abingdon and New York: Routledge.

References

Allen, E. J., Mesik, J., Kay, K. N., & Oxenham, A. J. (2022). 'Distinct representations of tonotopy and pitch in human auditory cortex.' *Journal of Neuroscience*, 42(3), 416–434. https://doi.org/10.1523/JNEUROSCI.0960-21.2021

Auerbach, B. D., & Gritton, H. J. (2022). 'Hearing in complex environments: Auditory gain control, attention, and hearing loss.' In *Frontiers in Neuroscience* (Vol. 16). Frontiers Media SA https://doi.org/10.3389/fnins.2022.799787

Behler, O., & Uppenkamp, S. (2016). 'The representation of level and loudness in the central auditory system for unilateral stimulation.' *NeuroImage*, 139, 176–188. https://doi.org/10.1016/J.NEUROIMAGE.2016.06.025

Bizley, J. K., & Cohen, Y. E. (2013). 'The what, where and how of auditory-object perception.' *Nature Reviews Neuroscience*, 14(10), 693–707. https://doi.org/10.1038/nrn3565

Briley, P. M., Goman, A. M., & Summerfield, A. Q. (2016). 'Physiological evidence for a midline spatial channel in human auditory cortex.' *JARO—Journal of the Association for Research in Otolaryngology*, 17(4), 331–340. https://doi.org/10.1007/s10162-016-0571-y

Briley, P. M., Kitterick, P. T., & Summerfield, A. Q. (2013). 'Evidence for opponent process analysis of sound source location in humans.' *JARO—Journal of the Association for Research in Otolaryngology*, 14(1), 83–101. https://doi.org/10.1007/s10162-012-0356-x

Caruso, V. C., Mohl, J. T., Glynn, C., Lee, J., Willett, S. M., Zaman, A., Ebihara, A. F., Estrada, R., Freiwald, W. A., Tokdar, S. T., & Groh, J. M. (2018). 'Single neurons may encode simultaneous stimuli by switching between activity patterns.' *Nature Communications*, 9(1). https://doi.org/10.1038/s41467-018-05121-8

Epstein, M., & Florentine, M. (2005). 'A test of the equal-loudness-ratio hypothesis using cross-modality matching functions.' *Journal of the Acoustical Society of America*, 118(2), 907–913. https://doi.org/10.1121/1.1954547

Epstein, M., & Florentine, M. (2006). 'Loudness of brief tones measured by magnitude estimation and loudness matching.' *Journal of the Acoustical Society of America*, 119(4), 1943–1945. https://doi.org/10.1121/1.2177592

Gockel, H. E., Carlyon, R. P., & Plack, C. J. (2011). 'Combination of spectral and binaurally created harmonics in a common central pitch processor.' *JARO—Journal of the Association for Research in Otolaryngology*, 12(2), 253–260. https://doi.org/10.1007/s10162-010-0250-3

Grantham, D. W. (1995). 'Spatial hearing and related phenomena.' In Moore, B. C. J. (ed.) *Hearing* (pp. 297–345). San Diego, CA: Academic Press. https://doi.org/10.1016/B978-012505626-7/50011-X

Hofman, P. M., Van Riswick, J. G. A., & Van Opstal, A. J. (1998). 'Relearning sound localization with new ears.' *Nature Neuroscience*, 1(5), 417–421. https://doi.org/10.1038/1633

Humphries, C., Liebenthal, E., & Binder, J. R. (2010). 'Tonotopic organization of human auditory cortex.' *NeuroImage*, 50(3), 1202–1211. https://doi.org/10.1016/j.neuroimage.2010.01.046

Jeffress, L. A. (1948). 'A place theory of sound localization.' *Journal of Comparative and Physiological Psychology*, 41(1), 35–39. https://doi.org/10.1037/h0061495

Litovsky, R. Y., & Macmillan, N. A. (1994). 'Sound localization precision under conditions of the precedence effect: Effects of azimuth and standard stimuli.' *Journal of the Acoustical Society of America*, 96, 752–758. https://doi.org/10.1121/1.411390

Litovsky, R. Y., Colburn, H. S., Yost, W. A., & Guzman, S. J. (1999). 'The precedence effect.' *Journal of the Acoustical Society of America*, 106(4), 1633–1654. https://doi.org/10.1121/1.427914

McAlpine, D., & Grothe, B. (2003). 'Sound localization and delay lines—Do mammals fit the model?' *Trends in Neurosciences*, 26(7), 347–350. https://doi.org/10.1016/S0166-2236(03)00140-1

McPherson, M. J., & McDermott, J. H. (2018). 'Diversity in pitch perception revealed by task dependence.' *Nature Human Behaviour*, 2, 52–66. http://dx.doi.org/10.1038/s41562-017-0261-8

Middlebrooks, J. C. (2021). 'A search for a cortical map of auditory space.' *Journal of Neuroscience*, 41(27), 5772–5778. https://doi.org/10.1523/JNEUROSCI.0501-21.2021

Moore, B. C. J. (2003). *An Introduction to the Psychology of Hearing*. Leiden: Academic Press.

Natarajan, N., Batts, S., & Stankovic, K. M. (2023). 'Noise-induced hearing loss.' In *Journal of Clinical Medicine*, 12(6), 2347. https://doi.org/10.3390/jcm12062347

Norman-Haignere, S., Kanwisher, N., & McDermott, J. H. (2013). 'Cortical pitch regions in humans respond primarily to resolved harmonics and are located in specific tonotopic regions of anterior auditory cortex.' *Journal of Neuroscience*, 33(50), 19451–19469. https://doi.org/10.1523/JNEUROSCI.2880-13.2013

Oxenham, A. J. (2013). 'Revisiting place and temporal theories of pitch.' *Acoustical Science and Technology*, 34(6), 388–396. https://doi.org/10.1250/ast.34.388

Oxenham, A. J. (2018). 'How we hear: The perception and neural coding of sound.' *Annual Review of Psychology*, 69(1), 27–50. https://doi.org/10.1146/annurev-psych-122216-011635

Oxenham, A. J. (2023). 'Questions and controversies surrounding the perception and neural coding of pitch.' *Frontiers in Neuroscience*, 16. https://doi.org/10.3389/fnins.2022.1074752

Oxenham, A. J., Micheyl, C., Keebler, M. V, Loper, A., & Santurette, S. (2011). 'Pitch perception beyond the traditional existence region of pitch.' *Proceedings of the National Academy of Sciences of the United States of America*, 108(18), 7629–7634. https://doi.org/10.1073/pnas.1015291108

Ozmeral, E. J., Eddins, D. A., & Eddins, A. C. (2021). 'Selective auditory attention modulates cortical responses to sound location change in younger and older adults.' *Journal of Neurophysiology*, 126(3), 803–815. https://doi.org/10.1152/jn.00609.2020

Perrott, D. R., & Saberi, K. (1990). 'Minimum audible angle thresholds for sources varying in both elevation and azimuth.' *Journal of the Acoustical Society of America*, 87(4), 1728–1731. https://doi.org/10.1121/1.399421

Plack, C. J., Barker, D., & Hall, D. A. (2014). 'Pitch coding and pitch processing in the human brain.' *Hearing Research*, 307, 53–64. https://doi.org/10.1016/j.heares.2013.07.020

Rayleigh, L. (1907). 'On our perception of sound direction.' *Philosophical Magazine Series 6*, 13(74), 214–232.

Smith, Z. M., Delgutte, B., & Oxenham, A. J. (2002). 'Chimaeric sounds reveal dichotomies in auditory perception.' *Nature*, 416(6876), 87–90. https://doi.org/10.1038/416087a

Song, P., Zhai, Y., & Yu, X. (2023). 'Stimulus-specific adaptation (SSA) in the auditory system: Functional relevance and underlying mechanisms.' *Neuroscience and Biobehavioral Reviews*, 149, 105190. https://doi.org/10.1016/j.neubiorev.2023.105190

Uppenkamp, S., & Röhl, M. (2014). 'Human auditory neuroimaging of intensity and loudness.' *Hearing Research*, 307, 65–73. https://doi.org/10.1016/j.heares.2013.08.005

Perceiving Multiple Sounds

So far, this book has focused on individual sounds—but how do people perceive multiple sounds? Recall from **Chapter 1** that the source of sound is an object that vibrates. What if several objects vibrate at the same time? For example, a car engine, a drill digging up a road, and an aeroplane flying overhead, all at the same time. Each object that vibrates produces sound pressure waves, but the sound pressure waves from different objects don't arrive separately at the ears. Instead, the waves from all sources arrive together—and the auditory system faces the challenge of teasing apart which parts of sounds belong to different objects. This chapter examines the different ways that people group sounds together—or perceive them separately—and how this might be accomplished by the auditory system.

> You can review sound pressure waves in **Chapter 1**.

3.1 The challenge of overlapping sounds

One challenge faced by the auditory system is separating the sources of the sounds that reach the ears, when multiple objects are vibrating at the same time. Another challenge is that most objects produce multiple vibrations that continue over time. Imagine a phone ringing. How does someone link the second ring with the first, or work out when the phone has stopped ringing? Ultimately, the auditory system has to make a best guess about the sources of the sounds. This section explains what determines how people perceive the sources of multiple sounds.

3.1.1 Assigning sounds to sources

Imagine you're given a box that contains the pieces of two different jigsaw puzzles. To construct the two puzzles, you would need to work out which pieces belong to one puzzle and which pieces belong to the other puzzle. The auditory system faces a challenge like this on a daily basis: the ears receive a mixture of sounds that are overlapping and the goal is to work out what sounds are present (Figure 3.1). This involves **grouping** (i.e. assigning to the same source) components of sounds that go together, and **segregating** (i.e. assigning to separate sources) components of sounds that belong to different sources. For example, if someone is in a café, they might want to group components of sounds that all belong to background music that's playing from a

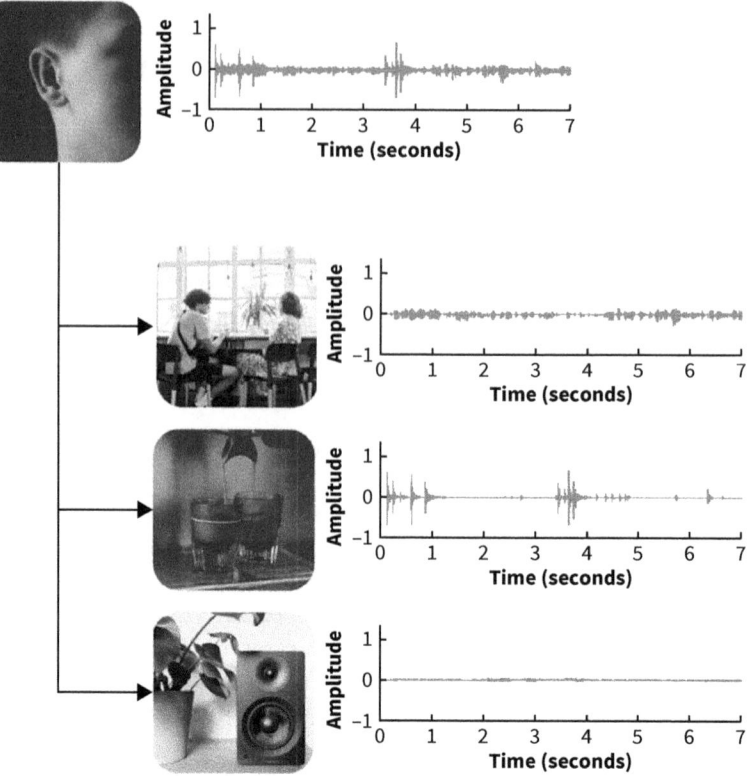

Figure 3.1 Example of the challenge faced by the auditory system when multiple sounds are present in our surroundings. The ears receive a mixture of sounds (left panel) and the auditory system is faced with the task of working out which objects are present in the environment (right panels). In a café, this could include the chatter of other people talking (upper right panel), the sounds of glasses knocking together (middle right panel), and some background music (lower right panel).

loudspeaker, and segregate them from the sounds of glasses knocking together in the kitchen (Figure 3.1). Grouping and segregation are two sides of the same coin, because segregating one sound from another means that they aren't grouped. Together, they are known as **perceptual organisation**. Another term that's commonly used to refer to grouping and segregating sounds is **auditory scene analysis** (Bregman, 1990).

> In visual perception, several Gestalt principles have been used to describe visual scene analysis, including the principles of 'proximity', 'similarity', and 'common fate'. Some aspects of auditory scene analysis can be considered as analogous to Gestalt principles for visual scene analysis, although there's no perfect correspondence. Nevertheless, researchers commonly assume that the goal of both auditory and visual scene analysis is to infer the simplest and most accurate explanation of sensory information, and rely on certain heuristics. In this chapter, we make some links to relevant principles of visual scene analysis.

3.1.2 Dealing with ambiguity

The challenge faced by the auditory system is more complex than sorting the pieces of two different jigsaw puzzles; sounds vary in many ways (e.g. location, intensity), so there are infinite combinations of sources that could have produced any sound wave that reaches the ears. In other words, the sound pressure wave that reaches the ears is ambiguous and doesn't tell someone exactly which objects vibrated.

> You can review location and intensity in **Chapter 2**.

To appreciate the scale of this challenge, imagine being given a box that contains pieces from lots of different jigsaw puzzles. There could be three, four, or many more different puzzles in the box, but you're not told how many; in addition, some of the jigsaw pieces are missing or damaged. It would be very difficult to sort the pieces into separate puzzles! Similarly, the auditory system isn't told how many different objects are vibrating in its surroundings, and often, different sounds occur at the same time. Further, some sounds are much louder than others, and can partially hide quieter sounds; these quieter sounds are a bit like pieces of a puzzle that are missing or damaged. Fortunately, the auditory system is quite good at guessing the sources of sounds when it's presented with a sound wave, and it can do so extremely quickly.

Sometimes, there are several guesses that make sense. When constructing a jigsaw puzzle, you might be able to make a piece fit in several different places. Depending on where you choose to place it, you might change the picture that you're constructing. Often, parts of sounds can be put in different places too (i.e. they can be grouped differently) and this can change someone's perception of the sounds in their surroundings. For example, a bird may chirp once or three times in succession: if someone hears three chirps in a row, they could either perceive this as one bird chirping three times, or as three different birds that each chirp once.

3.1.3 Focusing on one sound

It would be very difficult to enjoy a party if you listened carefully to every sound around you. Most often, people aren't aware of all of the sounds that are going on around them. Take a moment now to actively listen to each of the sounds you can hear. Even if you're in a quiet room, you might be able to hear a clock ticking, a fan whirring, or birds or traffic outside. At a party, someone might hear the sounds of glasses knocking together, people talking, and music playing—and they might only want to focus on one of these sounds at a time. For example, sometimes they might want to listen to a friend who's talking to them, whereas other times they might want to listen to their favourite song. Generally, people can focus on a sound within a mixture by directing their attention towards it.

> Attention isn't a single entity and **Chapter 5** revisits attention in the context of perceiving speech in noisy places—which is a more natural setting in which people encounter multiple sounds. In everyday settings, someone might want to focus their attention on the person who's speaking to them or, alternatively, try to listen in on the conversation next to them while also listening to the person who's speaking to them.

3.2 Perceptual organisation

Given there are infinite ways that sounds can be grouped and segregated, which factors influence what someone perceives? Researchers have typically studied this by breaking it into two components, known as **simultaneous grouping** and **sequential grouping**. Simultaneous grouping refers to the challenge of how people perceive sounds that overlap in time, like when two people talk over each other: how could someone work out who's saying what? Sequential grouping refers to how people group sounds that are separated in time, like a phone that rings 10 times before it stops: each ring is separated from the previous one by a brief silent pause, so how could a listener identify that they're all coming from the same phone?

The distinction between simultaneous grouping and sequential grouping is artificial, because perceiving most sounds in everyday life involves using both at the same time. Nevertheless, this distinction appears to be useful, because different factors seem to influence simultaneous and sequential grouping. To study these processes, researchers typically use very simple sounds, like artificial tones, and capitalise on the fact that these sounds are often ambiguous. Intriguingly, when sounds are ambiguous, even small changes in the acoustics of the sounds can quite dramatically alter what someone perceives.

3.2.1 Simultaneous grouping

First, let's consider perceptual organisation for two or more sounds that overlap in time. Even though most natural sounds continue over time (like two people talking over each other), the auditory system analyses sound on a moment-by-moment basis. Under this conceptualisation, we can think of taking a snapshot in time (e.g. a few hundred milliseconds when both people are talking), and trying to work out—within that time—which components of the sound belong together (i.e. both to the same voice) and which components belong apart (i.e. some components to one voice, and other components to the second voice).

Recall from **Chapter 1** that most natural sounds aren't pure tones, but rather contain several different frequencies. The cochlea separates a sound wave into its frequencies—so the frequencies within the sound mixture are sorted as they ascend the auditory pathway. Let's imagine that a sound mixture contains 10 different frequencies. How does someone work out whether the sound mixture was produced by one object that produced all 10 frequencies (e.g. a harmonic complex tone) or 10 different objects that each produced one frequency (e.g. 10 pure tones)? This is akin to picking 10 jigsaw pieces out of a box and trying to work out how many different puzzles they belong to. To do this, someone might try to find patterns among the set of pieces or look for clues in order to group them together. Similarly, the auditory system looks for 'cues' within a sound mixture.

> You can review how the cochlea separates sounds into frequencies in **Chapter 1**.

One cue (i.e. pattern) is that frequencies from the same object typically follow a harmonic series. Therefore, frequencies that follow a harmonic series (e.g. 100, 200, 300, and 400 Hz) are quite likely to originate from the same object, whereas frequencies that don't belong to the harmonic series (e.g. 217 Hz in a mixture of 100, 200, 300, and 400 Hz) are more likely to originate from a different object.

Indeed, studies show that harmonicity affects the perception of simultaneous sounds (Rajappa et al., 2023). Frequencies within a harmonic complex tone are usually perceived as a coherent whole, rather than as separate frequencies. When one of the frequencies in a harmonic complex tone is altered to a different frequency, the tone is still perceived as a coherent whole—but when its frequency is moved further away (more than about 3%), people tend to perceive it as a separate tone (Darwin & Ciocca, 1992).

> You can review harmonic complex tones in **Chapter 2**.

Another cue is timing. If different frequencies are produced by the same object, then these frequencies are likely to begin and end at the same time (which is sometimes called 'common onset'). In addition, if the amplitude of the sound changes over time, then the amplitudes of components that were produced by the same object are likely to increase and decrease at the same times. For example, all of the frequencies coming from a music player will stop at the same time when the music is turned off, and this might help people to separate the frequencies that belong to the music from the frequencies that belong to a cooling fan. People can sometimes identify different objects *within* music too—for example, the sounds made by different instruments—and this can also be based on timing. For example, the frequencies produced by a saxophone start and stop together, and if they usually occur at different times to the frequencies produced by a piano, then it is usually possible to segregate the sounds from the two instruments.

> Grouping of components that change amplitude together can be compared to the Gestalt principle of 'common fate' in vision, which refers to the idea that components that change in the same way at the same time are more likely to be grouped.

Studies using simple tones show that when frequencies all begin at the same time, people are more likely to group them, whereas they often segregate frequencies that start later than others (Darwin & Ciocca, 1992) (Figure 3.2). In addition, components that are modulated in amplitude can be segregated from components that are *not* modulated in amplitude (i.e. that have a flat envelope) (Moore & Bacon, 1998).

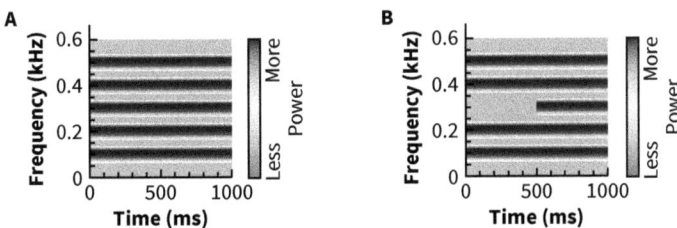

Figure 3.2 Spectrograms of two complex tones. Panel a shows a harmonic complex tone with a fundamental frequency of 100 Hz. In panel b, notice how the third harmonic (300 Hz) starts later than the other frequencies. Perceptually, the third harmonic is usually perceived as being segregated from the other harmonics when it starts later.

> Curiously, timing is such a strong cue for segregation that, sometimes, adding more noise to a mixture makes some frequencies easier to hear, provided it's added with the correct timing. When a target tone is presented at the same time as amplitude-modulated noise at a similar frequency, it can be difficult to hear the tone—but adding more noise at a higher frequency makes the target tone easier to hear if it has exactly the same amplitude modulation. This phenomenon is called 'co-modulation masking release', because the tone is easier to hear when the noise is modulated in the same way.

Researchers have also studied whether spatial location contributes to simultaneous grouping. While it does seem to contribute, sound components are unlikely to be segregated if location is the *only* cue for segregation (i.e. if the frequencies and timings are congruent) (Darwin & Ciocca, 1992). It's unclear why location is a weak cue for simultaneous grouping—but it could be because location isn't always reliable in everyday, reverberant settings (because sounds reach the ears from several different directions when they're reflected off surfaces). Another possible reason is that information about frequency and timing is already available at the cochlea, whereas only neurons much further along the auditory pathway—after the signals from the two ears have been combined—seem to be sensitive to location.

> You can review reverberation in **Chapter 2**.

Ultimately, simultaneous grouping doesn't depend on any individual cue, but arises from combining all of the cues that are available. Similarly, even if the shape of a puzzle piece appears to fit with that of another piece, they're unlikely to belong together if the colours are entirely different. It's for this reason that frequency, timing, and location are considered as 'cues' rather than rules. Perceptual organisation is simply the auditory system's best guess of which components of sounds belong together and which belong apart—and sometimes small changes in these acoustic cues have a large influence on whether someone perceives one object or two.

3.2.2 Sequential grouping

In the previous section, we considered grouping during a 'snapshot' in time. Yet, natural auditory signals evolve over time. For example, when a phone rings, most people usually have no difficulty working out that it's the same phone that produces each ring, even though the rings are separated by brief silent pauses. This challenge becomes even more difficult if another sound—like an alarm—occurs at the same time. If we return to our jigsaw puzzle analogy, imagine that you've started constructing two different jigsaw puzzles from the pieces in the box. If you take a new piece from the box, how do you work out whether it belongs to the first puzzle, the second puzzle, or a third puzzle that you've not yet started? Interestingly, the balance of cues that are involved in sequential grouping appear to differ from those that are involved in simultaneous grouping.

An influential paradigm that's been used to study sequential grouping is known as 'streaming' (van Noorden, 1975). The 'streaming' paradigm is a simple example of sequential grouping that presents pure tones of two different frequencies. The pattern of tones is displayed in Figure 3.3(a). Notice that none of the pure tones overlap in time with one another,

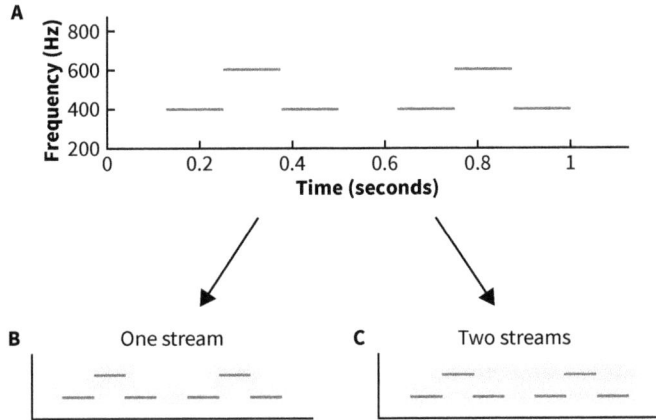

Figure 3.3 A schematic of the streaming paradigm. Tones of two different frequencies are presented at two different rates (panel a). Notice that the lower-frequency tones are presented at a faster rate than the higher-frequency tones. The figure only shows two repeats, but the same pattern is often repeated for tens of seconds. The sounds can either be perceived as one stream that contains the tones at both frequencies (panel b), or two streams, each containing the tones at the higher or lower frequency (panel c).

and—therefore—this is an example of sequential grouping, with no simultaneous grouping. Interestingly, these tones are commonly perceived in two different ways. Sometimes, all the tones are perceived as arising from a single object (i.e. as one stream, which is commonly described as a 'galloping' rhythm; Figure 3.3(b)); other times, they're perceived as two separate streams—one containing only the higher-frequency tones and the other containing only the lower-frequency tones (Figure 3.3(c)).

Interestingly, whether people perceive one stream or two depends on the acoustic properties of the tones. For example, when there's a greater difference in frequency between the higher and lower tones, people are more likely to perceive two streams than one, whereas, when the tones are close in frequency, people are more likely to perceive one stream.

The difference in frequency in the streaming paradigm can be compared to the Gestalt principle of proximity that's often described in relation to visual scene analysis (Figure 3.4).

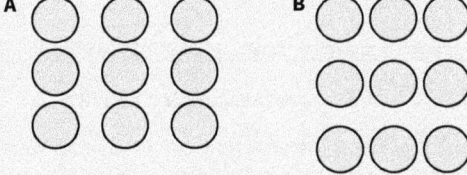

Figure 3.4 Panels a and b both consist of nine circles. The spatial proximity of the circles affects their grouping. In panel a, the circles are closer vertically than horizontally, and people are more likely to perceive three vertical objects (i.e. three columns of circles) than three horizontal objects (i.e. three rows of circles). In panel b, the circles are closer horizontally than vertically, and people are more likely to perceive three horizontal objects than three vertical objects.

The timing of the tones matters too. If the tones are presented at a slower rate—so there's a longer gap between them—people are more likely to perceive one stream. Whereas, when they're presented at a faster rate, people are more likely to perceive two streams. Rate is sometimes referred to as tempo and is directly related to the time between repetitions of the tones. When the unit is Hertz (as in Figure 3.5), the rate refers to the number of times a tone is presented per second.

Researchers have tested a variety of different rates to determine the combination of frequencies and rates that lead to different percepts (Figure 3.5). Tones that are presented with large frequency differences combined with slow rates are typically perceived as two streams, whereas tones that are presented with small frequency differences are typically perceived as one stream. In between, there lies a combination of frequencies and rates where perception is usually ambiguous—that is, the tones are sometimes perceived as one stream, and other times as two streams.

We can think of timing and frequency information as competing to determine how sounds are grouped (Bregman, 1994). When the tones in the 'streaming' paradigm are close in frequency, they are more likely to be grouped together and perceived as a single stream. However, when the tones are close in time, then subsequent tones at the same frequency are more likely to be grouped in time, creating the perception of two streams (Figure 3.5). Another way of thinking about this is that when playing a saxophone, someone can change the notes they play, but they would need some time to change the position of their fingers and mouth. If the notes are played slowly with silent gaps in between, then it's likely that a single musician can play all of the notes. Whereas, if the notes alternate rapidly with little gap in between, then it would be very difficult for one person to do, and it's more likely that two people are playing the notes—one who is playing the higher notes and the other who is playing the lower notes.

> Some composers have used streaming to their advantage. Highly proficient musicians are able to play complex sequences of tones, that switch between higher and lower tones, very quickly—and when these pieces of music are heard, they perceptually separate into two streams.

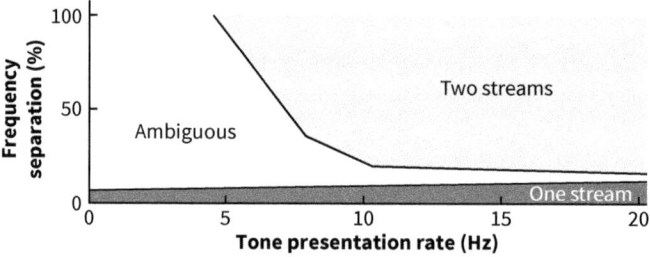

Figure 3.5 Schematic showing the percepts that arise from combinations of frequency differences (vertical axis) and rates (horizontal axis) in the streaming paradigm. Faster rates are shown towards the right of the graph. Different areas of the graph show how the percept is either usually perceived as two streams, usually perceived as one stream, or ambiguous (i.e. sometimes perceived as one stream and sometimes perceived as two streams). Notice the change in percept from one stream to two streams as the rate becomes faster and the frequency separation increases (i.e. compare the lower left to the upper right of the figure).

Source: adapted from Fishman, Y. I., & Steinschneider, M. (2010). 'Formation of auditory streams'. In A. R. Palmer & A. Rees (Eds.), *The Oxford handbook of auditory science: The auditory brain* (pp. 215–245).

When the stimulus is ambiguous and continues for a long time, people's perception often switches back and forth between one and two streams. When the tones first start, people are more likely to hear one stream, but—as the pattern continues for longer (about 10 seconds)—their perception often switches to two streams (Pressnitzer & Hupé, 2006). This has led to the idea that streaming 'builds up' over time. In other words, most people more likely to *group* sounds initially but, when they're exposed to them for longer, they're more likely to *segregate* them.

As the pattern continues for longer, however, people's perception typically switches back and forth between one and two streams—seemingly at random. When the stimulus is ambiguous, there appears to be a role of intention (van Noorden, 1975). In other words, people can choose whether to perceive one or two streams. Also, perception may depend on whether the person is directing attention to the sounds (Carlyon et al., 2001), although the role of attention in sequential grouping is hotly debated (Further insights 3.1).

> **Further insights 3.1** Attention
>
> Perceptual organisation can be affected by attention, but the role of attention in auditory perceptual organisation is still debated. Some researchers argue that only attended objects can be segregated (Cusack et al., 2004), whereas others suggest that segregation occurs automatically without attention (Macken et al., 2003). Based on the balance of evidence, it seems likely that segregation *can* occur without attention, but attention nevertheless influences how sounds are grouped and segregated—and this may depend on properties of the sounds. For example, when sounds are separated by a large difference in frequency and small difference in time, then the sounds may be segregated even if they're not attended, because the percept is unambiguous. Whereas, when the sound mixture is ambiguous, attention might have a greater effect on what someone perceives (Sussman et al., 2007).

Other than frequency and timing, several other acoustic cues are also important for sequential grouping. Unlike simultaneous grouping, spatial location has a strong effect on sequential grouping: people are more likely to perceive two streams if sounds come from two different locations (Dowling, 1968). Grouping by spatial location can be compared to the Gestalt principle of 'proximity' in visual scene analysis. While people are more likely to perceive two steams if sounds come from two different locations, grouping by frequency can override grouping by location. For an example, see Diana Deutsch's scale illusion (Deutsch, 2021).

Also, when two or more complex tones are in a sound mixture, people are more likely to segregate them if they differ in fundamental frequency or timbre (i.e. they have different spectra) (Vliegen & Oxenham, 1999).

> A difference in timbre can be compared to the Gestalt principle of similarity that's often described in relation to visual scene analysis (Figure 3.6).

(continued...)

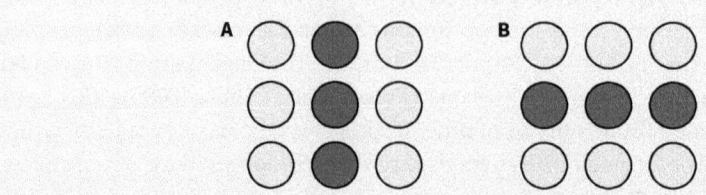

Figure 3.6 Panels a and b both consist of nine circles. The colour of the circles affects their grouping. In panel a, the circles in the middle column are a darker colour than the other circles, and people are more likely to perceive three vertical objects (i.e. three columns of circles) than three horizontal objects (i.e. three rows of circles). In panel b, the circles in the middle row are darker than the other circles, and people are more likely to perceive three horizontal objects than three vertical objects.

Sequential grouping becomes more difficult when sounds don't merely repeat, but change over time. In this situation, people are more likely to group sounds that have smooth transitions in acoustic properties over time—such as a gradual increase in frequency or a gradual change in location—and segregate sounds that change suddenly. This is because natural sounds typically change smoothly, and sudden changes are rare. Think back to the example of a musician who plays tones of different frequencies. If the tone glides smoothly from one frequency to another, it's likely that one musician played the tone, so people are likely to group all parts of the tone as belonging to one source; whereas, if the tone suddenly changes frequency by a large amount, it's more likely that the tone after the frequency change was played by a second musician, and people are more likely to segregate the tone before and after it changes frequency (Bregman & Dannenbring, 1973).

3.2.3 Prior knowledge

The cues we've introduced so far in this chapter can be considered as expectations about sounds based on properties of the world that are fixed. However, perceptual organisation can also be influenced by short-term expectations that change over time and when listening in different settings. Simply repeating a pattern of tones multiple times can be sufficient for the tones to group together as one stream and become segregated from other sounds (McDermott et al., 2011)—suggesting that the repeated sounds are perceived as originating from a single object. This might occur because the combined sounds from two or more sources are unlikely to repeat in exactly the same way, so a regular pattern is more likely to originate from a single object. Possibly, detecting repeating patterns may even be how people learn about the sounds made by new objects.

Other studies have shown that the context that occurs *before* a sound mixture has begun affects how those sounds are perceived. For example, when presented with an ambiguous version of the streaming paradigm, people are more likely to hear two streams if they previously heard a mixture with a small frequency difference that was unambiguously perceived as one stream (Snyder et al., 2008). This phenomenon is assumed to reflect a contrastive effect that emphasises differences between two sets of sounds.

3.3 Multiple sounds in the brain

It is often assumed that early stages of the auditory pathway process individual features (e.g. particular frequencies at the cochlea), whereas later stages of the pathway respond to objects. Yet, precisely which part of the auditory pathway integrates features into objects remains a mystery. This is a difficult challenge, because we're looking for responses in the auditory pathway that describe someone's perceptual experience of sounds, beyond simply encoding the acoustic features of the sounds they hear—in other words, which part(s) of the auditory pathway contains information about how sounds are grouped, and whether the person perceives two streams or one.

3.3.1 How are sounds 'bound' together?

It was once assumed that sounds can only be segregated if they generate responses in different groups of neurons early in the auditory pathway, called the 'peripheral channelling theory' (Hartmann & Johnson, 1991); for example, if their frequencies are sufficiently distinct. However, researchers now know that even sounds that have highly similar spectra can be segregated (Vliegen & Oxenham, 1999). From the opposite perspective, sounds can be grouped even if they generate responses in distinct groups of neurons. For example, even frequencies that are far apart tend to be grouped if they belong to a harmonic series (see Section 3.2.1). This raises the question: If generating responses in similar groups of neurons isn't necessary or sufficient, how are sounds 'bound' together into a unified percept?

One possibility is that the *timing* of neural firing determines perceptual organisation. Let's imagine that one group of neurons responds best to frequencies of 100 Hz and another group of neurons responds best to frequencies of 800 Hz. If tones at 100 Hz and 800 Hz are repeated and, on every repeat, they occur at exactly the same time, the two groups of neurons will always respond at the same time (Figure 3.7(a)). If 100-Hz tones always occur exactly 50 milliseconds before every 800-Hz tone, then the responses of the two groups of neurons will always have a fixed delay between them (Figure 3.7(b)). However, if the 100-Hz and 800-Hz tones occur at different times and don't always follow one another in the same way, then there will be no systematic relationship between the timing of responses in the two groups of neurons (Figure 3.7(c)). One prominent theory—called 'temporal coherence'

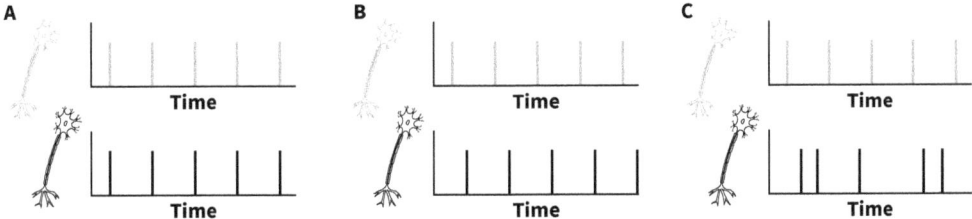

Figure 3.7 Schematics showing example response patterns for two groups of neurons—one illustrated by the upper plots, and one illustrated by the lower plots. In panel a, the two groups of neurons respond at the same time. In panel b, the lower group of neurons always responds a fixed length of time after the upper group of neurons responds. In panel c, the responses of the lower group of neurons are unrelated to the responses of the upper group of neurons.

theory—assumes that the tones at 100 Hz and the tones at 800 Hz will be grouped together if responses in the two groups of neurons are correlated, and segregated if they're not correlated. Therefore, in the first two examples (Figure 3.7(a) and (b)) the theory predicts that the tones would be grouped together, and in the third example (Figure 3.7(c)) it predicts they'd be segregated. Temporal coherence theory is consistent with the results from several studies (e.g. O'Sullivan et al., 2015), but some questions remain unanswered. For example, neurons in many parts of the auditory pathway are sensitive to sounds at particular frequencies—so, in *which part* of the auditory pathway is the timing of neural responses compared?

> The intra-parietal sulcus is also thought to contribute to perceptual organisation in vision and in other sensory modalities.

3.3.2 Where does segregation occur?

Regardless of *how* grouping occurs, some researchers have been interested in *where* in the brain grouping and segregation occurs. In other words, is there an area of the brain that responds differently when sounds are segregated compared to when they're grouped together?

Historically, researchers have often assumed that perceptual organisation must occur further along the auditory pathway than primary auditory cortex, because primary auditory cortex responds best to individual features of sounds. Indeed, one influential brain imaging study found no evidence for perceptual segregation in auditory cortex, and instead found relevant activity in an area of parietal cortex: the intra-parietal sulcus (Cusack, 2005). This study used a version of the streaming paradigm (see Section 3.2.2) in which the stimulus was ambiguous: people sometimes perceived it as one stream and sometimes perceived it as two streams. When people reported perceiving two streams, the intra-parietal sulcus was more active than when they reported perceiving one stream—even though the sounds they heard were identical in both cases. Thus, activity in the intra-parietal sulcus seems to relate to perceptual organisation of sounds, regardless of the acoustics of the sounds themselves.

> The 'temporal coherence' theory also proposes that attention can enhance the coherence of neural firing, which offers an explanation for how attention affects perceptual organisation.

However, other studies have observed responses related to perceptual organisation in auditory cortex—although the precise location within auditory cortex differs among studies. When perceptual organisation is manipulated by changing the frequencies of sounds in the streaming paradigm, responses have been observed in planum temporale, the superior temporal gyrus, and primary auditory cortex. A study in rhesus monkeys showed that neurons in primary auditory cortex change their responses during the streaming paradigm, consistent with the build-up of streaming that's reported by human listeners (i.e. the change from perceiving one stream to two streams) (Micheyl et al., 2005). In addition, a patient who experienced damage to auditory cortex subsequently had difficulty segregating sounds (Holmes et al., 2021)—although the damage was mainly in secondary auditory cortex and spared primary auditory cortex.

> You can learn about the different regions of auditory cortex in **Chapter 1**.

Ultimately, different studies have reported different findings and there doesn't appear to be one place in the auditory pathway that consistently links to perceptual organisation. Instead, responses may differ depending on which feature of sounds is used for grouping and segregation (e.g. frequency, timing, or prior knowledge). Also, given that perceptual organisation relies on encoding basic features of sounds as well as higher-level processes such as attention, multiple stages of the auditory pathway probably work together to determine people's perception.

> Attention is typically associated with responses in frontal and parietal cortex. When someone directs their attention to a sound they want to listen to, these areas are thought to send signals to auditory cortex, via descending connections.

3.3.3 Neural indicators of perceptual organisation

Some researchers have tried to look for other types of responses in the brain that only occur when sounds are segregated and not when they're grouped. In a similar way to how a fire alarm indicates that smoke is present, brain responses that show this pattern could be considered as indicators of perceptual segregation. Some researchers have tried to identify such responses using **electro-encephalography** (EEG), which measures brain activity using electrodes placed on the scalp and, therefore, reflects a combination of brain responses across cortex. When sounds are played, researchers can record EEG responses and identify how these responses differ when sounds are perceived in one way compared to another. This section covers two well-studied EEG responses that have been suggested to be neural indicators of perceptual organisation, which are known as the **mismatch negativity** and the **object-related negativity**.

> EEG measures electrical activity in the brain by recording via metal sensors placed on the scalp, which are sensitive to small voltage changes. This electrical activity arises due to the firing of neurons in the brain, and is detectable even after passing through the skull. The amplitude and timing of EEG responses can tell us about how stimuli are processed in the brain.

The mismatch negativity (Figure 3.8) occurs in a variety of settings and has been associated with sounds that are surprising. For example, it occurs when a sequence of tones suddenly changes to a different frequency; it also occurs when a change occurs within a repeating pattern of sounds. The mismatch negativity isn't specific to perceptual organisation, but one idea is that it highlights deviations in sounds that could indicate that a new object is present in the environment (Shinn-Cunningham, 2020). In addition, the mismatch negativity occurs when someone expects a sound but it doesn't occur, so it could also be useful for indicating that an object has disappeared from the environment (Yabe et al., 1997).

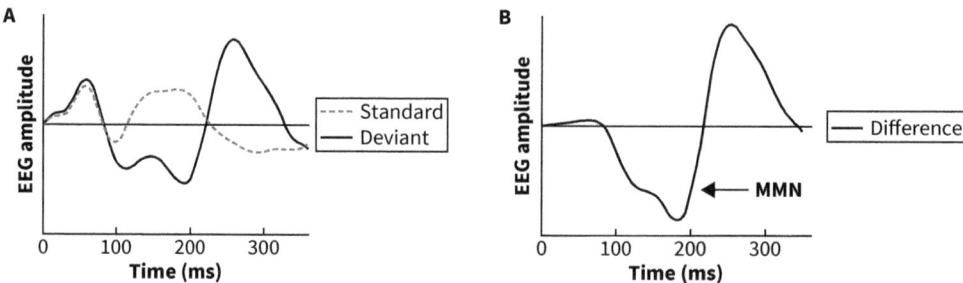

Figure 3.8 Schematic of the mismatch negativity (MMN) response. In panel a, the dashed line indicates electro-encephalography (EEG) responses to 'standard' (i.e. repeating) tones within a sequence, and the solid line indicates EEG responses to 'deviant' (i.e. surprising) tones in the sequence. Panel b shows the difference between the responses from panel a ('deviant' minus 'standard'): the negative peak between 150 and 200 ms in panel b is referred to as the MMN.

In the streaming paradigm, the mismatch negativity has been found to occur when people perceive two streams and not when they perceive one stream (Sussman et al., 2007)—yet its relationship to perceptual organisation isn't straightforward. For example, the mismatch negativity has sometimes been observed when sounds aren't segregated into multiple streams (Shinozaki et al., 2000). Therefore—in a similar way to how a fire alarm doesn't always indicate a fire, and could just as easily be set off when smoke comes from burnt toast—the mismatch negativity might not reflect perceptual organisation directly, but rather indicate deviations within a set of sounds that *could* lead to changes in perceptual organisation.

Conversely, the **object-related negativity** (Figure 3.9) has sometimes been assumed to reflect perceptual organisation more directly. It occurs when a complex tone is presented in which the frequency of one of the harmonics has been changed so that it's perceived separately (Alain et al., 2001). It also occurs when patterns of tones are segregated from other tones. Interestingly, the object-related negativity has been linked to brain responses in superior temporal cortex and the intra-parietal sulcus (Molloy et al., 2019). Nevertheless, the relationship between the object-related negativity and perception isn't entirely consistent either.

Overall, researchers have had limited success in identifying neural indicators of perceptual organisation. This could be because our auditory systems have evolved to deal with

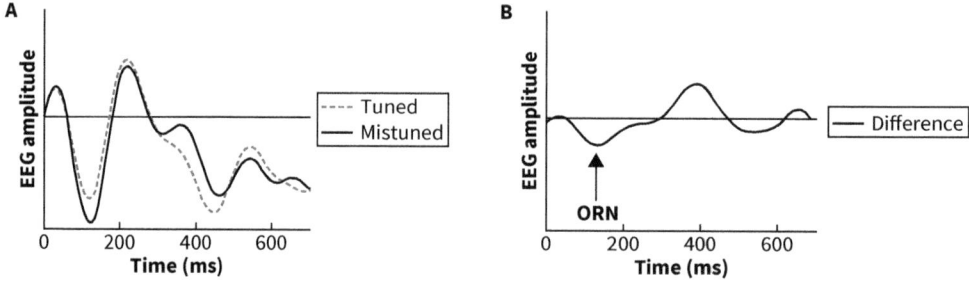

Figure 3.9 Schematic of the object-related negativity (ORN) response. In panel a, the dashed line indicates electro-encephalography (EEG) responses to a harmonic complex tone in which all of the harmonics are integer multiples of the fundamental frequency, and the solid line indicates EEG responses to a 'mistuned' complex tone, in which one of the harmonics has been shifted so it is no longer an integer multiple of the fundamental frequency. Panel b shows the difference between the responses from panel a ('mistuned' minus 'tuned'): the negative peak at approximately 100 ms in panel b is referred to as the ORN.

everyday listening scenarios that people frequently encounter, rather than the types of tasks that they're asked to do when they participate in experiments. How often have you tried to count how many objects are present in your surroundings? We're guessing the answer is not very often! Therefore, while the paradigms introduced in this chapter are useful for probing basic responses of the auditory system, they're a far stretch from everyday listening environments, where the goal is typically to listen to a particular sound, rather than identify how many sounds are present. The next chapters of this book deal with hearing in action. **Chapters 5 and 6** examine how people perceive multiple sounds from the perspectives of listening to speech and music. Studies investigating speech and music may be more similar to the listening challenges that people encounter in their everyday lives.

Summary

When multiple objects are vibrating in the environment, the signal that reaches the ears is ambiguous—and what someone perceives relies on their auditory system's best guess at the objects that are present. The best guess is based on several cues. Some of the cues reflect fixed properties of the world—such as plausible combinations of frequencies that an object emits. Other cues are more flexible: for example, perception depends on the context that someone is in and can change if they realise that some sounds are repeating. Researchers don't yet fully understand precisely how responses in the auditory pathway reflect perceptual organisation, and this remains a topic of ongoing research.

Further your understanding

Fishman, Y. I., & Steinschneider, M. (2010). 'Formation of auditory streams.' In A. Rees & A. R. Palmer (eds) *The Oxford Handbook of Auditory Science: The Auditory Brain* (pp. 215–245). Oxford, Oxford University Press.

Bregman, A. (2008). 'Audio demonstrations of auditory scene analysis.' https://themusiclab.github.io/bregman-archive/downloadstoc.htm

References

Alain, C., Arnott, S. R., & Picton, T. W. (2001). 'Bottom-up and top-down influences on auditory scene analysis: Evidence from event-related brain potentials.' *Journal of Experimental Psychology: Human Perception and Performance*, 27(5), 1072–1089. https://doi.org/10.1037/0096-1523.27.5.1072

Bregman, A. S. (1990). *Auditory Scene Analysis: The Perceptual Organization of Sound*. Cambridge, MA: MIT Press. https://doi.org/10.7551/mitpress/1486.001.0001

Bregman, A. (1994). 'Auditory scene analysis: The perceptual organization of sound.' Retrieved from https://books.google.co.uk/books?hl=en&lr=&id=jI8muSpAC5AC&oi=fnd&pg=PR11&dq=bregman+auditory+scene+analysis+the+perception+organization+of+sound&ots=SHmYLeDAAB&sig=wkFTZaQ2EAVQE2n-1weuQnMl5c0

Bregman, A. S., & Dannenbring, G. L. (1973). 'The effect of continuity on auditory stream segregation.' *Perception & Psychophysics*, 13(2), 308–312. https://doi.org/10.3758/BF03214144

Carlyon, R. P., Cusack, R., Foxton, J. M., & Robertson, I. H. (2001). 'Effects of attention and unilateral neglect on auditory stream segregation.' *Journal of Experimental Psychology: Human Perception and Performance*, 27(1), 115–127. https://doi.org/10.1037/0096-1523.27.1.115

Cusack, R. (2005). 'The intraparietal sulcus and perceptual organization.' *Journal of Cognitive Neuroscience*, 17(4), 641–651. https://doi.org/10.1162/0898929053467541

Cusack, R., Deeks, J., Aikman, G., & Carlyon, R. P. (2004). 'Effects of location, frequency region, and time course of selective attention on auditory scene analysis.' *Journal of Experimental Psychology: Human Perception and Performance*, 30(4), 643–656. https://doi.org/10.1037/0096-1523.30.4.643

Deutsch, D. (2021) 'Scale Illusion.' http://deutsch.ucsd.edu/psychology/pages.php?i=203

Darwin, C. J., & Ciocca, V. (1992). 'Grouping in pitch perception: Effects of onset asynchrony and ear of presentation of a mistuned component.' *Journal of the Acoustical Society of America*, 91(6), 3381–3390. https://doi.org/10.1121/1.402828

Dowling, W. J. (1968). 'Rhythmic fission and perceptual organization.' *Journal of the Acoustical Society of America*, 44(1), 369. https://doi.org/10.1121/1.1970461

Hartmann, W. M., & Johnson, D. (1991). 'Stream segregation and peripheral channeling.' *Music Perception*, 9(2), 155–183. https://doi.org/10.2307/40285527

Holmes, E., Utoomprurkporn, N., Hoskote, C., Warren, J. D., Bamiou, D. E., & Griffiths, T. D. (2021). 'Simultaneous auditory agnosia: Systematic description of a new type of auditory segregation deficit following a right hemisphere lesion.' *Cortex*, 135, 92–107. https://doi.org/10.1016/j.cortex.2020.10.023

Macken, W. J., Tremblay, S., Houghton, R. J., Nicholls, A. P., & Jones, D. M. (2003). 'Does auditory streaming require attention? Evidence from attentional selectivity in short-term memory.' *Journal of Experimental Psychology: Human Perception and Performance*, 29(1), 43–51. https://doi.org/10.1037/0096-1523.29.1.43

McAdams, S., & Bregman, A. (1979). 'Hearing musical streams.' *Computer Music Journal*, 3(4), 26–60. https://www.jstor.org/stable/4617866

McDermott, J. H., Wrobleski, D., & Oxenham, A. J. (2011). 'Recovering sound sources from embedded repetition.' *Proceedings of the National Academy of Sciences*, 108(3), 1188–1193. https://doi.org/10.1073/PNAS.1004765108

Micheyl, C., Tian, B., Carlyon, R. P., & Rauschecker, J. P. (2005). 'Perceptual organization of tone sequences in the auditory cortex of awake macaques.' *Neuron*, 48(1), 139–148. https://doi.org/10.1016/J.NEURON.2005.08.039

Molloy, K., Lavie, N., & Chait, M. (2019). 'Auditory figure-ground segregation is impaired by high visual load.' *Journal of Neuroscience*, 39(9), 1699–1708.

Moore, B. C. J., & Bacon, S. P. (1998). 'Detection and identification of a single modulated carrier in a complex sound.' *Journal of the Acoustical Society of America*, 94(2), 759. https://doi.org/10.1121/1.408205

O'Sullivan, J. A., Shamma, S. A., & Lalor, E. C. (2015). 'Evidence for neural computations of temporal coherence in an auditory scene and their enhancement during active listening.' *Journal of Neuroscience*, 35(18), 7256–7263. https://doi.org/10.1523/JNEUROSCI.4973-14.2015

Pressnitzer, D., & Hupé, J. M. (2006). 'Temporal dynamics of auditory and visual bistability reveal common principles of perceptual organization.' *Current Biology*, 16(13), 1351–1357. https://doi.org/10.1016/J.CUB.2006.05.054

Rajappa, N., Guest, D. R., & Oxenham, A. J., (2023). 'Benefits of harmonicity for hearing in noise are limited to detection and pitch-related discrimination tasks.' *Biology (Basel)*, 12(12), 1522. https://doi.org/10.3390/biology12121522

Shinn-Cunningham, B. G. (2020). 'Brain mechanisms of auditory scene analysis.' In D. Poeppel, G. R. Mangun, & M. S. Gazzaniga (eds) *The Cognitive Neurosciences* (pp. 159–166). Cambridge, MA: MIT Press. https://doi.org/10.7551/mitpress/11442.003.0020

Shinozaki, N., Yabe, H., Sato, Y., Sutoh, T., Hiruma, T., Nashida, T., & Kaneko, S. (2000). 'Mismatch negativity (MMN) reveals sound grouping in the human brain.' *Neuroreport*, 11(8), 1597–1601. https://doi.org/10.1097/00001756-200006050-00001

Snyder, J. S., Carter, O. L., Lee, S. K., Hannon, E. E., & Alain, C. (2008). 'Effects of context on auditory stream segregation.' *Journal of Experimental Psychology. Human Perception and Performance*, 34(4), 1007–1016. https://doi.org/10.1037/0096-1523.34.4.1007

Sussman, E. S., Horváth, J., Winkler, I., & Orr, M. (2007). 'The role of attention in the formation of auditory streams.' *Perception & Psychophysics*, 69(1), 136–152. https://doi.org/10.3758/BF03194460

van Noorden, L. P. A. S. (1975). 'Temporal coherence in random tone sequences' (Technische Hogeschool Eindhoven). https://research.tue.nl/en/publications/temporal-coherence-in-the-perception-of-tone-sequences

Vliegen, J., & Oxenham, A. J. (1999). 'Sequential stream segregation in the absence of spectral cues.' *Journal of the Acoustical Society of America*, 105(1), 97. https://doi.org/10.1121/1.424503

Yabe, H., Tervaniemi, M., Reinikainen, K., & Näätänen, R. (1997). 'Temporal window of integration revealed by MMN to sound omission.' *Neuroreport*, 8(8), 1971–1974.

Part 2
Hearing in Action

Perceiving Speech

Most good parties are filled with conversations. At a party, speech serves many purposes: calling a friend's name from across the room, getting to know someone new by talking to them, or alerting someone that they're about to knock over a drink. Spoken language is one of the main ways that most people communicate with one another—but how do people work out what someone is saying to them? This is a much bigger question than it may appear! The ears receive a continuous speech signal, yet—from this acoustic signal—a listener is able to extract information about *what's* being said, *who's* speaking, and *how* they're saying it. This chapter first describes the acoustic properties of speech in general terms, then examines how people work out what's being said, who's speaking, and how they're saying it. Finally, we consider how speech is represented in the auditory pathway.

4.1 What is speech?

Why do words sound different from one another? This section explains some key acoustic properties of speech. It also describes some acoustic differences between different types of speech sounds.

4.1.1 Speech as a sound pressure wave

Like other sounds, speech is simply a sound pressure wave (Figure 4.1). During conversations, people speak approximately 150–200 words every minute (Duchin & Mysak, 1987), producing a complex sound pressure wave that varies over time. As a result, speech changes quickly in both amplitude and frequency.

Recall from **Chapter 1** that the source of sound is an object that vibrates. If someone says 'hello' to another person at a party, their **vocal folds** (see Figure 4.2) vibrate. The vocal folds are two pieces of elastic tissue, controlled by muscle. When people exhale air from their lungs, the air passes through their vocal folds, and makes the vocal folds vibrate.

> You might have heard the vocal folds referred to as the 'vocal cords'. These two terms are interchangeable, although 'vocal folds' is usually preferred by auditory scientists.

After the vocal folds vibrate, the sound is then filtered by the **vocal tract**—which refers to the cavity above the vocal folds (Figure 4.2). The vocal tract changes shape when people

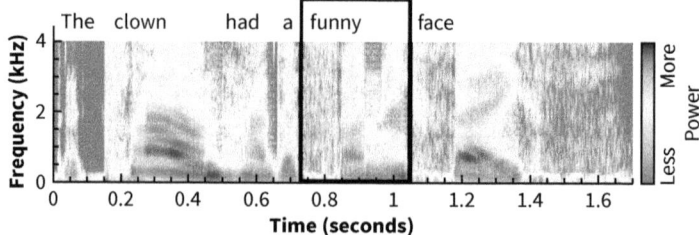

Figure 4.1 Spectrogram of a spoken sentence. Approximate locations of word onsets are indicated above the spectrogram. The black box shows the approximate location of the word 'funny': notice how much the spectrogram varies within the word.

move their mouths. Ultimately, most people can change the sounds that they produce in two ways: first, by controlling the tension of their vocal folds, and second, by changing the shape of their vocal tract. People can do this very rapidly within a word, which leads to the fast amplitude and frequency modulations that are characteristic of speech.

4.1.2 Variations within the speech signal

Different parts of speech have different acoustic properties, and most people use these acoustic properties to work out *what's* being said, *who's* speaking, and *how* they're saying it. For example, we can start by comparing vowels (e.g. the 'a' in 'party' and the 'i' in 'drink') and consonants (e.g. the 'f' in 'funny' and the 's' in 'snake').

Vowel sounds are harmonic complex tones, and the source of vowel sounds is the vibration of the vocal folds. When people whisper, they hold their vocal folds apart, so the

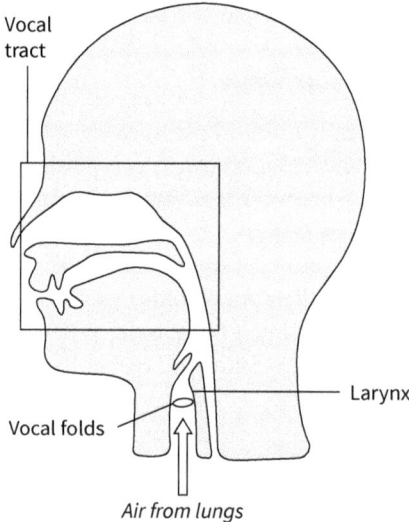

Figure 4.2 Illustration showing a cross-section of the articulatory system. Air from the lungs passes the vocal folds in the larynx, before reaching the vocal tract.

vocal folds don't vibrate when air passes through them. For this reason, whispered vowels are not harmonic complex tones, but are more similar to noise (like some consonants). To understand speech, people need to be sensitive to subtle differences in vowel sounds that distinguish one vowel from another. For example, if the friend who's sat next to them is getting up, they might need to work out if their friend said 'Can you pass me my *cup*?' or 'Can you pass me my *cap*?'.

There are two key properties of vowel sounds that affect the speech signal. The first is the fundamental frequency. Recall from **Chapter 2** that harmonic complex tones contain harmonics, which are integer multiples of the fundamental frequency (Figure 4.3(a)). Therefore, when the fundamental frequency changes, the frequencies of all of the harmonics change. A vowel's fundamental frequency is controlled by the tension of the vocal folds: if someone applies greater tension to their vocal folds, it makes the vocal folds vibrate faster, and they produce vowels with higher fundamental frequencies.

The second property is peaks in the spectrum (Figure 4.3(b)), which are known as **formants**. Formants are not related to vibrations of the vocal folds, but instead relate to the shape of the vocal tract. Most people can change the shape of their vocal tract by moving their **articulators**—which include the lips and tongue.

Have you ever noticed that beatboxers are able to produce a variety of sounds? They mimic other sounds by changing the positions of their articulators. Moving their articulators changes the frequencies of the formants. During continuous speech, like that shown in Figure 4.1, the formants are constantly changing, which happens because the shape of the vocal tract changes while people speak. It's these changes in formants that help people to convey what they want to say.

> Recall from **Chapter 1** (Further insights 1.1) that the shape of an object affects its resonant frequency. Moving the articulators affects the formants by altering the shape of the vocal tract. The formants in speech correspond to the resonant frequencies of the vocal tract.

You can think of the vocal tract as being a bit like a sieve. Just as a sieve lets through some objects and not others, the vocal tract transmits some frequencies and suppresses others. Yet,

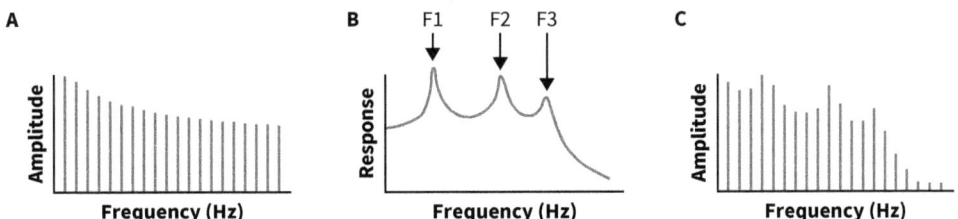

Figure 4.3 Graphs showing how harmonics (panel a) and formants (panel b) combine to produce the spectrum (panel c). We label the formant with the lowest frequency as the first formant (often abbreviated to F1), the formant with the second lowest frequency as the second formant (F2), and so on. Notice how the harmonics are equally spaced along the frequency axis (panel a), whereas the formants (F1, F2, F3: panel b) are not equally spaced.

unlike a sieve, the vocal tract is sensitive to several different frequencies at the same time: therefore, speech sounds contain several formants (Figure 4.3(b)).

> The vocal tract modifies the amplitude of the harmonics. People typically perceive changes to the amplitude of the harmonics as a change in 'timbre'. Timbre refers to the 'quality' of a sound, which differs between sounds with different spectra.

The positions of harmonics (Figure 4.3(a)) and formants (Figure 4.3(b)) are relatively independent. That's because harmonics are largely determined by how fast the vocal folds vibrate, whereas formants are mainly determined by the shape of the vocal tract. What falls through a sieve depends on both what's passed through it and the size and shape of the holes. Similarly, when a vowel sound reaches the ears, its acoustic properties depend on what entered the vocal tract of the person speaking—via their vocal folds—and the size and shape of their vocal tract. Try experimenting for yourself, if you can: try making a sustained 'ooh' sound, then—in the same breath—change the shape of your mouth so that you're producing an 'aah' sound. If you're able to do this, you should notice that you changed the sound you produced by changing the positions of your articulators (which affects the shape of your vocal tract), without changing pitch. You might find that you are also able to produce 'ooh' sounds with a different pitch while keeping your mouth still.

> The source-filter model (Chiba & Kajiyama, 1941; Fant, 1960) separates speech production into two components: the source (the vocal folds)—which determines the harmonics—and the filter (the vocal tract)—which determines the formants.

The resulting vowel sound (Figure 4.3(c)) reflects the combination of the harmonics (Figure 4.3(a)) and the formants (Figure 4.3(b)). Notice in Figure 4.3(c) that the positions of the formants affect the amplitude of each harmonic. Harmonics close to the formant frequencies have greater amplitudes than those further away from the formant frequencies.

Consonants sound a bit different, because they're produced by restricting the air flow from the lungs, which happens when people narrow—or sometimes completely obstruct—the vocal tract using their articulators (e.g. the tongue). For some consonants (like the 'f' in 'funny'), the vocal folds don't vibrate and the flow of air in the vocal tract is the sound source. For this reason, the consonant sounds more similar to noise (i.e. quite different from a harmonic complex tone!); whereas for other consonants (like the 'l' in 'clown' and the 'n' in 'clown'), the sound source is vocal fold vibration, similar to vowels. Other consonants (like the 'th' in 'the') have turbulence in the vocal tract *and* vocal fold vibration as the sound sources. These variations mean that different consonants have different acoustics (Further insights 4.1).

> The sound source that originates in the vocal tract is, essentially, a turbulent flow of air that's created by narrowing the vocal tract as air from the lungs passes through it. The vocal folds can be held open while the air passes through them, so they don't vibrate.

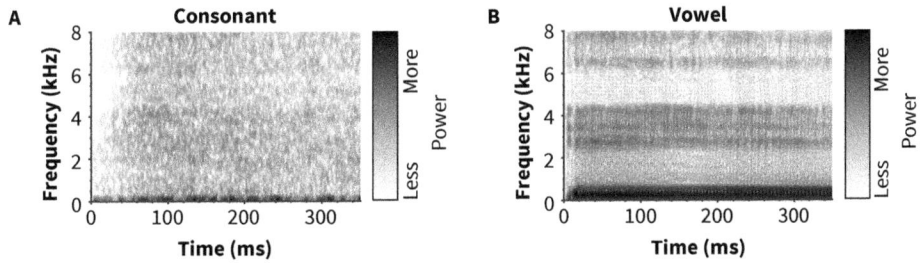

Figure 4.4 Spectrograms for consonant ('f' in 'funny'; panel a) and vowel ('y' in 'funny'; panel b) sounds when produced alone. Notice how the vowel sound has its power concentrated in specific frequency bands (i.e. the dark horizontal bands), whereas the consonant sound has its power spread more evenly across the frequency range.

> **Further insights 4.1** What differs among consonants?
>
> Consonants can be described according to three different attributes: (i) how the air is restricted (which is called the 'manner of articulation' and differentiates consonants that involve a complete obstruction—such as the 'p' in 'party'—from those that involve a narrowing of the vocal tract—such as the 'f' in 'funny'); (ii) where in the vocal tract the restriction of air flow occurs (which is called the 'place of articulation' and differentiates consonants that have a restriction around the lips—such as the 'f' in 'funny'—from those that have a restriction further back in the mouth—such as the 'c' in 'clown'); and (iii) whether the vocal folds vibrate (like the 'v' in 'van') or not (like the 'f' in 'funny') (see e.g. Zsiga, 2024 for more detail).

To hear the difference between different speech sounds, try saying the word 'funny' (Figure 4.1): if you hold the 'f' sound, you might notice that it sounds similar to noise (see Figure 4.4(a)). Most people produce an 'f' sound by placing their teeth close to their lips, which restricts the sound that comes out of their mouth, whereas you might notice that your vocal cavity opens up if you produce the 'u' sound (Figure 4.4(b)) in the middle of the word 'funny' and the 'y' sound at the end of 'funny'.

> Even though 'y' is often considered to be a consonant in written English, the 'y' sound at the end of the word 'funny' is considered as a vowel in phonetics: when produced with a British English accent, it sounds similar to the 'ee' sound in 'see'.

When people hear speech, they pick up on these types of acoustic variations, which ultimately help them to perceive words and sentences that convey meaning. But, there is much more to speech perception than piecing together vowel and consonant sounds—as the following section reveals.

4.2 How do people recognise words?

When someone listens to what their friend is saying to them at a party, they tend not to perceive a succession of modulated tones and noise bursts, but a unified percept of words and phrases. Speech **intelligibility** refers to the ability to extract words and sentences from the acoustic signal. This section examines how people recognise words and sentences in speech.

4.2.1 Speech segmentation

Have you ever walked past someone who's speaking in a different language? If you don't know the language, you might find it difficult to tell where words begin and end. That's because the acoustic signal contains surprisingly few cues for segmenting speech into words. In everyday life, people typically don't hear words spoken individually, but as part of a sentence or dialogue—and, when spoken naturally, words and syllables aren't always separated by pauses or dips in peak amplitude (i.e. places in which the amplitude envelope approaches zero). So how do people tell where words begin and end?

Certain acoustic cues have been identified as possible signals for word boundaries; for example, stress (which describes the level, duration, and pitch of the acoustic signal at some places relative to others), fundamental frequency contour, and duration. However, no single cue determines word boundaries in all contexts.

Fundamental frequency contour simply refers to changes in fundamental frequency over time. We can think of the contour as a line that goes up and down throughout a word, sentence, or longer passage of speech (Figure 4.5).

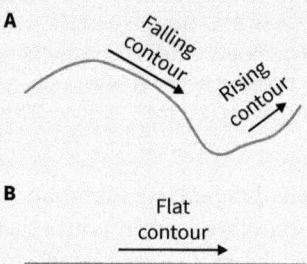

Figure 4.5 Illustrations of different fundamental frequency contours. Panel a shows a varying contour, with rising and falling portions. Panel b shows a flat contour with no variation.

Rather than relying solely on acoustics, speech segmentation depends on prior knowledge (Norris et al., 1997). As someone learns a language, it becomes easier to identify word boundaries. Their knowledge of the possible words in a language influences speech segmentation: segmentations are more likely to contain words (such as 'stem') than non-words (such as 'dems') (Billig et al., 2013). Thus, while it might seem intuitive to think that words are only recognised *after* they've been segmented, word recognition instead happens *alongside* speech segmentation.

Have you ever misheard a sentence as an entirely different sentence? Sometimes, several different segmentations of speech are possible. For example, most people find that the sentence 'Let's recognise speech' can also be interpreted as 'Let's wreck a nice beach'.

Figure 4.6 shows the time-series representation of this sentence spoken aloud and the word boundaries when it's interpreted as each of the two sentences. Curiously, not only do these sentences have entirely different meanings, but the word boundaries are also in different positions.

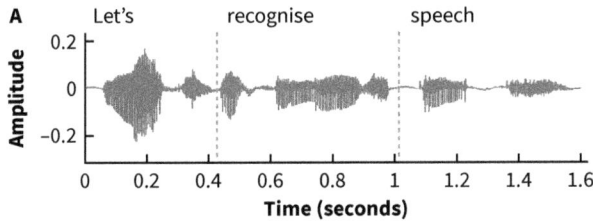

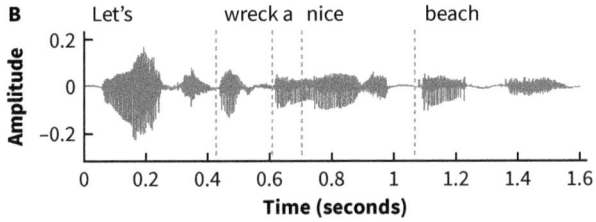

Figure 4.6 Time series of a spoken phrase. Both panels show an identical acoustic signal, but the two panels show different interpretations: 'Let's recognise speech' (panel a) and 'Let's wreck a nice beach' (panel b). Notice how the word boundaries (approximated by the vertical dashed lines) differ between the two interpretations.

When several different segmentations are plausible, context plays an important role in how people perceive speech. For example, knowing the context of a conversation can help someone to guess whether their friend is more likely to be talking about speech (e.g. if they're attending the same auditory perception classes) or going to the beach (if they are anyone else!).

4.2.2 The building blocks of speech

When someone arrives at a party, the first word they'll usually hear is 'hello'. When someone hears the 'e' sound in the word 'hello', do they: (a) perceive only the 'e'; (b) perceive it as part of the syllable 'he'; or (c) perceive as part of the whole word 'hello'? This simple example illustrates how we can consider speech at different timescales. Researchers have long debated which timescale people perceive when they hear speech—in other words, what is the 'unit' or 'building block' of speech perception?

So far in this chapter, we've discussed speech with reference to vowels and consonants—but the way that people usually learn vowels and consonants in school tends to reflect written language, rather than spoken language. When we talk about spoken language, we usually talk about **phonemes**, which describe how language *sounds*, rather than how it's written.

Phonemes are defined as the smallest unit that distinguishes one spoken word from another in a given language. For example, the 'b' in 'bet' distinguishes it from 'pet'. A phoneme can correspond either to an individual written letter as it sounds in particular words (e.g. the 'e' in 'bet') or to how several letters sound when they're spoken together (e.g. the 'ea' in 'peat' distinguishes it from 'pet'—the 'e' and the 'a' in 'peat' aren't pronounced separately).

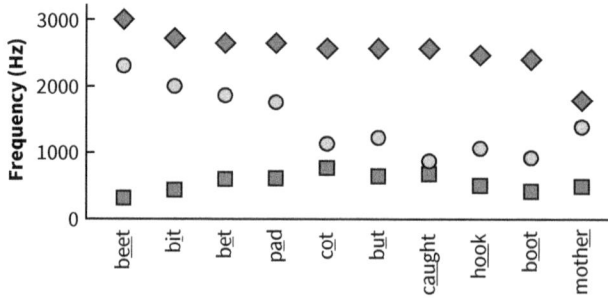

Figure 4.7 Schematic showing average frequencies (spoken by 50 males) for the first three formants of American English vowels (first formant displayed as squares; second formant displayed as circles; third formant displayed as diamonds). Different vowel categories are shown along the horizontal axis: the vowel category is underlined within an example word. Notice that each vowel category is associated with a different combination of formant frequencies.

Source: adapted from Reetz, H., & Jongman, A. (2009). *Acoustic characteristics of speech sounds.* In Phonetics: Transcription, production, acoustics, and perception (pp. 182–207).

Different phonemes have been associated with different formant frequencies (Reetz & Jongman, 2009) (Figure 4.7). Therefore, we might assume that we recognise each phoneme individually, then piece them together into words, much like constructing a jigsaw puzzle. However, if you tried to extract individual phonemes from different sentences and piece them together to make a new sentence, you'd find that the resulting sentence would be very difficult to understand! That's because the acoustic properties of phonemes depend on the word it's in, because of a phenomenon of speech production called **coarticulation**. To appreciate coarticulation for yourself, try saying 'list' then 'lost' and notice how your mouth is in a different position when you say the two words. Even though the 'l' sound is common to the two words, the acoustics of the 'l' sound differ between the two words (Figure 4.8). Therefore, when people hear a segment of speech, they can't simply match its acoustics to a particular phoneme.

Coarticulation occurs because speech is spoken quickly, and people continuously move their articulators to produce different speech sounds. This means that the formant frequencies of any spoken phoneme are influenced by where the articulators were before, and where they need to move to next. For this reason, there are few acoustic aspects of phonemes that remain constant in different speech contexts—and people cannot accurately recognise words when several phonemes have been artificially joined together (Harris, 1953). This suggests that phonemes are *not* the unit of speech perception.

Several researchers have argued that *syllables* are the unit of speech perception (Greenberg, 2006). Removing part of a syllable from a word (e.g. the 'd' from 'hands') doesn't reduce intelligibility, whereas removing an entire syllable does. However, even syllables vary acoustically between different utterances, and some researchers propose that *words* are the unit of perception (e.g. Osgood, 1963). Nevertheless, words are also perceived differently in different contexts: if someone hears the sentence 'Check the time and the . . .', they're more likely to hear the word 'date' than 'bait' when the acoustic signal is ambiguous (Bond & Garnes, 1980). This occurs for two reasons: first, 'date' is more frequently heard in the English language than 'bait'; second, 'date' is more consistent with the topic of the sentence, because 'date' and 'time' are **semantically related**.

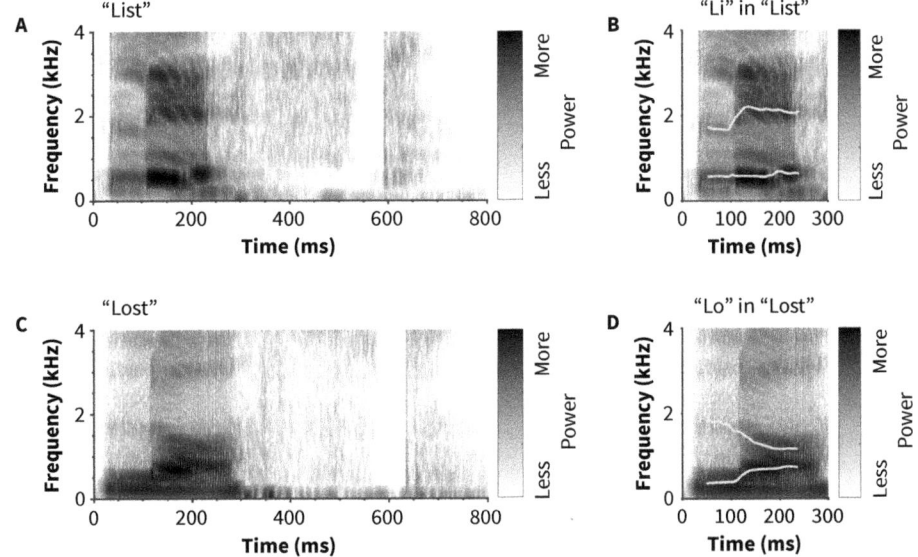

Figure 4.8 Spectrograms of 'list' (panels a and b) and 'lost' (panels c and d). The formants appear in the spectrograms as the darker horizontal bands of higher power. Panels b and d show the same spectrograms as in panels a and c, but the horizontal axis only shows the timing of the first syllable ('li' and 'lo'), and the frequencies of the first two formants are superimposed on the spectrograms. Notice in panel b how the first formant remains flat and the second formant becomes higher during the transition ('li'), whereas the two formants converge in panel d: the first formant becomes higher and the second formant becomes lower during the transition ('lo').

> If you search on the internet, you'll be able to find lots of everyday examples of how speech perception is influenced by context. For example, you could check out the 'Brainstorm / Green Needle' illusion, the 'Yanny or Laurel' illusion, or look for misheard song lyrics (which are called 'mondegreens').

So, if the acoustics of phonemes, syllables, and words all vary in different contexts, how do people perceive speech? Ultimately, there may be no single 'unit' of speech perception, but a flexible process in which context plays a big role, and speech segments are interpreted based on the context of an entire utterance (e.g. Friston et al., 2020).

4.2.3 Categorical perception

Notice in Figure 4.1 how the speech signal varies continuously. Yet, people often perceive speech categorically, which is known as **categorical perception**. That is, when the acoustic signal is between two perceptual categories (e.g. a sound they perceive as 'b' and a sound they perceive as 'p'), they usually perceive one option (e.g. either 'b' or 'p') and not something in between. In other words, the perception of speech is more similar to a light switch that can only be off or on, rather than a dimmer switch that varies the light level continuously. We can often pinpoint a perceptual boundary along the acoustic continuum where someone's perception changes, fairly suddenly, from one category to another (Figure 4.9).

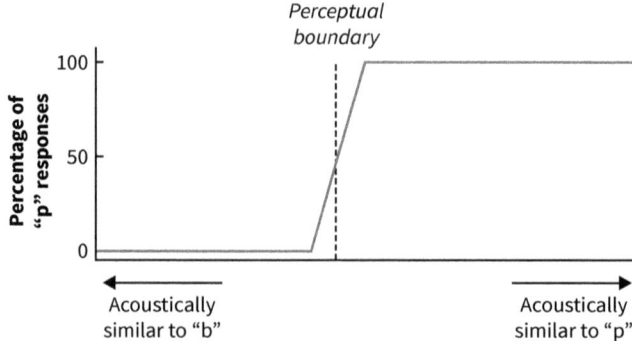

Figure 4.9 Schematic of typical experimental results that demonstrate categorical perception of speech stimuli. As the acoustic properties of the speech signal vary between two extremes (e.g. between 'b' and 'p', which differ in voice onset time; along the horizontal axis), perception changes: when given two different choices for how the sound is perceived ('b' and 'p'), the percentage of stimuli rated as 'p' increases rapidly at the perceptual boundary. Stimuli to the left of the perceptual boundary are typically perceived as 'b', whereas stimuli to the right are typically perceived as 'p'.

> The acoustic continuum between 'b' and 'p' (i.e. the x-axis of Figure 4.9) is known as voice onset time. Voice onset time refers to the time between the start of a spoken consonant and the time that the vocal folds start vibrating. While 'b' has a short voice onset time (i.e. the vocal folds start vibrating shortly after the consonant begins), 'p' has a longer voice onset time. We can change a sound from being 'b'-like to 'p'-like by artificially changing the voice onset time, so that it's longer.

> Traditional views of speech perception assumed that everyone perceives speech categorically, and any other continuous information (e.g. that distinguishes between one 'b' sound and another 'b' sound) is discarded. However, most people do seem to retain some of this continuous information. In addition, there is some evidence that children with dyslexia or specific language impairment perceive speech more continuously than typically developing children—suggesting that categorical perception differs among people (see e.g. Kapnoula et al., 2017).

The perceptual boundary is not fixed and varies in different contexts. When presented as part of a word, sounds close to the perceptual boundary are more likely to be perceived in a way that completes a real word. For example, an ambiguous sound between 'k' and 'g' is more likely to be perceived as 'g' when followed by 'ift' by an English listener, because 'gift' is a word and 'kift' isn't a word in English. In addition, when people listen to artificial speech sounds with computerised 'accents', their categorisation responses change, demonstrating that learning plays a role in categorical perception (Holt et al., 2018). The effect of a word's context on the perceptual boundary is known as the 'Ganong effect' (Ganong, 1980).

4.2.4 Lack of invariance

Imagine how the word 'hello' can sound very different when it's spoken by different people, or when someone is happy or sad. The acoustics of a word are affected not only by its linguistic composition (i.e. which syllables or phonemes it contains), but also by the person who speaks it, and the **prosody** they use. This has been called the 'lack of invariance' problem (Liberman et al., 1957), because the word 'hello' has different acoustics each time it's spoken.

> Prosody encompasses changes in pitch, level, and duration when someone speaks. Prosody is covered in more detail in **Section 4.4**.

Researchers have debated how information about what was said (i.e. linguistic content) is separated from *who* said it (i.e. voice information). For example, this could involve processes specific to speech perception that somehow involve removing voice information from the acoustic signal (Johnson & Sjerps, 2021). However, linguistic content and voice information are intermingled in the acoustic signal, and are very difficult to separate. Unlike a fingerprint, which looks very similar on different surfaces, a voice doesn't have a consistent effect on speech and instead varies with each spoken utterance.

Rather than using processes specific to speech perception, the 'lack of invariance' problem may instead be resolved by the same processes that people use to perceive non-speech sounds. Consistent with this idea, a listener's interpretation of speech is affected by the frequencies of sounds that came before it, even if those sounds are not speech (Huang & Holt, 2012). Figure 4.10 shows an experiment in which an ambiguous word—which could either be perceived as 'bet' or 'but'—was preceded by the phrase, 'Please say what this word is'. Participants were more likely to say 'but' if the frequencies of the phrase were shifted higher, and they were more likely to say 'bet' if the frequencies of the phrase were shifted lower—even though the word itself was acoustically identical in both cases! People's perception of the word changed in the same way when it was preceded by a sequence of tones that were higher or lower in frequency, instead of a spoken phrase. Therefore, when people perceive words, they take into account the context in which the word is heard—regardless of whether the context is someone's voice or another (seemingly irrelevant) sound.

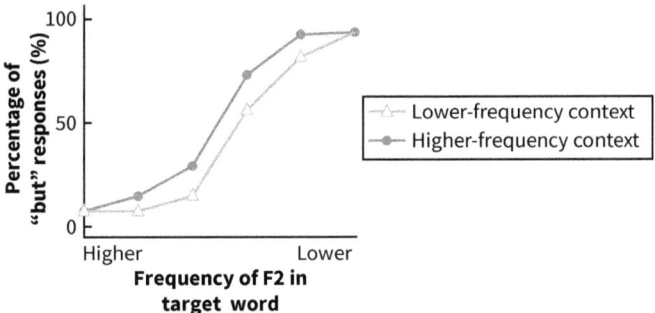

Figure 4.10 Results of Huang & Holt (2012), showing that spectral context affects speech perception. The percentage of 'but' responses (vertical axis) changes with the frequency of the second formant (F2) of 'bet' / 'but' (horizontal axis). Although, notice there are differences in the percentages of 'but' responses between two contexts: preceding the word 'bet' / 'but' was a spoken phrase ('Please say the word . . .') that was presented at a higher (circles) or lower (triangles) frequency. Participants were more likely to report 'but' in the higher-frequency context than in the lower-frequency context.

Source: data from Huang & Holt (2012). 'Listening for the norm: adaptive coding in speech categorization.' *Frontiers in Psychology*, 3(Feb), 10. https://doi.org/10.3389/fpsyg.2012.00010

4.3 Voices

Speech also contains information about *who's* talking. When you watch TV, you might notice that different people's voices sound different. Imagine hearing a new voice over the phone or on the radio: you might be able to guess some characteristics about the person talking just from hearing their voice. So, how do people use information from someone's voice to work out who they are? This section explains how people can identify who's speaking when they hear speech.

4.3.1 Size

Different people are different shapes and sizes. Just as the size and shape of people's feet differ—which affects their shoe size—so do the mass of their vocal folds and the size and shape of their vocal tract. Broadly speaking, people who are larger have bigger vocal folds and longer vocal tracts. These physical attributes have some systematic effects on the speech that they produce. Vocal folds with greater mass typically vibrate at slower rates, which gives a voice a lower fundamental frequency. For this reason, people tend to associate lower voices with people who are physically larger. Also, the length and shape of each person's vocal tract affects its resonant frequencies, which affects the formant frequencies in speech: formants are further apart (known as formant spacing) when speech is produced by someone with a longer rather than a shorter vocal tract (Turner et al., 2009).

> Most people perceive voices with a lower fundamental frequency as having a lower pitch. You can review pitch in **Chapter 2**.

Despite these physical associations, no voice is associated with just one fundamental frequency and one pattern of formant frequencies: the fundamental frequency and formant frequencies of a voice change as someone speaks different words (as described in Section 4.2). Also, imagine someone singing: even though they have a 'comfortable' fundamental frequency, they can produce sounds with a wide variety of fundamental frequencies. Ultimately, the speech that someone produces is a combination of their physical characteristics and flexible changes that arise when they move their articulators and adjust the tension of their vocal folds. Often, the extent to which someone can change their fundamental frequency and vocal tract is bigger than the differences between people (Markel & Davis, 1979)—which means that it's unlikely that someone will get an accurate estimate of a person's size from hearing them speak just one word.

4.3.2 Voice gender

Most research into the perception of voice gender has typically categorised voices into male and female (although see Further insights 4.2). Differences between the voices of men and women are typically attributed to differences in size and body mass. On average, women's voices have a higher fundamental frequency than men's voices: the average fundamental frequency of a woman's voice is 223 Hz and the average fundamental frequency of a man's voice is 132 Hz (Peterson & Barney, 1952). However, the distributions of fundamental frequencies overlap considerably between men and women. Also, formant frequencies are approximately 20% higher, on average, for women's voices compared to men's voices—but, again, this varies substantially across people (Fant, 1966).

> **Further insights 4.2** Non-binary voice gender
>
> In recent years, research on non-binary voice gender perception has become more prevalent. For example, some research has allowed people to choose among categories of 'masculine', 'feminine', and 'other', or to rate voices on continuous gender scales. In addition, some research has included participants with a variety of gender identities (e.g. those who describe themselves as transgender and/or non-binary) to examine how someone's gender identity affects their perception of voice gender. The results have revealed differences in voice gender classification among people who have different gender identities. For example, participants who reported a non-binary gender identity were more likely to categorise gender-neutral voices as non-binary, compared to people who reported they were cisgender (Hope & Lilley, 2022).
>
> Given that the perception of femininity often relates to a higher fundamental frequency and higher formant frequencies, transgender individuals tend to adjust these aspects of their voices. This phenomenon implies that voices are strongly related to an individual's perception of their identity.

In general, people can accurately recognise whether a person is male or female from fundamental frequency alone *or* from formant frequencies alone—and listeners misidentify the gender of a voice when either is artificially manipulated (Fellowes et al., 1997). Manipulating both the fundamental frequency and formant frequencies of speech leads to convincing changes in perceived gender (Skuk & Schweinberger, 2014).

4.3.3 Age

Imagine the voices of a 4-year-old, a 14-year-old, and a 40-year-old: they all sound different. Given that size impacts the properties of speech, it's not too surprising that people's voices change from childhood into adulthood. Children have average fundamental frequencies of approximately 264 Hz, whereas adults have lower fundamental frequencies: on average, around 178 Hz (Peterson & Barney, 1952). Children also have higher formant frequencies—which are approximately 20% higher than adult females (Fant, 1966)—because they have shorter vocal tracts.

4.3.4 Identity

When people hear a voice over the phone, how do they tell who it is? Every voice is different, and people can often recognise someone's identity from their voice, especially if they're familiar with the person who's speaking. However, recognising someone from their voice can be challenging, because voices sound different in different contexts—and no single acoustic property is unique to one person's voice.

Given that fundamental frequency and formant spacing convey information about someone's size, age, and voice gender, it seems intuitive that people use these same properties of speech to help work out someone's identity. People use both fundamental frequency and formant spacing to help them distinguish among several different voices that are unfamiliar to them. Most people can also use this information to recognise familiar people (e.g. friends or family) from their voices. Other acoustic properties—such as the shape of the spectrum—contribute too (Matsumoto et al., 1973).

Several studies have tried to work out which acoustic property contributes *most* to identity perception. Changing formant spacing seems to have a greater impact on familiar-voice recognition than changing fundamental frequency—suggesting that most people rely more heavily on formant spacing. This could be because formant spacing is more stable across contexts than fundamental frequency, making it a more reliable indicator of voice identity (Gaudrain et al., 2009). In other words, most people can change the fundamental frequency of their voice to a greater extent than they can change the size of their vocal tract. However, studies disagree on which properties contribute most to voice identity perception, and some researchers have proposed that properties people use to identify someone depend on which are most distinctive among the particular set of talkers that they're trying to distinguish (Lee et al., 2019). For example, your friend might have a distinctive fundamental frequency when compared with five people who have higher fundamental frequencies, whereas their low formant spacing may be more distinctive if you were trying to pick out their voice among people who have similarly low fundamental frequencies.

4.4 Prosody

How often have you been confused by a text message or email, only for the misunderstandings to be easily resolved in person? A possible reason is because speech doesn't only convey words, but also carries meaning that isn't conveyed by the words themselves. Spoken speech contains prosody, which encompasses changes in pitch, level, and duration—and can be thought of as *how* something is being said. This section describes how prosody can alter the meaning of speech and convey emotion.

4.4.1 Conveying meaning

Although the stereotypical professor has a reputation for speaking in monotone (i.e. with a stable fundamental frequency), most speech varies in fundamental frequency over time. **Intonation** refers to variations in fundamental frequency across a word, sentence, or longer passage of speech.

In British English, intonation is used to convey whether someone is speaking a question or a statement. Statements usually have a relatively flat fundamental frequency contour, whereas questions have a contour that rises on the last word. From the spectrograms in Figure 4.11, you might be able to see that the same word ('party') has a rising contour (i.e. the fundamental frequency gets higher towards the end of the word) at the end of a question ('You had a party?'; Figure 4.11(b)), but is flatter when it's at the end of a statement ('You had a party'; Figure 4.11(d)).

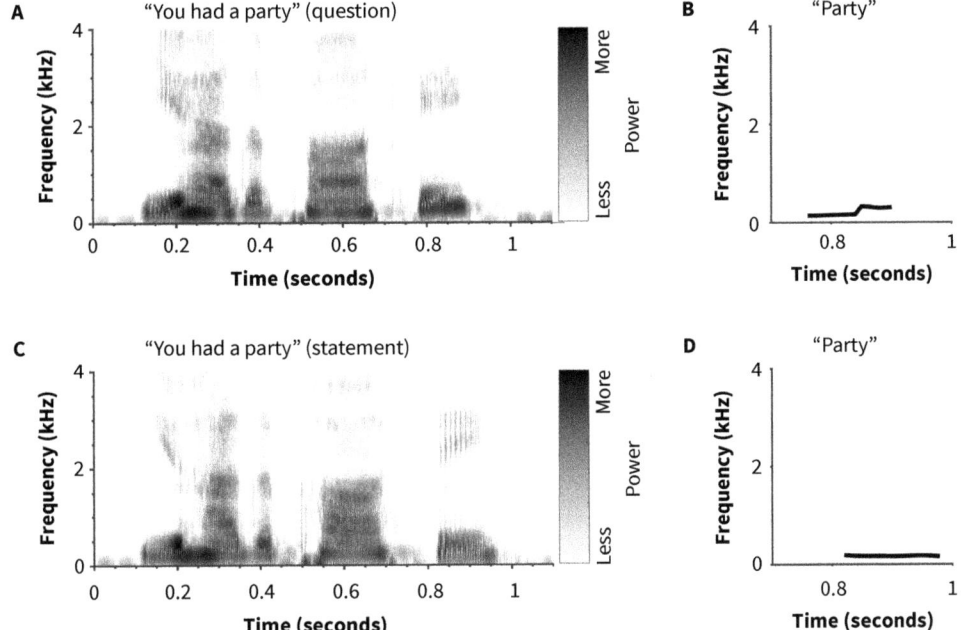

Figure 4.11 The spoken sentence 'You had a party' when spoken as a question (panels a and b) and as a statement (panels c and d). Panels a and c show spectrograms of the spoken sentences. Panels b and d show the corresponding fundamental frequency contours of the final word 'party'. Notice how the frequency contour of 'party' differs between the two panels depending on whether it is part of a question or part of a statement.

> In tonal languages, intonation affects a word's meaning. For example, in Mandarin Chinese, 'mā' is spoken with a flat pitch contour and means mother. Whereas, 'mǎ', which means horse, is spoken with a pitch contour that falls and then rises. Therefore, recognising the pitch contour of a word is particularly important in tonal languages—you wouldn't want to accidentally call your mother a horse!

Relative sound level can also emphasise particular words within a sentence. Compare the following two sentences: 'Do you have a *pen*', and 'Do *you* have a pen'. In the former, the level is greater for the word 'pen' than the other words in the sentence, emphasising that the talker is asking for a pen, rather than a pencil; in the latter, the level is greater for the word 'you', emphasising that the talker is asking the listener, rather than someone else in the room. Emphasis can also be conveyed by small changes in duration. Therefore, the word 'pen' may also have a longer duration in the sentence 'Do you have a *pen*' than 'Do *you* have a pen'; whereas, 'you' may have a longer duration in the second sentence than the first.

4.4.2 Conveying emotion

People also use prosody to convey emotion, such as happiness or fear. Imagine how someone might say, 'That dog's coming towards us', differently depending on whether they're happy or scared. If they're scared, they might speak faster and put emphasis on different words (e.g. 'dog' if they're happy or 'us' if they're scared).

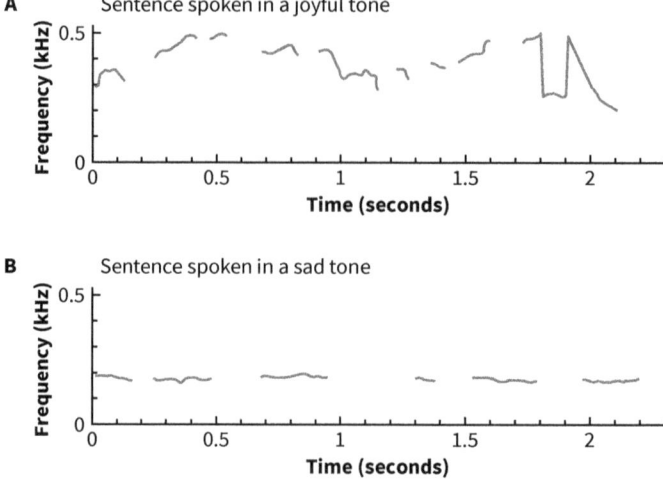

Figure 4.12 The fundamental frequency contours for a sentence spoken in a joyful tone (panel a) and a sad tone (panel b). Notice how the frequency contour varies more when the sentence is spoken in a joyful tone as opposed to a sad tone—the sad tone has a relatively flat frequency contour.

Different emotions are associated with different average fundamental frequencies (Figure 4.12), amplitudes, and **tempos**—and also different amounts of variability in these properties (Pittam & Scherer, 1993). However, the acoustic properties associated with different emotions overlap, and no individual acoustic cue is diagnostic of a particular emotion. For example, anger has some similar acoustic properties to happiness: a high fundamental frequency, large variability in fundamental frequency, and a high amplitude.

In the context of speech perception, 'tempo' refers to the speed at which speech is spoken.

In general, people are quite good at recognising emotion in voices. However, some emotions are recognised better than others: people are better at recognising joy, sadness, and anger than they are at recognising fear and disgust (Pittam & Scherer, 1993).

Like voice identity, some researchers have studied which acoustic properties are *most* important for recognising emotion. Several studies found that variability in fundamental frequency is the most important property (Ladd et al., 1985). However, one study found that **tempo** was more important than fundamental frequency (Breitenstein et al., 2001). Interestingly, people can still recognise emotion above chance following a range of manipulations that disrupt different acoustic properties. Overall, this suggests that people can use a variety of acoustic properties to provide clues about someone's emotions.

4.5 Speech processing in the brain

So far, this chapter has examined the ways in which most people perceive speech, but how is speech processed in the auditory pathway? Like other sounds, speech evokes responses at all stages of the auditory pathway, but it's usually associated with additional brain activity above and beyond simple tones. This section provides an overview of some brain responses that have been associated with speech perception.

> You can review the stages of the auditory pathway in **Chapter 1**.

4.5.1 Decoding speech from brain activity

Given that many people perceive speech categorically ('categorical perception'), we might expect to find brain responses that are categorical—in other words, brain responses that are more similar for speech that belongs to the same category than for speech that belongs to different categories, regardless of acoustics. Indeed, studies have shown that speech categories are present in brain responses (Formisano et al., 2008): different vowels can be 'decoded' from activity in **bilateral** superior temporal cortex, even when the vowels are spoken by different people and, therefore, have different acoustics. This result implies that the brain contains a representation of vowel content irrespective of talker identity. Similarly, different talker identities can be decoded from a different—but partly overlapping—area of cortex, regardless of which vowel is spoken.

> 'Decoding' refers to a method in cognitive neuroscience, in which an algorithm is trained to learn how brain activity relates to different stimuli (e.g. speech sounds). Once the algorithm has been trained to learn the relationship, we can give it new brain data and see whether it can work out (i.e. 'decode') which sounds were presented when that brain activity was recorded. If it can decode the sounds correctly, then we can say that the brain responses contain information about those stimuli. It's like playing a game in which you're trying to guess a celebrity's name based on clues provided by someone else—just as their responses allow you to guess the celebrity's name, in the game of 'decoding', brain responses allow us to guess which sounds were presented.

4.5.2 Are brain responses to speech special?

Recall from **Chapter 1** that some neurons in secondary auditory cortex respond more vigorously to vocalisations than to simpler stimuli. A hierarchy has been proposed in the brain, whereby early auditory cortex processes basic acoustic features and higher auditory areas process complex combinations of features, such as those present in speech. Like building a house, the basic foundations need to be laid first, before more complex structures can be built on top. Early stages of auditory cortex (Heschl's gyrus and planum temporale) respond similarly to speech and non-speech sounds and, therefore, can be considered as processing basic features that are common to a variety of sounds. In contrast, parts of superior temporal cortex—including the superior temporal gyrus and superior temporal sulcus, which are further along in the auditory pathway—respond more to speech than to non-speech sounds (i.e. tones and noise) and are thought to be particularly sensitive to complex combinations of features that are present in speech (Binder et al., 2000) (see Figure 4.13(a)).

Given that some areas of the brain show greater responses to speech than to other sounds, some researchers have claimed that speech is special and has a unique representation in the brain. However, this argument is hotly contested: some regions may respond more to speech simply because it is acoustically complex or because listeners are highly familiar with speech, and so these responses may not be unique to speech (Price, 2012).

> The left anterior superior temporal sulcus (STS) has been shown to relate to other acoustically complex stimuli, and other areas—such as the left posterior STS—are associated with the familiarity of words (Price, 2012).

4.5.3 Speech intelligibility in the brain

A related question is: What makes speech intelligible? In other words, if someone is listening to their friend speaking, how can they identify the words that their friend is saying?

Understanding where speech intelligibility occurs in the brain is a challenge, because a pure intelligibility representation would be independent of acoustics. Most studies addressing this question have compared intelligible speech with unintelligible sounds

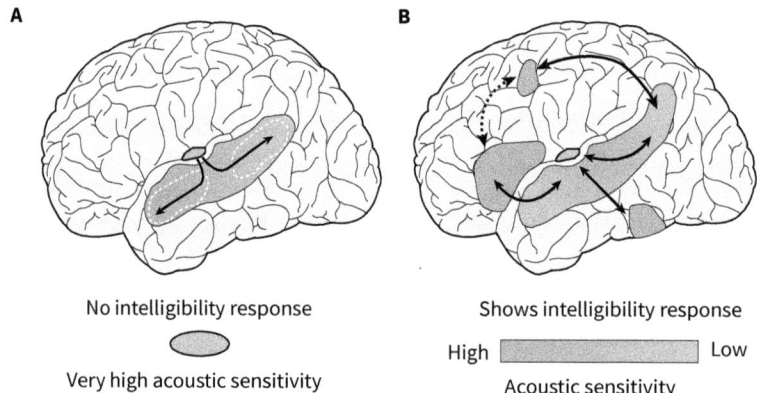

Figure 4.13 Schematic showing general patterns of brain imaging results, from Peelle et al. (2010). As illustrated in panel a, primary auditory cortex responds to auditory input (i.e. shows high acoustic sensitivity) but its response is largely unaffected by whether the input is intelligible or unintelligible (i.e. no intelligibility response). In contrast, responses in superior temporal cortex are sensitive to the intelligibility of speech. Panel b displays an extension of the speech hierarchy shown in panel a that goes beyond superior temporal cortex and includes areas that are sensitive to the intelligibility and not the acoustics of speech. In both panels, outlines show functional boundaries between areas of cortex and arrows indicate the proposed flow of information between areas.

Source: from Peelle, Johnsrude, & Davis (2010). 'Hierarchical processing for speech in human auditory cortex and beyond.' *Frontiers in Human Neuroscience*, 4, 1735.

(Further insights 4.3), but because the sounds differ in both intelligibility and acoustics, it's difficult to elucidate the reason for any differences in brain responses.

> **Further insights 4.3** **Degraded speech**
>
> In everyday life, people sometimes encounter degraded speech; for example, a bad telephone connection or listening to someone speak in a large, echoey room. In experiments, researchers can degrade speech deliberately—either to mimic everyday settings in which speech is degraded or to test the role that specific aspects of speech play in speech perception. People are surprisingly good at understanding speech after it's been degraded in different ways (Warren et al., 1995).
>
> One common stimulus used in experiments is **noise-vocoded speech**: the amplitude envelope is extracted in different frequency ranges, and the temporal fine structure within each range is replaced by noise that's modulated by the amplitude envelope (Shannon et al., 1995). Just as it's more difficult to tell what's shown in a picture when the image is pixelated, it's more difficult to understand speech when it's been noise-vocoded. Noise vocoding reduces the frequency resolution of speech, and removes the harmonic structure, because the temporal fine structure has been replaced by noise. Therefore, information about the fundamental frequency of speech is degraded. However, the amplitude modulations are preserved. Noise-vocoded speech can be used to test the role of detailed frequency information in perception.
>
> **Tone-vocoded speech** is similar to noise-vocoded speech, but the temporal fine structure is replaced by a pure tone, rather than noise.
>
> **Sine-wave speech** is a different type of manipulation: modulated tones are generated that track the frequencies of the formants of speech and the original speech signal is discarded. Therefore, much of the acoustic information is removed and sine-wave speech only contains information about speech formants. Interestingly, even though it's more difficult to understand sine-wave speech than natural speech, words and sentences in sine-wave speech can still often be recognised, which demonstrates that this limited formant information is enough for listeners to perceive the content of speech (Remez et al., 1981).

Davis and Johnsrude (2003) took a unique approach by comparing intelligible speech to various forms of less intelligible speech. Speech was made less intelligible by manipulating it in different ways: for example, by adding background noise or by using noise-vocoding (see Further insights 4.3). This method allowed them to separate out any specific acoustic manipulation from the decrease in intelligibility that was common to all of the manipulations. They found that responses in superior temporal cortex primarily depend on acoustics rather than intelligibility, whereas other regions in the temporal and frontal lobes show responses that vary with intelligibility, regardless of acoustics. Their results imply an extension of the speech hierarchy we introduced in Section 4.5.2: primary auditory cortex responds to basic acoustic features present in all sounds, superior temporal cortex responds most to complex combinations of acoustic features that are present in speech, and other areas of temporal and frontal cortex respond most when speech is intelligible (Figure 4.13(b)).

Other researchers have taken a different approach: rather than examining *where* in the brain responds to speech, they have investigated *how* the brain responds to speech. One aspect of speech that has been linked to intelligibility is the amplitude envelope. Most people's brains track the amplitude envelope of all sounds, including unintelligible sounds, such as speech played backwards and speech in a foreign language: brain responses increase when the amplitude of a sound increases, and they decrease when the amplitude of a sound decreases. However, some researchers have claimed that better tracking of the amplitude envelope is what makes speech intelligible: they find better tracking for intelligible than unintelligible speech (Vanthornhout et al., 2018). A brain imaging study found, more specifically, that envelope tracking in the superior temporal sulcus correlates with speech intelligibility (Hausfeld et al., 2024). Supporting the view that intelligibility is linked to brain responses for the amplitude envelope, people cannot understand speech as accurately when their brains are stimulated in a way that disrupts the ability to track the envelope (Wilsch et al., 2018). Yet, other research suggests that better tracking of the envelope doesn't always relate to better intelligibility: sometimes, better tracking is associated with *worse* intelligibility, for example in people with hearing loss and in older people (Zan et al., 2020). Therefore, how cortical tracking of the amplitude envelope relates to speech intelligibility is still debated.

4.5.4 Lateralisation of brain responses

Traditionally, speech processing was thought to be **lateralised** to the left hemisphere of the brain. This was based on studies in patients who had suffered brain damage (e.g. to Broca and Wernicke's areas, which are both in the left hemisphere; see Further insights 4.4): patients who have lesions that include the left superior temporal gyrus are more likely to have speech-processing deficits than patients who have only right-hemisphere lesions (Griffiths et al., 1999). However, the brain reorganises after damage, and it may simply be the case that one hemisphere is better at reorganising than the other. Neuroimaging studies in healthy people show responses in bilateral superior temporal cortex when people listen to speech, suggesting that both hemispheres are actively engaged in speech processing. Nevertheless, there are still ongoing debates about whether the left hemisphere plays a *greater* role than the right hemisphere in perceiving speech (Giroud et al., 2020).

We say that a response is lateralised if it only takes place in the left hemisphere or the right hemisphere of the brain, whereas we say that a response is bilateral if it takes place in both hemispheres. For a response that takes place in both hemispheres, we can say that one hemisphere is dominant, which means that responses are stronger (or more important) in that hemisphere than in the other.

Further insights 4.4   Broca's and Wernicke's areas

Broca's and Wernicke's areas are among the most widely known areas of the brain. These areas are based on seminal cases where patients seemingly lost particular aspects of speech production and/or perception. Broca (1861) noticed that patients who had damage to a posterior region of the left inferior frontal gyrus—which was subsequently dubbed **Broca's area** (Figure 4.14)—all had a common pattern of

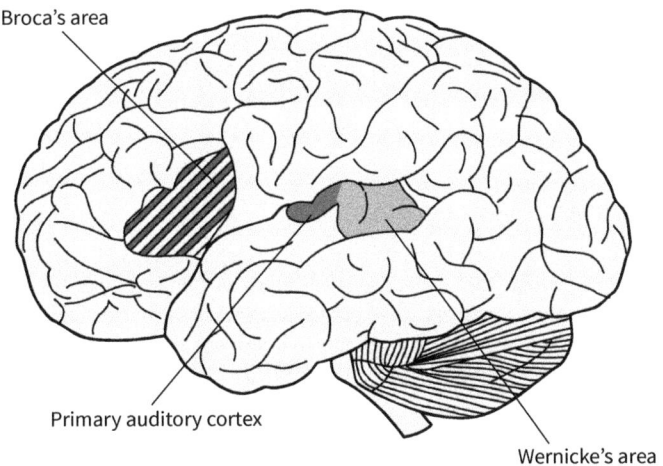

Figure 4.14 Anatomical locations of Broca's and Wernicke's areas. Notice how the two areas are located in different parts of the brain, which explains why patients with damage to each of these areas have different types of difficulties.

Source: adapted from Goldsmith, M., 'Hearing sound.' *Sound: A Very Short Introduction*, (Oxford, 2015; online edn, Oxford Academic, 17 Dec. 2015), https://doi.org/10.1093/actrade/9780198708445.003.0004

difficulties. These patients articulated speech very slowly, although they produced speech that was correct and meaningful, and their speech comprehension was only mildly affected. Interestingly, Wernicke (1874) identified a set of patients who seemed to display the opposite pattern: their speech production was grammatically correct, but the speech they produced was meaningless, and they also had difficulties comprehending speech. These patients had damage to the posterior portion of the left superior temporal gyrus, which is now known as **Wernicke's area**. Crucially, these cases demonstrate that different aspects of speech rely on separate brain areas, at least to a certain extent. This work has been highly influential, and subsequent research has examined the precise roles of these areas. Yet, researchers now know that speech perception and comprehension engage a much wider network of cortical areas.

Some theories (e.g. Hickok & Poeppel, 2000, 2007) propose that acoustic processing of speech is bilateral, but the process of extracting words is left-lateralised. Other theories propose that even acoustic processing of speech is left-dominant. For example, one idea is that the left hemisphere is specialised for fast temporal processing, whereas the right hemisphere is specialised for fine-grained spectral processing (Zatorre et al., 2002)—and because speech progresses quickly in time, it draws heavily on processes that occur in the left hemisphere. Yet, competing theories have not yet been fully resolved.

4.5.5 Involvement of motor cortex

Another debate in the literature is whether motor cortex (Further insights 4.5) plays an important role in speech perception. The motor theory assumes that speech perception occurs in motor space, rather than in acoustic space. According to this theory, a listener understands what their friend has said by working out how they themselves would have moved their articulators if they had produced the same sounds; by calculating these movements, the listener infers what their friend intended to say. Under this view, speech perception is argued to be heavily intertwined with speech production.

> **Further insights 4.5 Motor cortex**
>
> Motor cortex is in a different area of the brain than the other regions discussed so far (Figure 4.15). It is located in the frontal lobe next to the central sulcus, which is a division that separates the frontal lobe from the parietal lobe. Motor cortex is known to play an important role in speech production, but the extent to which it plays a key role in speech perception is hotly debated. By comparing Figures 4.13(b) and 4.15, notice that an area of premotor cortex is highlighted in Figure 4.13(b) as being sensitive to speech intelligibility.
>
>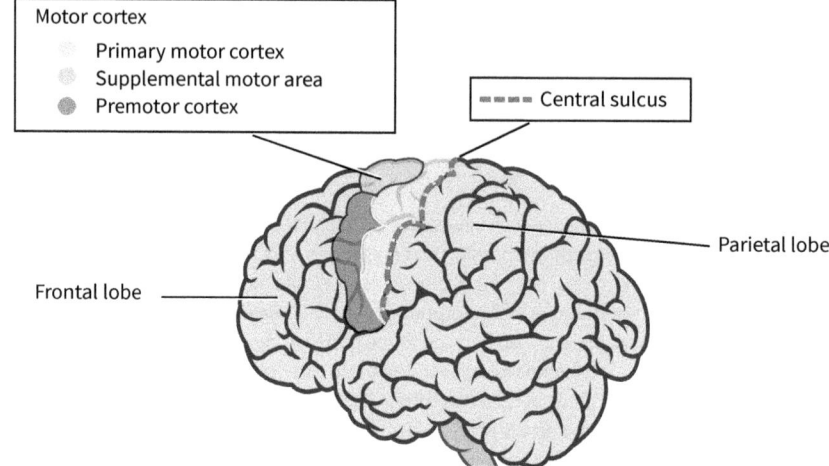
>
> **Figure 4.15** Motor cortex includes primary motor cortex, supplementary motor area, and premotor cortex. Only the left hemisphere of the brain is shown in the image, but motor cortex also includes the corresponding areas in the right hemisphere.

There is evidence that motor cortex responds when people passively listen to speech, and is associated with better speech comprehension. However, the strongest version of the motor theory assumes that motor areas are *critical* for speech perception, and several pieces of evidence speak against this. For example, infants can understand speech before they're able to produce it themselves (Eimas et al., 1971), and people who never develop the ability to speak fluently can still understand speech (Bishop et al., 1990).

Less extreme versions of the motor theory are still debated. Some researchers argue that motor representations are helpful for understanding speech, even if they're not critical—especially when speech is difficult to understand. Analysing the pattern of results across neuroimaging studies, researchers have found some overlap in frontal and temporal areas of the brain that respond during speech perception and production, regardless of the context; whereas overlap in motor cortex only occurs when speech perception is challenging (Perron et al., 2024). Consistent with the idea that motor representations are helpful for understanding speech, speech perception can be disrupted by stimulating motor areas of the brain (Smalle et al., 2015).

4.5.6 Brain processing of non-linguistic aspects of speech

So far in this section, we've mainly considered brain responses to the *content* of speech (i.e. extracting words or sentences from the acoustic signal)—but how are other aspects of speech covered in this chapter (such as voice identity and prosody) processed in the brain? For example, does a friend's voice elicit responses different to responses to the voice of a stranger?

The 'auditory face' model proposes that voice identity, speech content, and emotion are processed in distinct (albeit interacting) areas of the brain (Belin et al., 2004). This idea is consistent with findings from patient lesion studies, which show that voice identity, speech content, and emotion can each be selectively impacted (Roswandowitz et al., 2018). For example, patients who have difficulties with voice recognition can show typical comprehension of speech and intact emotional processing. On the other hand, neuroimaging studies in healthy people—including the one described in Section 4.5.1—show that areas of the brain that respond to speech content overlap with areas that respond to voice-specific content (von Kriegstein et al., 2010). Ultimately, this work implies that responses to the content of speech are not entirely separate from responses to voice identity and emotion in speech, and interact in the brain in people without brain damage.

> The 'auditory face' model is based on an influential model of face perception—as you may be able to guess, given its name. According to the 'auditory face' model, common low-level analysis of speech occurs in primary auditory cortex, and processing of voice identity occurs in the anterior portion of the superior temporal sulcus in the right hemisphere (Belin & Zatorre, 2003).

Summary

Recognising words would be straightforward if every word was associated with invariant acoustic properties, but the acoustic signal varies considerably in different contexts. Thus, speech recognition is not simply a case of recognising prescribed acoustic segments. To add to this complexity, speech also contains voice and prosody information, which affect the acoustic signal in various ways. All of these aspects of speech are represented in brain responses and are not processed entirely separately.

Further your understanding

Reetz, H., & Jongman, A. (2009). *Phonetics: Transcription, Production, Acoustics, and Perception* (Chapter 10: pp. 182–207). Chichester, Wiley-Blackwell.

Scott, S. K., & Wise, R. J. (2004). 'The functional neuroanatomy of prelexical processing in speech perception.' *Cognition*, 92(1–2), 13–45.

References

Belin, P., & Zatorre, R. J. (2003). 'Adaptation to speaker's voice in right anterior temporal lobe.' *Neuroreport*, 14(16), 2105–2109. https://doi.org/10.1097/00001756-200311140-00019

Belin, P., Fecteau, S., & Bédard, C. (2004). 'Thinking the voice: Neural correlates of voice perception.' *Trends in Cognitive Sciences*, 8(3), 129–135. https://doi.org/10.1016/j.tics.2004.01.008

Billig, A. J., Davis, M. H., Deeks, J. M., Monstrey, J., & Carlyon, R. P. (2013). 'Lexical influences on auditory streaming.' *Current Biology*, 23(16), 1585–1589. https://doi.org/10.1016/j.cub.2013.06.042

Binder, J. R., Frost, J. A., Hammeke, T. A., Bellgowan, P. S., Springer, J. A., Kaufman, J. N., & Possing, E. T. (2000). 'Human temporal lobe activation by speech and nonspeech sounds.' *Cerebral Cortex*, 10(5), 512–528. Retrieved from http://www.ncbi.nlm.nih.gov/pubmed/10847601

Bishop, D. V. M., Byers Brown, B., & Robson, J. (1990). 'The relationship between phoneme discrimination, speech production, and language comprehension in cerebral-palsied individuals.' *Journal of Speech and Hearing Research*, 33(2), 210–219. https://doi.org/10.1044/jshr.3302.210

Bond, Z. S., & Garnes, S. (2017). 'Misperceptions of fluent speech.' In R. A. Cole (ed.) *Perception and Production of Fluent Speech* (pp. 115–132). Abingdon and New York: Routledge.

Breitenstein, C., Van Lancker, D., & Daum, I. (2001). 'The contribution of speech rate and pitch variation to the perception of vocal emotions in a German and an American sample.' *Cognition and Emotion*, 15(1), 57–79. https://doi.org/10.1080/02699930126095

Broca, P. (1861). 'Nouvelle observation d'aphémie produite par une lésion de la moitié postérieure des deuxième et troisième circonvolutions frontales.' In *Bulletins de la Société Anatomique de Paris* (vol. 36), Paris.

Chiba, T. & Kajiyama, M. (1941). *The Vowel: Its Nature and Structure*. Tokyo: Tokyo-Kaiseikan.

Davis, M. H., & Johnsrude, I. S. (2003). 'Hierarchical processing in spoken language comprehension.' *Journal of Neuroscience*, 23(8), 3423–3431. https://doi.org/10.1523/jneurosci.23-08-03423.2003

Duchin, S. W., & Mysak, E. D. (1987). 'Disfluency and rate characteristics of young adult, middle-aged, and older males.' *Journal of Communication Disorders*, 20(3), 245–257. https://doi.org/10.1016/0021-9924(87)90022-0

Eimas, P. D., Siqueland, E. R., Jusczyk, P., & Vigorito, J. (1971). 'Speech perception in infants.' *Science*, 171(3968), 303–306. https://doi.org/10.1126/science.171.3968.303

Fant, G. (1960). *Acoustic Theory of Speech Production*. The Hague: De Gruyter Mouton.

Fant, G. (1966). 'A note on vocal tract size factors and non-uniform F-pattern scalings.' *STL-QPSR*, 7(4), 22–30.

Fellowes, J. M., Remez, R. E., & Rubin, P. E. (1997). 'Perceiving the sex and identity of a talker without natural vocal timbre.' *Perception and Psychophysics*, 59(6), 839–849. https://doi.org/10.3758/BF03205502

Formisano, E., Martino, F. De, Bonte, M., & Goebel, R. (2008). ' "Who" is saying "what"? Brain-based decoding of human voice and speech.' *Science*, 322(November), 970–973. Retrieved from http://www.sciencemag.org/content/322/5903/970.short

Friston, K. J., Parr, T., Yufik, Y., Sajid, N., Price, C. J., & Holmes, E. (2020). 'Generative models, linguistic communication and active inference.' *Neuroscience and Biobehavioral Reviews*, 118, 42–64. https://doi.org/10.1016/j.neubiorev.2020.07.005

Ganong, W. F. (1980). 'Phonetic categorization in auditory word perception.' *Journal of Experimental Psychology: Human Perception and Performance*, 6, 110–125.

Gaudrain, E., Li, S., Ban, V. S., & Patterson, R. D. (2009). 'The role of glottal pulse rate and vocal tract length in the perception of speaker identity.' *Proceedings of the Annual Conference of the International Speech Communication Association, INTERSPEECH*, 148–151.

Giroud, J., Trébuchon, A., Schön, D., Marquis, P., Liegeois-Chauvel, C., Poeppel, D., & Morillon, B. (2020). 'Asymmetric sampling in human auditory cortex reveals spectral processing hierarchy.' *PLoS Biology*, 18(3), e3000207. https://doi.org/10.1371/journal.pbio.3000207

Greenberg, S. (2006). 'Listening to speech: An auditory perspective.' In S. Greenberg & W. Ainsworth (eds) *Listening to Speech: An Auditory Perspective* (Mahwah, NJ: Lawrence Erlbaum Associates, p. 458). Retrieved from http://books.google.com/books?hl=en&lr=&id=wCBmWIGSRGcC&pgis=1

Griffiths, T. D., Rees, A., & Green, G. G. R. (1999). 'Disorders of human complex sound processing.' *Neurocase*, 5, 365–378. https://doi.org/10.1080/13554799908402733

Harris, C. M. (1953). 'A study of the building blocks in speech.' *Journal of the Acoustical Society of America*, 25(5), 962–969. https://doi.org/10.1121/1.1907227

Hausfeld, L., Hamers, I. M., & Formisano, E. (2024). 'FMRI speech tracking in primary and non-primary auditory cortex while listening to noisy scenes.' *Communications Biology*, 7(1), 1217. https://doi.org/10.1038/s42003-024-06913-z

Hickok, G., & Poeppel, D. (2007). 'The cortical organization of speech processing.' *Nature Reviews Neuroscience*, Vol. 8, pp. 393–402. https://doi.org/10.1038/nrn2113

Hickok, G., & Poeppel, D. (2000). 'Towards a functional neuroanatomy of speech perception.' *Trends in Cognitive Sciences*, Vol. 4, pp. 131–138. https://doi.org/10.1016/S1364-6613(00)01463-7

Holt, L. L., Tierney, A. T., Guerra, G., Laffere, A., & Dick, F. (2018). 'Dimension-selective attention as a possible driver of dynamic, context-dependent re-weighting in speech processing.' *Hearing Research*, 366, 50–64. https://doi.org/10.1016/j.heares.2018.06.014

Hope, M., & Lilley, J. (2022). 'Gender expansive listeners utilize a non-binary, multidimensional conception of gender to inform voice gender perception.' *Brain and Language*, 224. https://doi.org/10.1016/J.BANDL.2021.105049

Huang, J., & Holt, L. L. (2012). 'Listening for the norm: Adaptive coding in speech categorization.' *Frontiers in Psychology*, 3(Feb), 10. https://doi.org/10.3389/fpsyg.2012.00010

Johnson, K., & Sjerps, M. J. (2021). 'Speaker normalization in speech perception.' In J. S. Pardo, L. C. Nygaard, D. B. Pisoni, & R. E. Remez (eds) *The Handbook of Speech Perception* (pp. 145–176). Hoboken, NJ: Wiley-Blackwell.

Kapnoula, E. C., Winn, M. B., Kong, E. J., Edwards, J., & McMurray, B. (2017). 'Evaluating the sources and functions of gradiency in phoneme categorization: An individual differences approach.' *Journal of Experimental Psychology: Human Perception and Performance*, 43, 1594–1611.

Ladd, D. R., Silverman, K. E. A., Tolkmitt, F., Bergmann, G., & Scherer, K. R. (1985). 'Evidence for the independent function of intonation contour type, voice quality, and F0 range in signaling speaker affect.' *Journal of the Acoustical Society of America*, 78(2), 435–444. https://doi.org/10.1121/1.392466

Lee, Y., Keating, P., & Kreiman, J. (2019). 'Acoustic voice variation within and between speakers.' *Journal of the Acoustical Society of America*, 146(3), 1568–1579. https://doi.org/10.1121/1.5125134

Liberman, A. M., Harris, K. S., Hoffman, H. S., & Griffith, B. C. (1957). 'The discrimination of speech sounds within and across phoneme boundaries.' *Journal of Experimental Psychology*, 54(5), 358–368.

Markel, J. D., & Davis, S. B. (1979). 'Text-independent speaker recognition from a large linguistically unconstrained time-spaced data base.' *IEEE Transactions on Acoustics, Speech, and Signal Processing*, 27(1), 74–82. https://doi.org/10.1109/TASSP.1979.1163201

Matsumoto, H., Hiki, S., Sone, T., & Nimura, T. (1973). 'Multidimensional representation of personal quality of vowels and its acoustical correlates.' *IEEE Transactions on Audio and Electroacoustics*, 21(5), 428–436. https://doi.org/10.1109/TAU.1973.1162507

Norris, D., McQueen, J. M., Cutler, A., & Butterfield, S. (1997). 'The possible-word constraint in the segmentation of continuous speech.' *Cognitive Psychology*, 34(3), 191–243. https://doi.org/10.1006/COGP.1997.0671

Osgood, C. E. (1963). 'On understanding and creating sentences.' *American Psychologist*, 18(12), 735–751. https://doi.org/10.1037/h0047800

Peelle, J. E., Johnsrude, I., & Davis, M. H. (2010). 'Hierarchical processing for speech in human auditory cortex and beyond.' *Frontiers in Human Neuroscience*, 4, 1735.

Perron, M., Vuong, V., Grassi, M. W., Imran, A., & Alain, C. (2024). 'Engagement of the speech motor system in challenging speech perception: Activation likelihood estimation meta-analyses.' *Human Brain Mapping*, 45(13), e70023. https://doi.org/10.1002/hbm.70023

Peterson, G., & Barney, H. (1952). 'Control methods used in a study of the vowels.' *Journal of the Acoustical Society of America*, 24(2), 175–184. Retrieved from http://scitation.aip.org/content/asa/journal/jasa/24/2/10.1121/1.1906875

Pittam, J., & Scherer, K. R. (1993). 'Vocal expression and communication of emotion.' In M. Lewis & J. M. Haviland (eds) *Handbook of Emotions* (pp. 185–197). New York: Guilford Press.

Price, C. J. (2012). 'A review and synthesis of the first 20 years of PET and fMRI studies of heard speech, spoken language and reading.' *NeuroImage*, 62(2), 816–847. https://doi.org/10.1016/j.neuroimage.2012.04.062

Reetz, H., & Jongman, A. (2020). 'Acoustic characteristics of speech sounds.' In *Phonetics: Transcription, Production, Acoustics, and Perception* (pp. 206–233). Chichester: Wiley-Blackwell. https://doi.org/10.1007/s00424-011-1058-7

Remez, R. E., Rubin, P. E., Pisoni, D. B., & Carrell, T. D. (1981). 'Speech perception without traditional speech cues.' *Science*, 212(4497), 947–950. https://doi.org/10.1126/SCIENCE.7233191

Roswandowitz, C., Maguinness, C., & von Kriegstein, K., (2018). 'Deficits in voice-identity processing: Acquired and developmental phonagnosia.' In S. Frühholz & P. Belin (eds), *The Oxford Handbook of Voice Perception* (pp. 854–892). Oxford: Oxford University Press. https://doi.org/10.1093/oxfordhb/9780198743187.013.39

Shannon, R. V, Zeng, F. G., Kamath, V., Wygonski, J., & Ekelid, M. (1995). 'Speech recognition with primarily temporal cues.' *Science*, 270(5234), 303–304. https://doi.org/10.1126/science.270.5234.303

Skuk, V. G., & Schweinberger, S. R. (2014). 'Influences of fundamental frequency, formant frequencies, aperiodicity, and spectrum level on the perception of voice gender.' *Journal of Speech, Language, and Hearing Research*, 57(1), 285–296. https://doi.org/10.1044/1092-4388(2013/12-0314)

Smalle, E. H., Rogers, J., & Möttönen, R. (2015). 'Dissociating contributions of the motor cortex to speech perception and response bias by using transcranial magnetic stimulation.' *Cerebral Cortex*, 25(10), 3690–3698. https://doi.org/10.1093/cercor/bhu218

Turner, R. E., Walters, T. C., Monaghan, J. J. M., & Patterson, R. D. (2009). 'A statistical, formant-pattern model for segregating vowel type and vocal-tract length in developmental formant data.' *Journal of the Acoustical Society of America*, 125(4), 2374–2386. https://doi.org/10.1121/1.3079772

Vanthornhout, J., Decruy, L., Wouters, J., Simon, J. Z., & Francart, T. (2018). 'Speech intelligibility predicted from neural entrainment of the speech envelope.' *BioRxiv*, (637424), 246660. https://doi.org/10.1101/246660

von Kriegstein, K., Smith, D. R. R., Patterson, R. D., Kiebel, S. J., & Griffiths, T. D. (2010). 'How the human brain recognizes speech in the context of changing speakers.' *Journal of Neuroscience*, 30(2), 629–638. https://doi.org/10.1523/JNEUROSCI.2742-09.2010

Warren, R. M., Riener, K. R., Bashford, J. A., & Brubaker, B. S. (1995). 'Spectral redundancy: Intelligibility of sentences heard through narrow spectral slits.' *Perception & Psychophysics*, 57(2), 175–182. https://doi.org/10.3758/BF03206503

Wernicke, C. (1874). *Der aphasische Symptomencomplex: Eine psychologische Studie auf anatomischer Basis*. Breslau: Max Cohn & Weigert.

Wilsch, A., Neuling, T., Obleser, J., & Herrmann, C. S. (2018). 'Transcranial alternating current stimulation with speech envelopes modulates speech comprehension.' *Neuroimage*, 172, 766–774.

Zan, P., Presacco, A., Anderson, S., & Simon, J. Z. (2020). 'Exaggerated cortical representation of speech in older listeners: Mutual information analysis.' *Journal of Neurophysiology*, 124(4), 1152–1164. https://doi.org/10.1152/JN.00002.2020

Zatorre, R. J., Belin, P., & Penhune, V. B. (2002). 'Structure and function of auditory cortex: Music and speech.' *Trends in Cognitive Sciences*, 6(January), 37–46. https://doi.org/10.1016/S1364-6613(00)01816-7

Zsiga, E. C. (2024). *The Sounds of Language: An Introduction to Phonetics and Phonology*. Chichester: Wiley-Blackwell.

Perceiving Speech in Noisy Places

Can you recall a time when you were trying to listen to someone talking, but it was difficult to understand what they were saying because there were lots of other sounds in the background—for example at a loud party or a busy train station? When people hear speech, other sounds are often present in their surroundings, but they usually only notice them when the sounds are loud enough to interfere with the speech that they're trying to listen to. For many people, perceiving speech in noisy environments is very difficult, and can become more difficult with increasing age. This chapter combines topics from **Chapter 3** ('Perceiving multiple sounds') and **Chapter 4** ('Perceiving speech') to examine how people understand speech when other sounds are present in their environment. It starts by reviewing what types of sounds are present in the environment, then examines how a variety of factors affect speech intelligibility, and finally considers how people focus their attention on speech in noisy places. Ultimately, considering how people perceive speech in noisy places might help to inspire novel ways to improve speech perception in situations that are particularly noisy, and also for people who find this difficult.

5.1 Types of noise

People hear speech in a variety of places that contain different types of noise. Compare how someone might encounter speech at home, in a café, or while walking next to a busy road. Everyday noise comes in a variety of forms: it might be a loud fan nearby, the chatter of other people talking, or the sound of cars passing by. These sounds all have different acoustic properties. This section explains how the ability to understand speech depends on the type of noise that's present.

5.1.1 Steady-state noise

Imagine that someone is trying to watch TV, but someone else is standing in front of the TV screen, blocking their view. The viewer might be able to see some of the image on the screen, but other parts of the image would be covered from their view. As the image on the TV screen changes, the same part of the TV screen would be covered by the person who's standing there. Similarly, noise can cover parts of speech that someone is trying to listen to. **Steady-state noise** refers to noise that has a constant amplitude. In other words, like someone standing in front of a TV screen, the noise remains the same over time. If people are trying to listen to speech, steady-state noise can be problematic, because it covers (i.e. 'masks') part of the spectrum. The white noise and pink noise introduced in **Chapter 1** are both examples of steady-state noise.

When someone hears speech in a noisy place, the speech and the background noise enter the ear at the same time. Recall from **Chapter 1** that the cochlea separates sounds into different frequencies. When someone hears a sound mixture, the cochlea can't distinguish which parts of the sound mixture are speech and which parts are noise: if the noise contains similar frequencies to speech, the energy from the speech and the noise will overlap at the cochlea. This overlap is thought to be why steady-state noise makes it difficult to understand speech. When noise energy masks the energy in speech, it's called **energetic masking**.

Steady-state noise can contain different frequencies—and the frequencies that are present in the noise affect how easy it is to understand speech. Noise that has a similar spectrum to speech (e.g. pink noise, which contains more low than high frequencies, just like speech) produces energetic masking (Berglund et al., 1996). This is like someone standing in between a person and a TV screen, blocking the person's view. In contrast, when the frequencies of the noise are different to those in speech, it's much easier to understand speech, because there's little or no energetic masking—the speech and noise are separated at the cochlea (i.e. they don't overlap). In a similar way, if someone is standing to the left of a TV screen, they might not block someone's view of the TV.

> You can review different types of noise in **Chapter 1**.

Energetic masking isn't all or nothing: the amount of energetic masking depends on the extent to which the frequencies of the noise overlap with those in the speech. In general, greater overlap provides more energetic masking. The amount of energetic masking also depends on the **signal-to-noise ratio** (Further insights 5.1).

Further insights 5.1 Signal-to-noise ratio

Most people with normal hearing can understand speech when background noise has the same intensity (i.e. sound pressure level) as speech. The difference in the average intensity of speech and background noise is known as the signal-to-noise ratio (abbreviated to SNR). When speech (i.e. the 'signal') is 3 dB more intense than the background (i.e. the 'noise'), the SNR is +3 dB; when they're the same intensity, the SNR is 0 dB; and when the speech is 6 dB less intense than the background noise, the SNR is −6 dB. When steady-state noise is present, speech intelligibility decreases steadily as the SNR decreases (Hawkins Jr. & Stevens, 2005). In other words, speech intelligibility decreases as the level of the noise increases, relative to the speech.

The SNR can be defined either at particular frequencies, within short time windows, or as an average over time. These ways of defining SNR are useful because the frequency and intensity of speech and noise can change over time. The least intense parts of speech are most vulnerable to noise: some consonants have a lower intensity and a shorter duration than vowels, which makes them harder to hear as the level of the noise increases (i.e. as the SNR decreases) (Miller & Nicely, 2005).

The signal-to-noise ratio is sometimes called the target-to-masker ratio, particularly if the background is competing speech (covered in Section 5.1.3). However, these two terms are equivalent.

> **Chapter 8** contains more information about how 'normal hearing' is defined, and about how hearing loss affects speech understanding in background noise.

When people try to understand speech, they seem to rely most heavily on the frequencies of the formants—and, therefore, noise that's close to the formant frequencies may be most problematic. Recall from **Chapter 4** that formants provide clues to the identity of a speech segment; for example, whether a word is 'bet' or 'but'. One idea is that people have difficulty extracting the formant frequencies in speech if the noise is at a similar frequency to that of the formants—and this makes it more difficult to distinguish between different words (Roberts & Moore, 1990). In support of this idea, when noise is inserted at the frequency of the second formant, people are more likely to confuse one vowel sound with another than when the noise is further away from the formant (Pickett, 1957). Thus, when trying to identify what's being spoken, people seem to rely most heavily on the frequencies of formants rather than the entire spectrum. This strategy is likely to be sensible, given that formants are where the energy in speech is greatest and are, therefore, likely to have the greatest signal-to-noise ratio.

5.1.2 Amplitude-modulated noise

Imagine someone trying to watch their favourite TV show, but people around them are walking in front of the screen. When the people stand still in front of the TV, blocking the person's view, it's impossible to watch the show—whereas, if the people are walking around, someone might be able to work out what's happening in the show by piecing together the moments when their view of the TV is unobstructed.

Listening to speech when steady-state noise is present is a bit like someone trying to watch their favourite show when someone is standing still in front of the TV. In this analogy, the speech someone is trying to listen to is the TV show and the people in front of the screen are the background noise. However, when someone tries to listen to speech in amplitude-modulated noise, it's more akin to trying to watch a TV show when people are walking past the screen: when the amplitude of the noise is at its lowest (see Figure 5.1), they can sometimes get an unobstructed 'view' of speech. These 'views' are called **glimpses** in hearing science. As a result of these glimpses, speech is much easier to understand if the background noise is modulated in amplitude than if its amplitude is constant (Festen & Plomp, 1990).

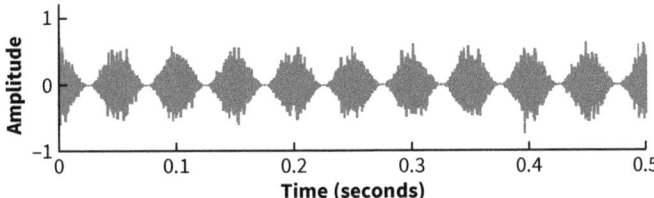

Figure 5.1 Time series plot showing amplitude-modulated white noise. Notice that the peak amplitude of the noise changes over time.

In general, it's easier to understand speech when there are more glimpses (Cooke, 2006). However, the timing of the glimpses also matters. When noise is turned on and off repeatedly, people find it difficult to understand speech when it's turned on and off once every second, but they find it easier when the noise is turned on and off 4–8 times every second (Fogerty et al., 2018)—even though the total amount of time that the noise is switched off is the same in both cases. It's thought that people piece glimpses together to get a good idea of what was spoken, in a similar way as constructing a jigsaw puzzle. When making a jigsaw, you might be able to get a good idea of the image you're creating even if you're only given a small set of the pieces—but, the more pieces you have, the better you may be able to imagine the full image. In other words, the amount of energetic masking is determined by not only the frequency of the noise, but also how its energy is distributed over time.

5.1.3 Competing speech

Have you ever been at a party, trying to listen to what your friend is saying, and heard lots of other conversations going on around you? Researchers often refer to this as the **cocktail party problem** (a term coined by Cherry, 1953). Yet, people don't need to be at a cocktail party to encounter these types of scenarios. For example, they might be at a busy restaurant or café and hear several conversations around them. While not technically 'noise', the sounds of other people talking can make it more difficult for someone to hear the speech that they're trying to listen to.

> You can find a technical description of 'noise' in **Chapter 1**.

> Researchers who study the ability to understand speech in background noise, usually call this 'speech-in-noise perception'. This is a broad term that refers to a variety of types of noise; it is sometimes even used to refer to speech in the presence of other speech—although, more specifically, when other speech is present, this is usually called 'speech-in-speech perception'.

Like noise, the sounds of other people talking produce energetic masking—and the amount of energetic masking depends on the frequencies of competing speech and, more specifically, how much they overlap with the frequencies in the speech that someone is trying to listen to (i.e. the 'target speech'). When the frequencies of the target and competing speech are more similar, it's more difficult to understand the target speech.

The average fundamental frequencies for voices of men and women differ. Consistent with this, a man's voice is more intelligible when competing speech is a woman's voice that has a different fundamental frequency than when competing speech is a man's voice that has a similar fundamental frequency. Similarly, a woman's voice is more intelligible when competing speech is a man's voice that has a different fundamental frequency than when it's a woman's voice that has a similar fundamental frequency. Yet, the difference in fundamental frequency doesn't need to be particularly large to benefit speech intelligibility: even small differences help people to understand target speech (Madsen et al., 2021). One reason is that the frequencies are separated by the cochlea (see Section 5.1.1). Also, when the target and competing speech have different fundamental frequencies, frequency and harmonicity cues may also help to segregate one voice from another due to simultaneous and sequential grouping (see **Chapter 3**).

> See **Chapter 4** for an overview of research into male, female, and non-binary voice gender.

Like amplitude-modulated noise, speech varies in amplitude over time. Therefore, when there's only one competing talker, there are typically lots of opportunities to 'glimpse' target speech when the amplitude of the competing speech is low. For this reason, we might expect speech to be easier to understand when competing speech is present than when noise is present. Yet, this isn't always the case, because there's another type of masking we need to consider.

In addition to energetic masking, competing speech also provides **informational masking** (Brungart et al., 2001). Informational masking is a catch-all term referring to any additional difficulty that isn't due to energetic masking—for example, due to similarity between the target and competing sounds (see Lutfi et al., 2013). Informational masking can arise if someone gets confused about which words were spoken by a target voice and which were spoken by a competing voice, in a similar way to how someone might get confused about which of two pieces belongs in a jigsaw puzzle if the pieces look very similar. For example, someone might perceive a sentence incorrectly if competing speech contains similar words that could plausibly be part of the sentence they're trying to listen to (which could lead to the percept 'He lost his cap' if the sentence 'That's a nice cap' is spoken while the sentence 'He lost his cup' is also spoken). Informational masking can also occur if the competing voice(s) resemble the target voice—for example, if the voices have indistinguishable pitches and accents. Researchers have demonstrated informational masking in the lab. In experiments in which people are played two voices and are asked to report the words from a target voice, they sometimes report words from the competing voice instead. As a result, speech can be less intelligible when competing speech is present than when noise is present, because competing speech provides informational masking as well as energetic masking, whereas noise only provides energetic masking.

Informational masking can be conceptualised as an additional challenge over and above energetic masking. It seems to engage some areas of the brain to a greater extent (Further insights 5.2). Rather than arising from overlap at the cochlea, informational masking is thought to arise from competition further along the auditory pathway (Scott et al., 2009). Consistent with this idea, the signal-to-noise ratio is not as important for informational masking as it is for energetic masking.

> **Further insights 5.2** How does noise affect brain responses to speech?
>
> Speech is more difficult to understand in noisy settings than in quiet settings. The additional challenge of listening in noisy settings is associated with greater responses in frontal and parietal areas of the brain (Scott & McGettigan, 2013). These responses are even stronger when competing speech is highly similar to target speech (Nakai et al., 2005). This could be for a variety of reasons. It could be due to informational masking, because these settings require greater effort, or because selective attention needs to be applied to help focus on target speech (which is covered in more detail in Section 5.3).

Rather than being all or nothing, the amount of informational masking varies in different settings. Competing speech provides the most informational masking when it's intelligible, because it's more likely to be confused with target speech. In contrast, unintelligible speech provides less informational masking: people are better at understanding target speech if competing speech is in a foreign language they don't understand than if it's in the same language as target speech (Iyer et al., 2010).

> Sometimes, researchers alter competing speech by playing it backwards, which makes it entirely unintelligible. Competing speech played backwards interferes even less with target speech than does speech in a foreign language. This is probably because some foreign languages contain similar phonemes to target speech in a different language, whereas the phonemes are unrecognisable when speech is played backwards. You can review phonemes in **Chapter 4**.

The number of competing voices also affects intelligibility: intelligibility is usually lower when there are more voices (Rosen et al., 2013). One reason is that increasing the number of voices increases the amount of energetic masking; you can think of increasing the number of voices as similar to someone trying to watch their favourite TV show when more and more people are walking in front of the TV screen! Increasing the number of competing voices matters, because the amplitude envelope of a sound becomes flatter when more voices are added to the mixture (see Figure 5.2); there are, therefore, fewer opportunities for glimpses (Bronkhorst & Plomp, 1992). In this sense, the masker begins to resemble steady-state noise as more voices are added. Beyond four competing voices, there's little change in intelligibility as the number increases further, because the sound mixture changes less and less as more voices are added.

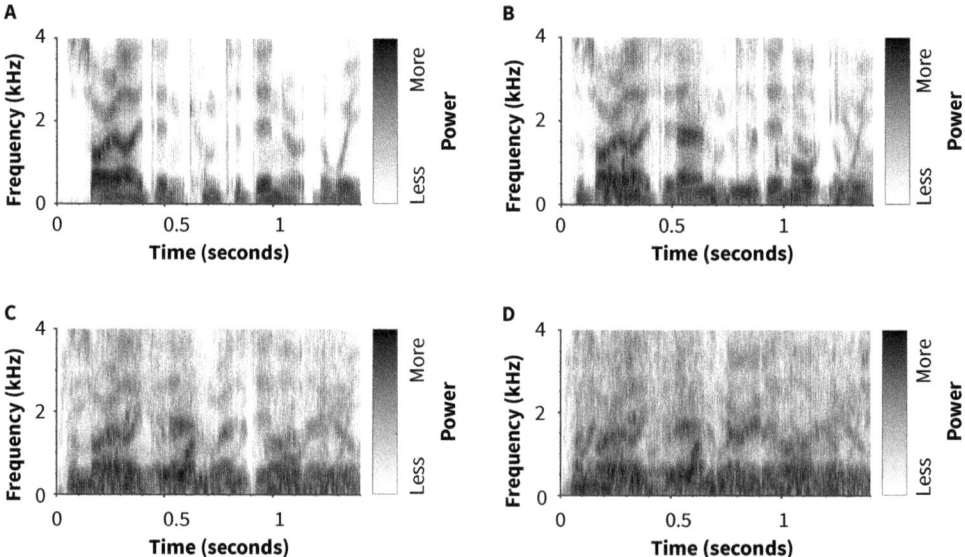

Figure 5.2 Spectrograms of one (panel a), two (panel b), four (panel c), and eight (panel d) voices. Notice how the energy is distributed more evenly across frequency and time in panel d than in panel a, and it more closely resembles steady-state noise.

> When the number of voices is high (e.g. 12 voices), competing speech is often called 'babble noise', because it's difficult to pick out individual voices in the mixture. Babble noise is often considered to be a more realistic type of noise than steady-state noise.

Overall, different types of sounds produce different combinations of energetic and informational masking (see Figure 5.3). For example, high-frequency noise (Figure 5.3(b)) provides low energetic masking (because it differs in frequency from target speech) and low informational masking (because it contains no speech content). Contrastingly, pink noise (Figure 5.3(c)) provides *high* energetic masking (because it overlaps with target speech in frequency and time) and low informational masking (because, again, it contains no speech content). If speech is heard with one competing talker (Figure 5.3(d)), this will produce low energetic masking (because target speech can be glimpsed when its amplitude is low) but high informational masking (because it contains competing speech content). However, if there are four competing talkers (Figure 5.3(e)), this will

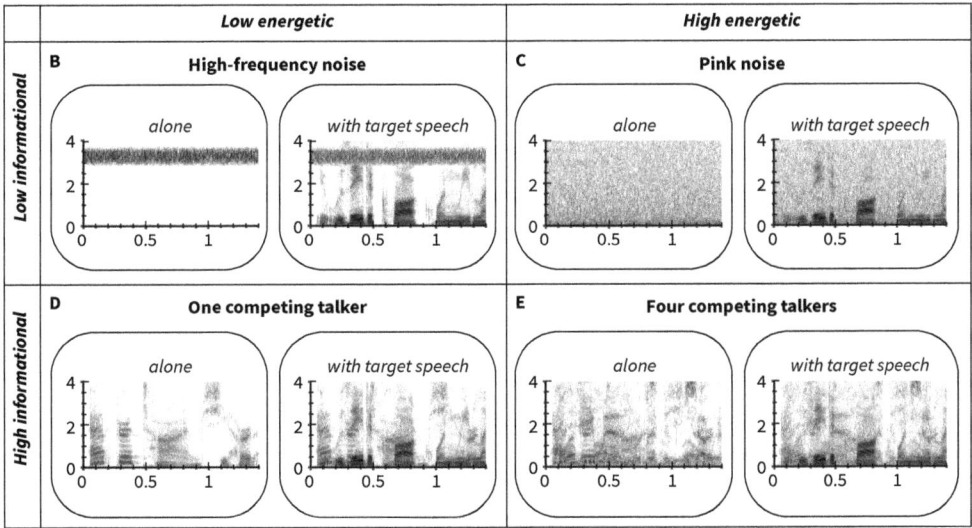

Figure 5.3 Masking of target speech (panel a) by different competing sounds that have different levels of energetic and informational masking. Within panels b–e, spectrograms of possible competing sounds are shown on the left and the spectrograms of the same competing sounds combined with the target speech are shown on the right.

produce *high* energetic masking (because the mixture overlaps with target speech in frequency and time) and high informational masking (because the talkers contain competing speech content).

5.2 Factors affecting intelligibility in noise

So far in this chapter, we've described why background noise makes it more difficult to understand speech—but how can we minimise its impact? People are often in places with background noise and, with the increase of mobile technology, the number of sounds in the environment is expanding. Therefore, it's useful to understand the factors that affect speech intelligibility in noisy places.

We've already reviewed two factors that affect speech intelligibility: the signal-to-noise ratio and differences in frequency. This section goes on to describe a variety of other factors that also have an influence. These include acoustic factors—such as separations in location, intensity, and timing—and cognitive factors—such as context, prior knowledge, and familiarity. The effect of each factor isn't all or nothing, but rather their contributions vary on a continuum. For this reason, speech intelligibility can be considered as the output of a mixing deck—on which different dials correspond to different factors—rather than as a switch that's either on or off. Each factor contributes to the level of intelligibility that people can achieve.

5.2.1 Spatial separation

It's easier to understand speech when competing sounds are presented from a different location. In an extreme case—in which sounds are presented through headphones—speech can be presented to one ear and competing sounds can be presented to the other ear. This provides a large improvement in speech intelligibility, compared to when speech and competing sounds are presented to the same ear.

> The phrase 'spatial release from masking' is often used to describe the benefit to speech intelligibility from separating target speech from competing sounds—in other words, the difference in performance when they're presented from different locations compared to when they're presented from the same location.

It is also true that smaller separations in location improve intelligibility. For example, if target speech is coming from straight ahead, positioning competing speech 30 degrees to the side leads to a substantial advantage over presenting it from the same location as the target speech (Figure 5.4). The *amount* of spatial separation also affects the intelligibility benefit. In general, when target speech is separated from competing sounds by a larger difference in location, intelligibility is better (compare Figure 5.4(b) and (c)). For example, a separation of 90 degrees leads to better intelligibility than a separation of 30 degrees (Marrone et al., 2008).

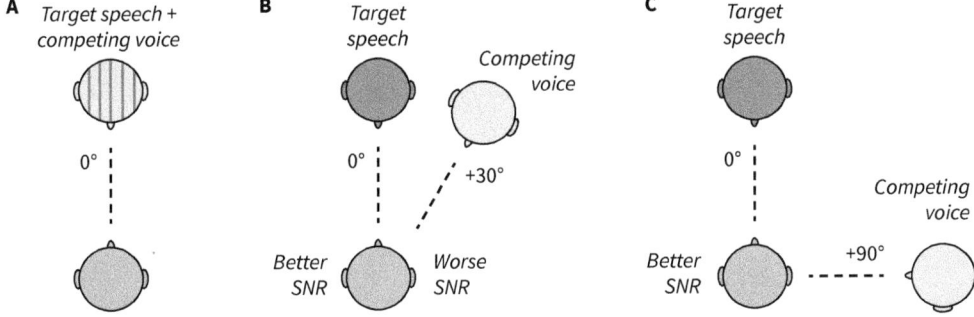

Figure 5.4 Moving a competing voice further away from a target improves speech intelligibility. All three panels show a birds-eye view of a simplified listening scenario. When a listener (displayed in the lower part of the figure) tries to understand speech spoken by a target talker (displayed in front of the listener), speech intelligibility is worse when a competing voice is at the same location as the target (e.g. 0°, as in panel a) than when it's at a different location (e.g. 30° or 90°, as in panels b and c). In panel a, the signal-to-noise ratio (SNR) is the same in both ears, whereas in panels b and c, the SNR is better at the left ear than at the right ear. In these contexts, the target talker can be considered as the 'signal' and the competing talker as the 'noise'.

The benefit of spatial separation can be attributed to several factors. First, most people can benefit from the head shadow effect. Recall from **Chapter 2** that the head acts as an acoustic barrier, reducing the transmission of sound energy from one side of the head to the ear on the other side. This head shadow means that when competing speech is presented at a different location to target speech, there's a better signal-to-noise ratio at the ear that's furthest away from the competing speech (Figure 5.4(b) and (c)). The improvement in signal-to-noise ratio at one ear is likely to be one factor that underlies the benefit from spatial separation (Plomp, 1976).

Second, binaural cues (i.e. interaural time and level differences; ITDs and ILDs, respectively) contribute to the improvement in intelligibility. We know that binaural cues are important, because people can benefit from spatial separation even when the signal-to-noise ratio at both ears is worse after spatial separation (as in Figure 5.5)—although ILDs seem to contribute more than ITDs (Culling & Summerfield, 1998), possibly because ITDs are less robust than ILDs in reverberant places (Shinn-Cunningham et al., 2005). These binaural cues may help with simultaneous and sequential grouping (see **Chapter 3**), enabling listeners to segregate target from competing speech. They may also help listeners to direct their attention to target speech (which is covered in more detail in Section 5.3).

> You can review interaural time differences, interaural level differences, and reverberation in **Chapter 2**.

5.2.2 Level differences

Signal-to-noise ratio (SNR) refers to the difference in level between target speech (the 'signal') and competing sounds (the 'noise'). In general, more positive SNRs lead to better intelligibility and more negative SNRs lead to poorer intelligibility (Further insights 5.1)—but

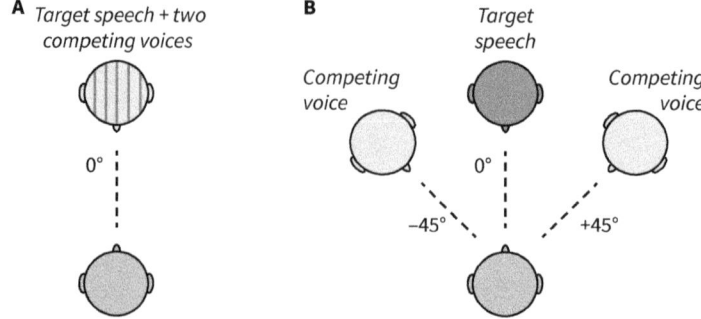

Figure 5.5 Effects of separating two competing voices from a target. Both panels show a birds-eye view of a simplified listening scenario: a listener tries to understand speech spoken by a target talker when two competing voices are present. In panel a, the two competing voices are co-located with the target. In panel b, the competing voices are at different locations to the target: one is to the left and the other is to the right. The target speech is more intelligible when the voices are separated (i.e. in panel b) than when they are co-located (i.e. in panel a). Interestingly, unlike Figure 5.4, the signal-to-noise ratio (SNR) at both ears is worse when the three voices are separated than when they are co-located (because at each ear in panel b there is a competing voice that's closer to the ear than the target speech, so the level of the competing voice will be greater than the level of the target speech; whereas, the target speech and competing voices are the same distance from each ear in panel a, so they will be the same level at each ear). Thus, the finding that target speech is more intelligible when the voices are separated (like in panel b) demonstrates that people benefit from spatial separation even when it doesn't improve SNR (e.g. due to binaural cues).

this isn't always true! Crucially, a *difference* in level between target speech and competing sounds can produce better intelligibility. So, interestingly, when the masker is competing speech, a difference in level can produce better intelligibility even if target speech is *less intense* than the competing speech. In general, intelligibility is poorer when the SNR is lowered below 0 dB, but, when the masker is competing speech, intelligibility can sometimes *improve* when the SNR is just below 0 dB (Brungart, 2001). This occurs because the difference in intensity acts as a cue to separate target and competing speech when masking is mainly informational, rather than energetic.

5.2.3 Timing differences

Recall from **Chapter 3** that timing is an important cue for simultaneous and sequential grouping of sounds. This principle comes into action when we consider how people understand speech in noisy environments. Differences in timing help people to perceptually separate speech from competing sounds: it's easier to understand speech when the background noise starts before the speech than when it starts at the same time. One reason is that the frequencies that belong to target speech start at a different time to those that belong to competing sounds, so the difference in timing allows people to distinguish which frequencies belong to target speech and which belong to competing sounds. In addition, the onsets of sounds are salient, so separating the onset of speech from competing sounds can help people to direct their attention to target speech.

5.2.4 Context

Recall from **Chapter 4** that the context of speech influences how people perceive it. Context has an even stronger influence on perception when competing sounds are present, because target speech is more ambiguous when it's masked by competing sounds.

Have you ever tried to listen to someone talking when someone else is coughing loudly nearby? Coughing sounds are types of noise and provide energetic masking. When the coughs are sufficiently loud, the SNR can be extremely low, such that the speech isn't perceptible above the noise. Like amplitude-modulated noise, most people can glimpse parts of the speech signal between the coughs—and context is important for helping people to 'fill in the gaps' in the speech signal that are masked by noise.

Interestingly, when people listen to speech that's interrupted by short bursts of noise, they usually don't feel as though they're making a guess about interrupted speech. Rather, they typically perceive a continuous speech signal that persists 'behind' the noise (Miller & Licklider, 2005). This phenomenon is called the **phonemic restoration effect**. Curiously, they may even be unaware that parts of the speech signal have been masked and that they've filled in the gaps themselves.

> Phonemic restoration occurs more generally when the target is not speech, but other (non-speech) sounds. Phonemic restoration is specific to the phonemes in speech and, when applied to other sounds, is sometimes called perceptual restoration (Warren, 1970) or auditory induction (Warren et al., 1972). Figure 5.6 illustrates an analogous example from visual perception, which can be linked to the Gestalt principles of closure and figure-ground.
>
>
>
> **Figure 5.6** Look at panel a first, and then look at panel b. Both panels consist of the same shapes, which can be combined to form the word 'sound'. The only difference is that some of the white space between the shapes has been filled with other shapes in panel b. Most people find it easier to see the word 'sound' in panel b than in panel a (and find it easier to see the word 'sound' in panel a after looking at panel b!). This is thought to occur because people assume the darker shapes are covering the word in panel b, and that the word 'sound' exists underneath it, so people perceptually 'fill in the gaps' between the shapes.

Phonemic restoration is such a strong effect that it occurs when researchers entirely remove chunks of the speech signal and replace them with steady-state noise—which ensures that there's no speech signal for people to hear among the noise.

If you listen to an audio demo of a spoken sentence from which some chunks of the speech signal have been removed, and then a demo in which the silent gaps have been replaced

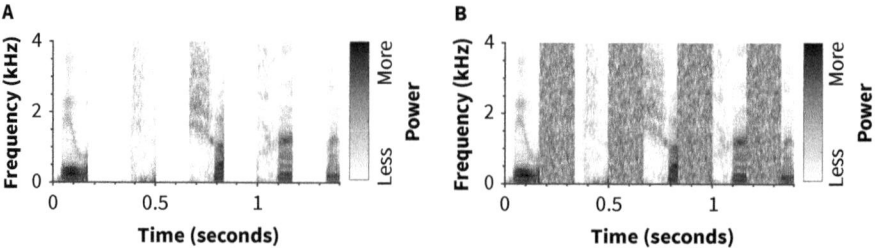

Figure 5.7 Spectrograms of excerpts from a spoken sentence that's interrupted by silent gaps (panel a) or white noise (panel b) three times per second.

with steady-state noise, you will notice that the latter (i.e. when noise covers the silent gaps) sounds more continuous and complete than the former (Figure 5.7).

Given that chunks of the speech have been removed (and, therefore, there's no speech behind the noise), the fact that people perceive speech continuing through the segments of noise means they must be actively filling in the speech that was removed. Interestingly, people don't perceive the sound as simply remaining the same as it was before the noise occurred, but as changing in a way that would be expected if the speech wasn't masked. This implies that people actively predict spectral and temporal properties of upcoming speech (e.g. predicting the spectrogram). These predictions are so strong that people often can't pinpoint exactly which parts of the speech were covered by noise and which were intact (Warren, 1970)!

> Phonemic restoration doesn't often occur when chunks of the speech signal are removed and left silent. Interestingly, it's most prominent when the noise is more intense than the speech. Thus, in order for the auditory system to restore a speech signal, the noise should be intense enough that it's capable of masking the speech signal.

Sometimes, people may rely on coarticulation to fill in the gaps during phonemic restoration. In other words, they can guess what phoneme is coming next based on the acoustics of the previous phoneme. Yet, people often also make predictions at longer timescales than individual phonemes—and these predictions can be so strong that they override the cues provided by coarticulation. For example, the 'each' in 'peach' and 'beach' have different acoustics. Yet, after hearing 'Let's go to the . . .', most people are more likely to perceive 'beach' than 'peach'—even if the original sentence is 'Let's go to the peach' and the 'p' sound is replaced with noise. In this example, the coarticulation cues are more consistent with the word 'peach', but the content of the sentence (i.e. the semantics) is more consistent with 'beach'. This phenomenon demonstrates that semantic context can strongly influence what people perceive. For this reason, when competing sounds are present, words are often more intelligible when they occur at the end of a sentence that provides context for the final word than when the same individual words are presented alone (i.e. without context).

> You can review coarticulation in **Chapter 4**.

5.2.5 Prior knowledge

Most people can also benefit from knowing what the target speech will sound like before it begins. For example, hearing a 'preview' of the person who's speaking (which might involve hearing them say a different word or sentence) can help people to subsequently identify the words they're saying (Freyman et al., 2004). More generally, simply being told *who* will speak or *where* their voice is going to come from (i.e. whether their voice will be on the left or the right) improves speech intelligibility when competing sounds are present (Kitterick et al., 2010). Similarly, intelligibility is better when people are told what gender a target voice will be, or when they've seen the beginning of the sentence written down (Freyman et al., 2004). These findings demonstrate that people can use a variety of different types of prior knowledge to improve their understanding of speech in noisy environments.

The effects of different types of prior knowledge may each be underpinned by different processes along the auditory pathway. Nevertheless, in general, prior knowledge may improve intelligibility by helping people to better segregate—or more quickly identify—target speech among competing sounds.

5.2.6 Familiarity

The effects described in Section 5.2.5 can be considered as short-term prior knowledge that occurs 'in the moment'. Yet, long-term familiarity with particular sounds—developed over months or years—also affects intelligibility in noisy environments. For example, people are better at understanding target speech if it's in their native language (i.e. the language they learnt first) than if it's in another language, even if they're highly proficient in the other language (Cooke et al., 2008). Possibly, when people hear speech in their native language, it helps them to use context (such as semantic context or knowledge about the words in that language) to improve speech intelligibility—and these cues aren't as readily available for a second language.

Generally, people also become highly familiar with other people's voices, such as those of their close friends, romantic partners, and family members. People are much better at understanding what someone is saying when they're listening to a voice that's familiar to them, as compared to a stranger's voice. The benefit of long-term familiarity with someone's voice is much larger than the benefit people get from a short-term 'preview' of someone's voice (like that described in Section 5.2.5). That said, the amount of benefit differs among different types of noise: people get a large benefit from a familiar voice in the presence of a competing talker, but little or no benefit in amplitude-modulated noise (Holmes & Johnsrude, 2020), which suggests that the main benefit of a familiar voice is to reduce informational masking (because informational masking is provided by a competing talker but not by amplitude-modulated noise) rather than energetic masking (which is provided by a competing talker *and* by amplitude-modulated noise).

Finally, people are familiar with accents that they usually encounter. Even if an unfamiliar accent is very easy to understand in quiet places, it's often less intelligible than a familiar accent when competing sounds are present (Adank et al., 2009).

5.3 Directing attention in noisy places

Have you ever found that you haven't noticed a sound until someone else pointed it out? When many sounds are present in the environment, people are not always aware of them all. Listening in noisy places typically relies on the ability to direct attention to a sound of interest and ignore other sounds in the environment. As this section describes, attention isn't a single process, but is rather a set of related processes (Allport, 1993). Sometimes, someone might want to focus their attention on one person's voice at a party (**selective attention**), but then they might want to turn their attention to a different person's voice (switching attention), or try to listen to two people at once (**divided attention**). This section outlines different ways that people direct their attention in noisy places and explains how this affects the perception of speech.

5.3.1 Selective attention

Perhaps the most intuitive type of attention is selective attention, which refers to the ability to focus on one sound when other sounds are present (Figure 5.8(a)). Selective attention is flexible and voluntary: most people can selectively attend to a sound that they're interested in listening to, like the sound of a friend's voice at a party.

Many researchers have asked what happens to competing speech that's not attended: how extensively is it processed by the auditory system? For example, are only basic acoustic properties of unattended speech analysed, or does it undergo the same level of semantic processing as attended speech? A seminal study that was published in the 1950s examined this question.

In this study (Cherry, 1953), the researcher presented two different speech passages to participants through headphones. One passage was presented to their left ear while, at the same time, an entirely different passage was presented to their right ear. The participants were asked to repeat one of the passages as it was heard; for example, the passage presented to their left ear. In general, people were able to successfully repeat speech that was presented to one ear, but they couldn't recall much about unattended speech that was presented to their other ear. They could recall some things about the unattended speech—for example, whether the voice was male or female—but they couldn't recall much about its content (e.g. the topic of speech, or which words were spoken). Most people also failed to notice when the unattended speech changed to a different language! This influential study implies that only basic acoustic properties of unattended speech are processed, and the semantic content of unattended speech isn't analysed. Nevertheless, this conclusion has been hotly debated and—as it turns out—isn't quite as straightforward as it appears (Har-Shai et al., 2021).

> You can review how male and female voices differ acoustically in **Chapter 4**.

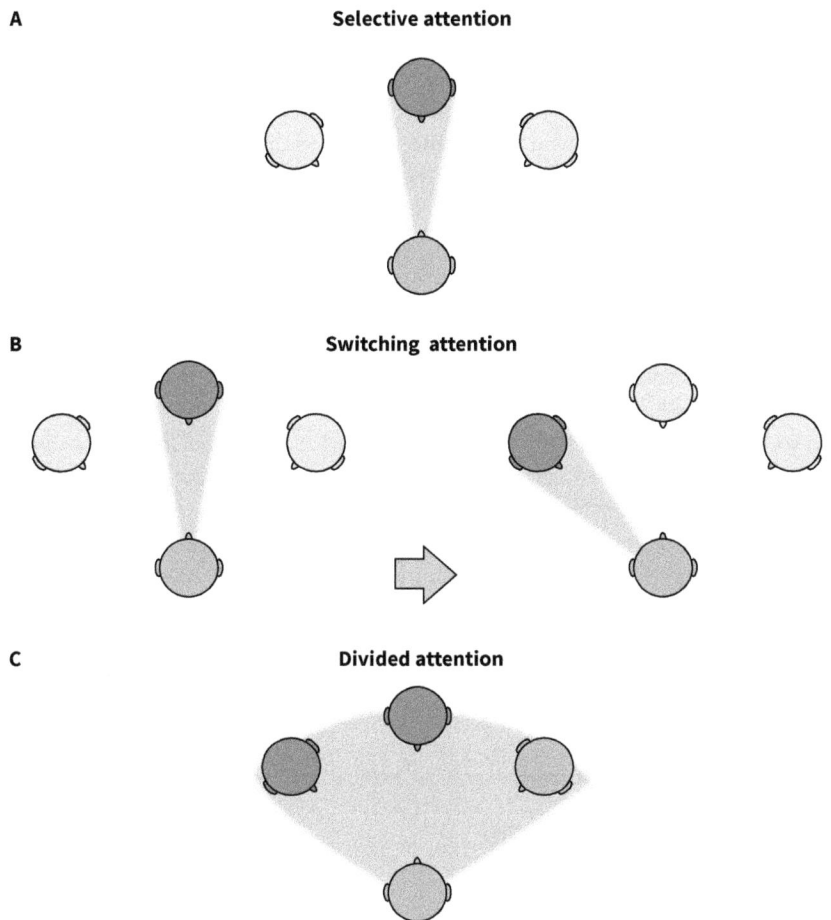

Figure 5.8 Schematics of the types of attention discussed in this section: selective attention (panel a), switching attention (panel b), and divided attention (panel c). In this figure, the listener is displayed in the lower part of each panel, and the shaded area illustrates the listener's focus of attention. Notice how the arc is directed at one talker in panel a but, in panel b, the focus switches from the middle talker to the left talker over time. In panel c, multiple talkers are attended.

The idea that the content of unattended speech isn't processed led to the 'early selection' theory of attention (Broadbent, 1958). This theory assumes that people only have a limited capacity for processing information in their surroundings. Therefore, speech that's attended is processed fully, whereas speech that's unattended is processed less extensively. In other words, there's a 'bottleneck' early in the auditory pathway, and only attended sounds are sent for further (e.g. semantic) processing. This is a bit like trying to fill a bottle from a tap: if there's lots of water coming out of the tap, then only some of it will make it into the bottle and the rest will run down the sink.

Other evidence, however, suggests that unattended sounds *can* be processed semantically— for example, people often notice their own name when it's in the unattended speech (Pinto et al., 2023)—and this evidence supports theories of 'late selection' (Deutsch & Deutsch, 1963).

Late selection theories assume that both attended and unattended sounds are processed fully, but the 'bottleneck' occurs when responses are made about sounds: only sounds that are attended are responded to.

Unfortunately, neither early nor late selection theories fully account for the results of experiments on attention. We can consider these theories as two extremes on a continuum: on one end of the continuum is early selection, on the other, late selection. In contrast, 'perceptual load theory' proposes that the 'bottleneck' is flexible and depends on the task demands (Lavie & Tsal, 1994). In other words, the 'bottleneck' varies along this continuum, depending on the setting. This theory assumes that when perceptual load is low (e.g. when there are few sounds in the environment and target sounds do not require much processing), the auditory system has spare resources and irrelevant sounds are processed. In contrast, when perceptual load is high (e.g. when there are lots of sounds that are presented rapidly or the target requires careful scrutiny), irrelevant sounds aren't fully processed because more resources are used to process attended sounds. Many results seem to be consistent with perceptual load theory, supporting the idea of a flexible 'bottleneck' that depends on the setting (see Murphy et al., 2016).

More recently, researchers have considered the idea that someone's resources for processing sounds don't only depend on the task demands. Instead, resources may vary across people, depending on their working memory capacity (Röer & Cowan, 2021). In addition, the same person may allocate different amounts of resources at different times, depending on their motivation to complete a task (Pichora-Fuller et al., 2016). This further aligns with the idea that the 'bottleneck' isn't fixed.

> Working memory is a type of short-term memory, for 'holding things in mind', that is assumed to have a limited capacity. Working memory capacity can be tested in a variety of ways, such as testing how many digits or words someone can recall from a list.

If there's some type of 'bottleneck', then presumably researchers should be able to find evidence for this when they look at responses in the auditory pathway. In general, selective attention is associated with responses in frontal and parietal areas of the brain, which send signals to auditory cortex that affect the responses of neurons there. Auditory cortex shows greater and more synchronised neural responses for attended than for unattended stimuli, such that the attended stimulus dominates the cortical response (O'Sullivan et al., 2019). However, the region of auditory cortex that's most active depends on what people are instructed to attend to (see Further insights 5.3). For example, one study presented vowel sounds from two different locations and asked participants to attend to either the location or the identity of the vowel (Ahveninen et al., 2006). When people attended to location, there was greater activity in areas that are specialised for processing a sound's location, whereas when people attended to the vowel identity, there was greater activity in areas that are specialised for processing speech content. These findings are consistent with the flexible nature of selective attention.

Areas of the brain that have been associated with selective attention include the superior parietal lobule, intraparietal sulcus, frontal eye fields, and inferior and medial frontal gyri (see e.g. Salmi et al., 2009).

Attention operates in a similar way when directing attention to non-speech sounds, and most theories of attention assume that it also operates similarly in the visual modality.

Processing the content of sounds has been associated with a ventral ('what') pathway, which starts in front of Heschl's gyrus, and leads to inferior temporal cortex—whereas processing a sound's location has been associated with a dorsal ('where') pathway, which begins behind Heschl's gyrus and leads to posterior parietal cortex (Figure 5.9). However, this distinction into two pathways is controversial (Bizley & Cohen, 2013; Perrodin et al., 2015).

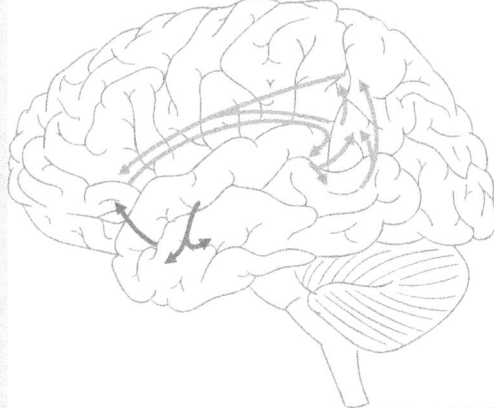

Figure 5.9 Proposed auditory ventral and dorsal streams, which are sometimes known as the 'what' and 'where' pathways.

Source: adapted from Figure 1 of Poliva (2016). 'From mimicry to language: A neuroanatomically based evolutionary model of the emergence of vocal language.' *Frontiers in Neuroscience*, 10, 307.

> **Further insights 5.3   What do people attend to?**
>
> We know that most people can successfully direct their attention to a sound that they're instructed to listen to. But how do they do this? Some researchers assume that people attend to features of sounds (e.g. frequency) or to spatial locations (i.e. sounds originating from a particular place), whereas others propose that people attend to entire 'objects' (Simon, 2015). In other words, they propose that attending to one feature of an object (e.g. its frequency) enhances processing of other properties of the same object (e.g. sounds at other frequencies that originate from the same location). The evidence is equivocal and, in many experiments, it's difficult to distinguish between these accounts—so this question remains hotly debated. Nevertheless, Driver (2001) suggests that this debate is a reinterpretation of the longer-lasting debate between early and late selection. Following this idea, whether objects, features, or spatial locations are attended to may depend on perceptual load and someone's capacity for processing sounds.

5.3.2 Switching attention

Have you ever had a conversation with someone, but noticed another, more interesting conversation happening nearby? If so, you might have stopped paying attention to the person speaking to you and started paying attention to the other conversation. In hearing science, changing the focus of attention is known as switching attention (Figure 5.8(b)).

Switching attention requires several processes. To do this, someone needs to disengage from the current conversation and focus their attention on the new conversation that they want to listen to—and this comes at a cost. This cost can manifest as a decrease in intelligibility or an increase in response time (or both) when someone switches their attention to another sound. The cost can be reduced by warning someone, in advance, that they will need to switch their attention; although, this doesn't entirely eliminate the cost of switching attention, possibly due to an 'inertia' from attending to the previous sound (Koch et al., 2011).

> Response time (also known as reaction time) is the length of time it takes someone to respond in an experiment, for example the time between a sound starting and the person pressing a button.

When people voluntarily switch their attention between one conversation and another, researchers have found responses in similar frontal and parietal areas of the brain that are involved in selective attention—implying that these areas need to 'work harder' when someone redirects their attention and focuses on a new conversation. Interestingly, people who have greater responses in these areas of the brain experience a smaller cost of switching attention (Larson & Lee, 2013).

5.3.3 Divided attention

When someone overhears something interesting in a nearby conversation, they might not want to switch their attention to it entirely, but instead they might try to listen to two conversations at once: the person who's speaking to them, and the new conversation that they've overheard. In hearing science, this is known as divided attention, and it can be measured by asking people to report words from two speech streams that are presented at the same time (Figure 5.8(c)).

The term 'divided attention' has often been taken to imply that, at each moment in time, people can split their attention between two or more sounds. However, researchers have long debated whether people can actually attend to two inputs simultaneously. Many have proposed that, instead, when someone divides their attention, they actually switch back and forth—very rapidly—between monitoring different sounds (Ihlefeld & Shinn-Cunningham, 2008). In other words, they can't listen to two conversations at exactly the same time—but can nevertheless keep track of two different conversations by listening to some pieces of one conversation and other pieces of another conversation.

Summary

When people encounter speech in everyday life, it's often accompanied by background noise—for example other conversations going on in a restaurant, the whir of a coffee machine in a café, or the sound of traffic as we walk down the street. What enters someone's ears is the continuous acoustic signal, and their auditory system faces the challenge of separating target speech from competing sounds. In these noisy settings, speech intelligibility is affected by a variety of acoustic and cognitive factors.

Whether someone wants to ignore competing sounds depends on their goal. Sometimes, they might want to selectively focus their attention on one voice, but other times they might want to switch their attention to another voice or try to listen to two voices at once.

As well as engaging the initial stages of the auditory pathway, listening in noisy settings is associated with greater responses in higher cortical areas, compared to listening in quiet settings.

Further your understanding

Assmann, P., & Summerfield, Q. (2004). 'The perception of speech under adverse conditions.' In *Speech Processing in the Auditory System. Springer Handbook of Auditory Research*, vol 18. New York, Springer. https://doi.org/10.1007/0-387-21575-1_5

Scott, S. K., & McGettigan, C. (2013). 'The neural processing of masked speech.' *Hearing Research*, 303, 58–66. https://doi.org/10.1016/j.heares.2013.05.001

References

Adank, P., Evans, B. G., Stuart-Smith, J., & Scott, S. K. (2009). 'Comprehension of familiar and unfamiliar native accents under adverse listening conditions.' *Journal of Experimental Psychology: Human Perception and Performance*, 35(2), 520–529. https://doi.org/10.1037/a0013552

Ahveninen, J., Jääskeläinen, I. P., Raij, T., Bonmassar, G., Devore, S., Hämäläinen, M. S., Belliveau, J. W., et al. (2006). 'Task-modulated "what" and "where" pathways in human auditory cortex.' *Proceedings of the National Academy of Sciences of the United States of America*, 103(39), 14608–14613. https://doi.org/10.1073/pnas.0510480103

Allport, D. A. (1993). 'Attention and control: Have we been asking the wrong questions? A critical review of twenty-five years.' In D. E. Meyer & S. Kornblum (eds.) *Attention and Performance XIV: Synergies in Experimental Psychology, Artificial Intelligence, and Cognitive Neuroscience* (pp. 183–218). Cambridge, MA: MIT Press.

Berglund, B., Hassmén, P., & Job, R. F. S. (1996). 'Sources and effects of low-frequency noise.' *Journal of the Acoustical Society of America*, 99(5), 2985. https://doi.org/10.1121/1.414863

Bizley, J. K., & Cohen, Y. E. (2013). 'The what, where and how of auditory-object perception.' *Nature Reviews Neuroscience*, 14(10), 693–707. https://doi.org/10.1038/nrn3565

Broadbent, D. E. (1958). 'Perception and communication.' Retrieved from http://books.google.co.uk/books/about/Perception_and_communication.html?id=GwtKAAAAMAAJ&pgis=1

Bronkhorst, A. W., & Plomp, R. (1992). 'Effect of multiple speechlike maskers on binaural speech recognition in normal and impaired hearing.' *Journal of the Acoustical Society of America*, 92(6), 3132. https://doi.org/10.1121/1.404209

Brungart, D. S. (2001). 'Informational and energetic masking effects in the perception of two simultaneous talkers.' *Journal of the Acoustical Society of America*, 109(3), 1101. https://doi.org/10.1121/1.1345696

Brungart, D. S., Simpson, B. D., Ericson, M. A., & Scott, K. R. (2001). 'Informational and energetic masking effects in the perception of multiple simultaneous talkers.' *Journal of the Acoustical*

Society of America, 110(5 Pt 1), 2527–2538. https://doi.org/10.1121/1.1408946

Cherry, E. C. (1953). 'Some experiments on the recognition of speech, with one and two ears.' *Journal of the Acoustical Society of America*, 25(5), 975. https://doi.org/10.1121/1.1907229

Cooke, M. (2006). 'A glimpsing model of speech perception in noise.' *Journal of the Acoustical Society of America*, 119(3), 1562–1573. https://doi.org/10.1121/1.2166600

Cooke, M., Lecumberri, M. L. G., & Barker, J. (2008). 'The foreign language cocktail party problem: Energetic and informational masking effects in non-native speech perception.' *Journal of the Acoustical Society of America*, 123(1), 414. https://doi.org/10.1121/1.2804952

Culling, J. F., & Summerfield, Q. (1998). 'Perceptual separation of concurrent speech sounds: Absence of across-frequency grouping by common interaural delay.' *Journal of the Acoustical Society of America*, 98(2), 785. https://doi.org/10.1121/1.413571

Deutsch, J. A., & Deutsch, D. (1963). 'Attention: Some theoretical considerations.' *Psychological Review*, 70(1), 80–90. https://doi.org/10.2147/NDT.S27447

Driver, J. (2001). 'A selective review of selective attention research from the past century.' *British Journal of Psychology*, 92, 53–78. Retrieved from http://www.ncbi.nlm.nih.gov/pubmed/11802865

Festen, J. M., & Plomp, R. (1990). 'Effects of fluctuating noise and interfering speech on the speech-reception threshold for impaired and normal hearing.' *Journal of the Acoustical Society of America*, 88(4), 1725–1736. https://doi.org/10.1121/1.400247

Fogerty, D., Carter, B. L., & Healy, E. W. (2018). 'Glimpsing speech in temporally and spectro-temporally modulated noise.' *Journal of the Acoustical Society of America*, 143(5), 3047–3057. https://doi.org/10.1121/1.5038266

Freyman, R. L., Balakrishnan, U., & Helfer, K. S. (2004). 'Effect of number of masking talkers and auditory priming on informational masking in speech recognition.' *Journal of the Acoustical Society of America*, 115(5), 2246–2256. https://doi.org/10.1121/1.1689343

Har-Shai Yahav, P., & Zion Golumbic, E. (2021). 'Linguistic processing of task-irrelevant speech at a cocktail party.' *eLife*, 10, e65096. https://doi.org/10.7554/eLife.65096

Hawkins Jr., J. E., & Stevens, S. S. (2005). 'The masking of pure tones and of speech by white noise.' *Journal of the Acoustical Society of America*, 22(1), 6. https://doi.org/10.1121/1.1906581

Holmes, E., & Johnsrude, I. S. (2020). 'Speech spoken by familiar people is more resistant to interference by linguistically similar speech.' *Journal of Experimental Psychology: Learning, Memory, and Cognition*, 46(8), 1465–1476. Retrieved from https://doi.org/10.31234/osf.io/2ebrs

Ihlefeld, A., & Shinn-Cunningham, B. G. (2008). 'Spatial release from energetic and informational masking in a divided speech identification task.' *Journal of the Acoustical Society of America*, 123(6), 4380. https://doi.org/10.1121/1.2904825

Iyer, N., Brungart, D. S., & Simpson, B. D. (2010). 'Effects of target-masker contextual similarity on the multimasker penalty in a three-talker diotic listening task.' *Journal of the Acoustical Society of America*, 128(5), 2998–3010. https://doi.org/10.1121/1.3479547

Kitterick, P. T., Bailey, P. J., & Summerfield, A. Q. (2010). 'Benefits of knowing who, where, and when in multi-talker listening.' *Journal of the Acoustical Society of America*, 127(4), 2498–2508. https://doi.org/10.1121/1.3327507

Koch, I., Lawo, V., Fels, J., & Vorländer, M. (2011). 'Switching in the cocktail party: exploring intentional control of auditory selective attention.' *Journal of Experimental Psychology: Human Perception and Performance*, 37(4), 1140–1147. https://doi.org/10.1037/a0022189

Larson, E., & Lee, A. K. C. (2013). 'The cortical dynamics underlying effective switching of auditory spatial attention.' *NeuroImage*, 64, 365–370. https://doi.org/10.1016/j.neuroimage.2012.09.006

Lavie, N., & Tsal, Y. (1994). 'Perceptual load as a major determinant of the locus of selection in visual attention.' *Perception & Psychophysics*, 56(2), 183–197. Retrieved from http://www.ncbi.nlm.nih.gov/pubmed/7971119

Lutfi, R. A., Gilbertson, L., Heo, I., Chang, A. C., & Stamas, J. (2013). 'The information-divergence hypothesis of informational masking.' *Journal of the Acoustical Society of America*, 134(3), 2160–2170. https://doi.org/10.1121/1.4817875

Madsen, S. M. K., Dau, T., & Oxenham, A. J. (2021). 'No interaction between fundamental-frequency differences and spectral region when perceiving speech in a speech background.' *PLoS ONE*, 16(4), e0249654. https://doi.org/10.1371/journal.pone.0249654

Marrone, N., Mason, C. R., & Kidd, G. (2008). 'Tuning in the spatial dimension: Evidence from a masked speech identification task.' *Journal of the Acoustical Society of America*, 124(2), 1146. https://doi.org/10.1121/1.2945710

Miller, G. A., & Licklider, J. C. R. (2005). 'The intelligibility of interrupted speech.' *Journal of the*

Acoustical Society of America, 22(2), 167. https://doi.org/10.1121/1.1906584

Miller, G. A., & Nicely, P. E. (2005). 'An analysis of perceptual confusions among some English consonants.' *Journal of the Acoustical Society of America*, 27(2), 338. https://doi.org/10.1121/1.1907526

Murphy, G., Groeger, J. A., & Greene, C. M. (2016). 'Twenty years of load theory—Where are we now, and where should we go next?' *Psychonomic Bulletin & Review*, 23(5), 1316–1340. https://doi.org/10.3758/S13423-015-0982-5

Nakai, T., Kato, C., & Matsuo, K. (2005). 'An fMRI study to investigate auditory attention: A model of the cocktail party phenomenon.' *Magnetic Resonance in Medical Sciences*, 4(2), 75–82. https://doi.org/10.2463/MRMS.4.75

O'Sullivan, J. A., Herrero, J., Smith, E., Schevon, C., McKhann, G. M., Sheth, S. A., Mesgarani, N., et al. (2019). 'Hierarchical encoding of attended auditory objects in multi-talker speech perception.' *Neuron*, 104(6), 1195–1209.e3. https://doi.org/10.1016/j.neuron.2019.09.007

Perrodin, C., Kayser, C., Abel, T. J., Logothetis, N. K., & Petkov, C. I. (2015). 'Who is that? Brain networks and mechanisms for identifying individuals.' *Trends in Cognitive Sciences*, 19(12), 783–796. https://doi.org/10.1016/j.tics.2015.09.002

Pichora-Fuller, M. K., Kramer, S. E., Eckert, M. A., Edwards, B., Hornsby, B. W. Y., Humes, L. E., Lemke, U., Lunner, T., Matthen, M., Mackersie, C. L., Naylor, G., Phillips, N. A., Righter, M., Rudner, M., Sommers, M. S., Tremblay, K. L., & Wingfield, A. (2016). 'Hearing impairment and cognitive energy: The framework for understanding effortful listening (FUEL).' *Ear and Hearing*, 37, 5S–27S. https://doi.org/10.1097/AUD.0000000000000312

Pickett, J. M. (1957). 'Perception of vowels heard in noises of various spectra.' *Journal of the Acoustical Society of America*, 29(5), 613–620. https://doi.org/10.1121/1.1908983

Pinto, D., Kaufman, M., Brown, A., & Zion Golumbic, E. (2023). 'An ecological investigation of the capacity to follow simultaneous speech and preferential detection of one's own name.' *Cerebral Cortex*, 33(9), 5361–5374. https://doi.org/10.1093/cercor/bhac424

Plomp, R. (1976). 'Binaural and monaural speech intelligibility of connected discourse in reverberation as a function of azimuth of a single competing sound source (speech or noise).' *Acustica*, 34(4), 200–211.

Poliva, O. (2016). 'From mimicry to language: A neuroanatomically based evolutionary model of the emergence of vocal language.' *Frontiers in Neuroscience*, 10, 307. https://doi.org/10.3389/fnins.2016.00307

Roberts, B., & Moore, B. C. (1990). 'The influence of extraneous sounds on the perceptual estimation of first-formant frequency in vowels.' *Journal of the Acoustical Society of America*, 88(6), 2571–2583. https://doi.org/10.1121/1.399978

Röer, J. P., & Cowan, N. (2021). 'A preregistered replication and extension of the cocktail party phenomenon: One's name captures attention, unexpected words do not.' *Journal of Experimental Psychology: Learning, Memory, and Cognition*, 47(2), 234–242. https://doi.org/10.1037/xlm0000874

Rosen, S., Souza, P., Ekelund, C., & Majeed, A. A. (2013). 'Listening to speech in a background of other talkers: Effects of talker number and noise vocoding.' *Journal of the Acoustical Society of America*, 133(4), 2431–2443. https://doi.org/10.1121/1.4794379

Salmi, J., Rinne, T., Koistinen, S., Salonen, O., & Alho, K. (2009). 'Brain networks of bottom-up triggered and top-down controlled shifting of auditory attention.' *Brain Research*, 1286, 155–164.

Scott, S. K., & McGettigan, C. (2013). 'The neural processing of masked speech.' *Hearing Research*, 303, 58–66. https://doi.org/10.1016/j.heares.2013.05.001

Scott, S. K., Rosen, S., Beaman, C. P., Davis, J. P., & Wise, R. J. (2009). 'The neural processing of masked speech: Evidence for different mechanisms in the left and right temporal lobes.' *Journal of the Acoustical Society of America*, 125(3), 1737–1743. https://doi.org/10.1121/1.3050255

Shinn-Cunningham, B. G., Kopco, N., & Martin, T. J. (2005). 'Localizing nearby sound sources in a classroom: Binaural room impulse responses.' *Journal of the Acoustical Society of America*, 117(5), 3100. https://doi.org/10.1121/1.1872572

Simon, J. Z. (2015). 'The encoding of auditory objects in auditory cortex: Insights from magnetoencephalography.' *International Journal of Psychophysiology*, 95(2), 184–190. https://doi.org/10.1016/j.ijpsycho.2014.05.005

Warren, R. M. (1970). 'Perceptual restoration of missing speech sounds.' *Science*, 167(3917), 392–393. https://doi.org/10.1126/SCIENCE.167.3917.392

Warren, R. M., Obusek, C. J., & Ackroff, J. M. (1972). 'Auditory induction: Perceptual synthesis of absent sounds.' *Science*, 176, 1149–1151.

6 Perceiving Music

People listen to music for a variety of reasons: because they like how it sounds, because they experience a particular emotion when they listen to it, or perhaps simply because someone else happens to be playing it. Music often comprises many different sounds that overlap, yet—remarkably—the auditory system can interpret it. This chapter draws on the fundamental aspects of hearing covered in **Chapters 2 and 3** to explain how people perceive music. It also examines how music is processed in the brain. Finally, this chapter addresses how music perception differs among people: for example, how is the way someone perceives music influenced by the culture they grew up in, the language they speak, or their experience of musical training?

6.1 Making sense of music

Acoustically, music is simply a series of sounds—but what makes these sounds *musical*? This section introduces some key attributes of music and describes how the acoustic properties of music contribute to perceptual organisation and to the emotions that people perceive in music.

6.1.1 Pitch in music

Imagine a well-known tune, such as 'Happy Birthday to You': you can probably imagine it played on the piano, the violin, or perhaps sung out loud by your friends! Yet, while each of these versions has a different 'quality' about it, most people would be able to recognise that the tune is 'Happy Birthday to You' in all cases. This is because all three versions have the same **melody** and **rhythm**. Melody describes how sounds are arranged to create a tune; specifically, it reflects the sequence of pitches that most people perceive. Rhythm describes the timing of sounds within music: it refers to the pattern of sounds over time.

You don't need to be trained in music to understand how the auditory system makes sense of music, but some basic familiarity with musical notes can be useful for understanding the acoustic properties of music. One convention in 'Western' music is that musical notes are named according to letters of the alphabet: A, B, C, D, E, F, and G. Figure 6.1 shows part of a piano keyboard, upon which the note names are labelled. The white keys are named with the letters of the alphabet, whereas the black keys have an additional qualifier: they also have a sharp (♯) or a flat (♭) symbol to indicate whether their pitch is usually perceived as higher (i.e. 'sharper') or lower (i.e. 'flatter') than the white note with the same letter. The separation between two adjacent notes on the piano is 1 **semitone** (Figure 6.1).

> 'Western' music refers to music from North American and Western European cultures. The musical notes that are used in 'Western' music are assigned to keys on the piano, as shown in Figure 6.1, whereas some music from other cultures doesn't use these musical notes. Most research examining music perception has focused on 'Western' music and listeners who are familiar with this type of music. However, musical styles differ across cultures—and what is perceived as music in one culture might not be perceived as music in another (Jacoby et al., 2020).

If you were to play the keys on a piano, one at a time, from the left side to the right side, you might notice that the pitch of the notes gradually gets higher with each note that you play.

Recall from **Chapter 2** that pitch is related to fundamental frequency. Musical notes are harmonic complex tones and, as we move from left to right on the piano keyboard, the fundamental frequency of the notes increases, and people usually perceive the notes as rising in pitch. The increase in fundamental frequency can be compared to walking up a spiral staircase. As someone walks up each step of a spiral staircase, they get higher off the ground—and, as we 'walk' up the notes on the piano, the notes become higher in fundamental frequency.

Notice in Figure 6.1 that the note names each appear twice. For example, find the two 'A' notes in Figure 6.1: these 'A' notes are one **octave** apart, which means that the fundamental frequency of the 'A' on the right of the figure is *double* the fundamental frequency of the 'A' to its left. Similarly, the 'C' in the middle of the figure has double the fundamental frequency of the 'C' on the left of the figure.

Even though these notes differ in fundamental frequency, notes with the same name are perceptually similar. For example, two 'A's from different octaves will sound more similar to each other than an 'A' and a 'B'—but why? Recall from **Chapter 2** that harmonic complex tones are made up of frequencies that are integer multiples of a single fundamental frequency. We can see this principle in action when we examine musical notes: one of the 'A' notes on the piano (depicted on the left side of Figure 6.1) has a fundamental frequency of

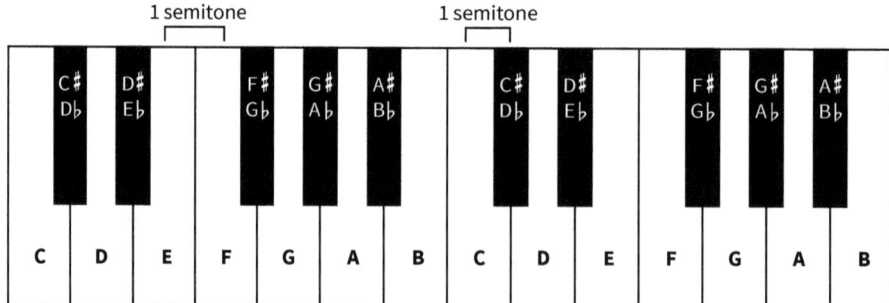

Figure 6.1 Section of a piano keyboard with the note names labelled. Each black note can be referred to as a sharp (♯) or a flat (♭). There is one semitone difference between each adjacent note, irrespective of whether the two notes are a black note and a white note, or two white notes. Notice how the pattern of note names repeats twice within the figure.

440 Hz and, therefore, the second harmonic is 880 Hz, the third harmonic is 1,320 Hz, the fourth harmonic is 1,760 Hz, and so on. The 'A' note that is one octave higher (depicted on the right side of Figure 6.1) has a fundamental frequency of 880 Hz, a second harmonic of 1,760 Hz, a third harmonic of 2,640 Hz, and so on. Notice how most of the frequencies in the two 'A' notes are the same. Whereas, the 'B' note depicted in the middle of Figure 6.1 has a fundamental frequency of 494 Hz, a second harmonic of 988 Hz, and a third harmonic of 1,482 Hz—which do not overlap with the harmonics in the 'A' notes. The overlap in harmonics is why people usually perceive two notes of the same name (e.g. two 'A's) as sounding more similar to each other than two notes with different names (e.g. an 'A' and a 'B').

Returning to the spiral staircase analogy, we can represent the perceptual relationship between two notes of the same name by imagining the relationship between different levels of the staircase. As someone walks up the spiral staircase, they might reach a door at the same position on each 'level' of the building—and we can compare this to reaching a note with the same name as we go from left to right on the piano in Figure 6.1. Figure 6.2 depicts the note names as a spiral. Each rotation of the spiral represents one octave. Notice how in this illustration 'A' is always on the left side of the spiral and 'D' is always on the right. The consistent positions of the note names illustrate the idea that notes with the same name are perceptually similar.

Ultimately, we can consider pitch in music as having two components (Deutsch et al., 2008): the first is the 'height' of the pitch as it changes from low to high; the second is the perceptual quality of the pitch, which is similar for sounds that have the same pitch label (e.g. 'A'). As an example, the two 'A' notes described in the previous paragraph have the same pitch label but the second is higher than the first.

> Using computer-generated tones, it's possible to create an illusion in which a sound is perceived to have an ever-increasing (or ever-decreasing) pitch. These sounds are known as 'Shepard tones', named after the person who first created them (Roger Shepard). Shepard tones are complex tones in which the constituent frequencies differ in sound level, in a particular way that makes the octave ambiguous.

6.1.2 Timing in music

Timing plays an important role in the perception of music. If you've ever tapped your foot along to music, it's likely that you've picked up the 'beat' (Further insights 6.1). The 'beat' is sometimes described as a pulse within music that repeats. You will already be familiar with the concept of a beat: your heart*beat* has a repeating pulse and you can probably feel it on your wrist. In music, the beat sets the tempo (i.e. speed) of the music, and tempo is sometimes defined as the number of beats per minute (abbreviated to 'bpm'). Music with a high number of beats per minute (e.g. 140 bpm) often sounds energetic, and you might expect to hear music with this tempo in a high-intensity exercise class. Music with a low number of beats per minute (e.g. 60 bpm) is much slower and you would be more likely to hear music with this tempo at a yoga class.

> Some beats are perceived as being stronger than others, which gives rise to 'meter'; meter is another perceptual attribute of music that reflects the organisation of beats over time.

> **Chapter 4** introduced tempo for speech, but tempo is also used to refer to the speed of music.

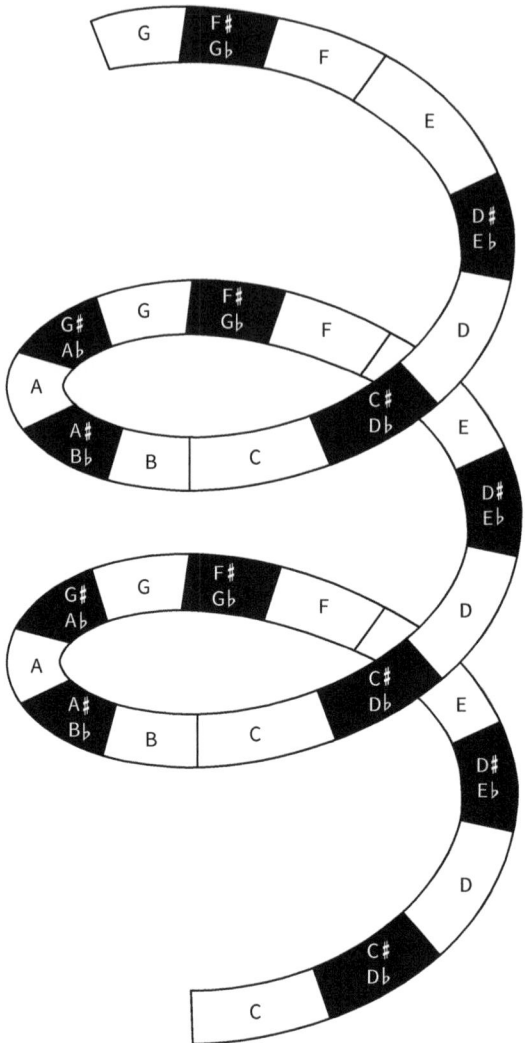

Figure 6.2 A schematic illustrating the two components of musical pitch perception: first, pitch increases from low to high, as depicted by the height of the spiral; second, there are similarities in pitch for notes with the same name, as depicted by the notes of the same name aligning vertically on the spiral. In this illustration, the spiral depicts two and a half octaves of note names. Notice how each rotation of the model includes one octave of notes, with notes of the same name stacked above each other.

Source: based on data from Elliott, T. M., Hamilton, L. S., & Theunissen, F. E. (2013). 'Acoustic structure of the five perceptual dimensions of timbre in orchestral instrument tones'. The *Journal of the Acoustical Society of America*, 133(1), 389–404. https://doi.org/10.1121/1.4770244

> **Further insights 6.1** Assessing rhythm perception
>
> One way to assess someone's perception of timing in music is to ask them to move in response to the music—for example by tapping their finger along to the beat. Tapping is a type of rhythm-production task, because people are asked to produce the rhythm by moving. Other tests focus on rhythm perception and don't require movement; for example, someone can be asked whether two rhythms are the same or different. Importantly, the type of task can influence the results: some people are good at rhythm perception but not rhythm production, and vice versa (Fiveash et al., 2022). In addition, some people perform well on some rhythm-perception tasks but not others; for example, someone might be able to detect that music has a regular compared to an irregular pulse, but struggle to identify if a series of rhythms are identical or different (Fiveash et al., 2022). These differences in performance could arise because some tests require additional skills. For example, some rhythm-perception tests require listeners to consider rhythm over long timescales, which means that people also need to have sufficient memory skills to complete the test successfully, in addition to good rhythm perception; therefore, individual differences in other skills, such as memory, could explain differences in performance among tests.

6.1.3 Timbre in music

If 'Happy Birthday to You' contains the same notes and has the same rhythm when it's played on the piano or violin, why doesn't it sound identical? Another important attribute of music is timbre, which is a sensation of the quality of sound. If you listen to two different musical notes that are matched for pitch, duration, location, and sound level, the remaining differences that you might perceive are due to differences in **timbre**. Different instruments produce notes with different timbres, because they are different shapes, sizes, and are made of different materials—which all affect the types of sounds they make.

Timbre can be difficult to describe because a variety of acoustic attributes (spectral, temporal, and spectro-temporal) affect the quality of a sound. Nevertheless, if someone describes a sound as 'bright', 'dull', or 'brassy', they're referring to the sound's timbre.

To quantify the difference in timbre between sounds, researchers have played pairs of sounds to people and asked them to rate the degree of similarity (or dissimilarity) between the sounds. After this is done for many sound pairs, the ratings can be analysed and visualised as a 'timbre space'. The timbre space is similar to a map, but rather than showing geographical distance, it shows the distance in perceived 'timbre space' between various sounds: sounds that are perceived to have similar timbres are close together in the 'timbre space', whereas sounds that are perceived to have dissimilar timbres are further apart.

6.1.4 Perceptual organisation of music

The principles of perceptual organisation come into action when people listen to music. For example, if you've ever listened to an orchestra or a live band, you'll know that several instruments often play at the same time: a listener might be able to tell apart the notes played by the trumpets and those played by the flutes or the violins. Other times, they might perceive a blended or 'unified' sound when they hear a piece played by multiple instruments, which could have a different quality, or timbre, to the individual instruments that make up the sound. So, why does this occur? **Chapter 3** compared perceptual organisation to selecting jigsaw pieces from a box and trying to work out how many puzzles they belong to. When applied to music, the sources within the music are the puzzles. When listening to a piece of music, someone might want to work out how many different sources of sounds (i.e. instruments) are present in the piece. Or, they might simply want to work out which sounds to group into the same stream, and which to segregate into separate streams.

> You can review **Chapter 3** for an overview of perceptual organisation, simultaneous grouping, and sequential grouping.

Perceptual organisation of music involves both simultaneous and sequential grouping. Remember that musical notes are harmonic complex tones, so multiple frequencies will reach the ears—even when only one instrument is playing. Therefore, someone needs to determine which frequencies in the sound that reaches their ears belong together (e.g. if they are played by the same instrument)—which relies on simultaneous grouping—and which should be segregated (e.g. if two instruments are playing notes from different melodies). Also, when listening to a musical tune such as 'Happy Birthday to You', people use sequential grouping to connect the successive notes. So, which factors influence perceptual grouping of music?

Similar to more basic, non-musical tones (covered in **Chapter 3**), the auditory system uses various cues—including frequency—to infer which sounds to group together and which to segregate. Harmonicity can sometimes be used to group the frequencies of one musical note (e.g. the harmonics of an 'A' note) and segregate them from another note (e.g. the harmonics of a 'B' note). Another cue is fundamental frequency: people tend to group sounds which are close in fundamental frequency and segregate sounds that are different in fundamental frequency. For example, a double bass has a fundamental frequency range of 41–392 Hz, whereas a piccolo has a much higher fundamental frequency range of 587–4,200 Hz. If someone has been listening to smooth changes in fundamental frequencies between 100 and 200 Hz and they suddenly hear a 4,000-Hz tone, it probably came from a different source than the lower tones, so they're likely to perceptually segregate it from the lower tones.

Timbre also contributes to the perceptual organisation of music. If you've ever listened to an orchestral piece of music, you might have noticed that it's easier to separate the notes played by the trumpets from those played by the violins, compared to separating the notes played by the violins from those played by the cellos. That's because the violin and cello come from the same 'family' of musical instruments (i.e. they're both part of the 'string' family) and they have similar timbres.

The similarity in timbre occurs because the violin and cello have a similar shape and are made from similar materials, whereas the trumpet is part of a different 'family' of musical instruments (the 'brass' family) and its timbre is quite different to that of a violin. In general, a greater difference in timbre has been associated with a more segregated percept (Fischer et al., 2021). Yet sometimes, when someone listens to an orchestral piece of music, they don't hear the instruments separately; instead, they might perceive a blended sound that has a different timbre to the individual instruments alone. In these cases, the sounds have been grouped together. Researchers have shown that a blended (i.e. fully grouped) percept is more likely to arise when sounds are harmonically related and start at the same time (McAdams et al., 2022).

At an orchestral concert, the musicians who play different instruments are often seated in different places. Higher-pitched string instruments, such as violins, are typically on the left side of the stage, whereas lower-pitched string instruments, such as double basses, are typically on the right side of the stage. The difference in spatial location helps people to segregate the notes played by different musicians. Spatial location is a cue for perceptual organisation of music, even when someone can't see the positions of the musicians; in other words, most people could separate a musical note played from their left side from one that's played on their right side by using cues for sound location, such as interaural differences in timing, interaural differences in level, and monaural spectral cues. That said, spatial location isn't a strong enough cue to override other cues; for example, a common illusion—described in Further insights 6.2—shows how people can sometimes be tricked into perceiving sounds as coming from a different location to where they originated, if other cues for perceptual organisation conflict with spatial location.

> To review cues for spatial localisation, see **Chapter 2**.

Further insights 6.2   The scale illusion

In a musical scale, the notes are ordered by fundamental frequency. In an ascending scale, the notes increase in fundamental frequency, whereas in a descending scale, the notes decrease in fundamental frequency. An interesting illusion—known as the 'scale illusion'—occurs when a listener is played two musical scales over headphones, but the notes alternate between being presented to the left and the right ears (Deutsch, 1975). The two scales are played at the same time, with one ascending (Figure 6.3(a)) and the other descending (Figure 6.3(b)). The first note of the ascending scale is played to the left ear at the same time as the first note of the descending scale is played to the right ear. The notes of each scale then alternate between the left and right ears, as illustrated in Figure 6.3(c). Interestingly, most listeners perceive the higher notes of both scales as coming from the left ear and the lower notes of both scales as coming from the right ear (Figure 6.3(d)). This percept differs from the physical locations of the notes because, in reality, both ears are presented with high and low notes. The scale illusion is thought to occur because listeners group the higher tones together and the lower tones together. Given that sounds with a similar fundamental frequency usually originate from the same sound source, and a sound source is unlikely to undergo large changes in location, the tones that are grouped together are usually perceived as originating from the same location.

(continued...)

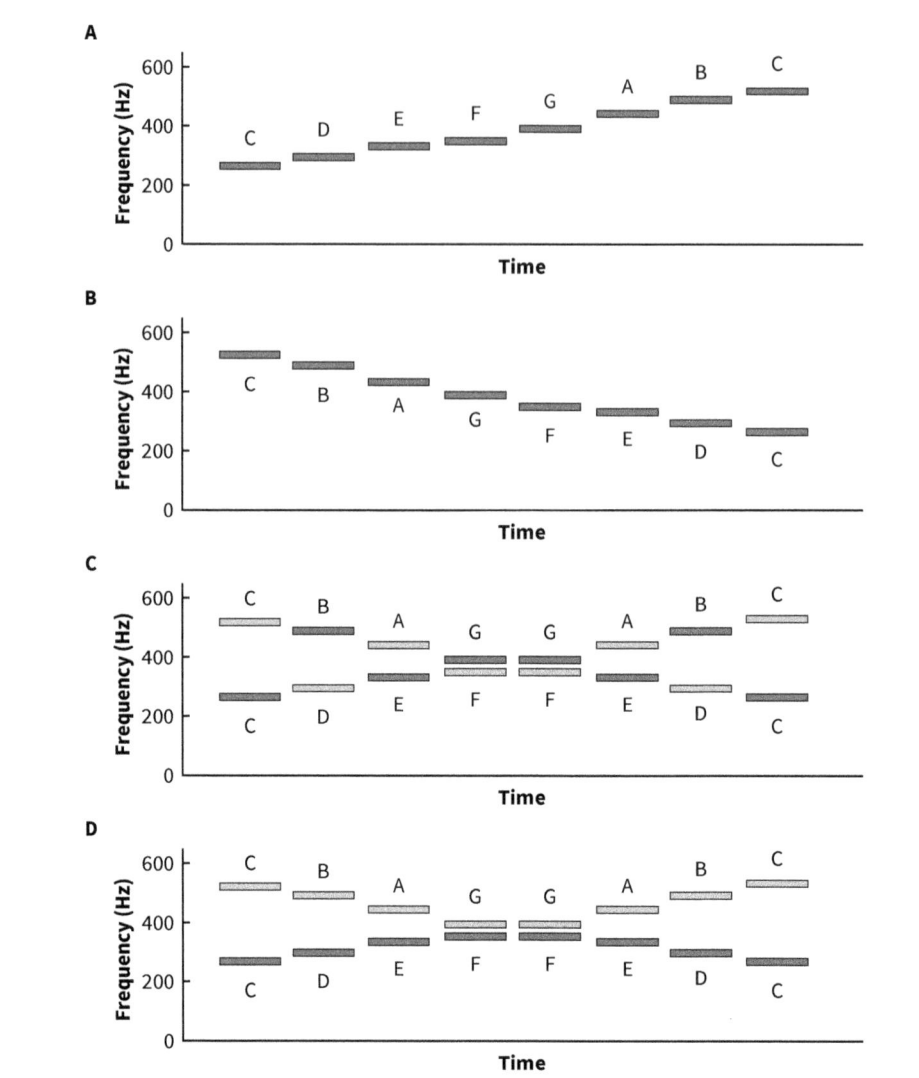

Figure 6.3 Illustration of the scale illusion. Examples of note names in ascending (panel a) and descending (panel b) scales. Panel c displays the notes presented to left (darker) and right (lighter) ears in the scale illusion. Panel d illustrates the illusory percept for left (darker) and right (lighter) ears.

Perceptual organisation in music is also biased by context and prior knowledge. For example, many people can still recognise a familiar tune like 'Happy Birthday to You' if it's played with a rhythm different to how they've heard before (particularly if they're hearing it while standing next to a cake that has candles on it!). Someone's previous experience with music also influences what they expect to hear. For example, music from North American and Western European cultures is usually written in a musical key, which indicates that some notes are more likely to occur in the music than others. The musical key of C contains the white notes on the piano (Figure 6.1), so listeners who are familiar with music from North American and Western European cultures will expect that music in this key will contain more white notes than black notes. To help understand what musical keys are, imagine that you're in a restaurant and you're trying to decide which dish to order. If you have a food allergy, you might look for symbols next to each item that indicate what ingredients it contains (e.g. vegan, contains fish, contains dairy). Similarly, a musical key indicates what notes the music is going to contain. If you order fish soup, you probably expect to find fish in it and, similarly, listeners expect to hear notes that are from the musical key that the music begins in. However, unlike restaurant menus, which should adhere to their descriptions (e.g. you might be annoyed to find fish in your vegan soup!), composers will sometimes use notes outside the specified key to create interest and surprise in music. People often learn about musical keys when they undertake formal music training, but a listener doesn't need to know the theory behind musical keys for them to influence their perception: many people also become familiar with musical keys—and, therefore, with which notes to expect—just by hearing music throughout their lives.

It's interesting to consider that there's no 'correct' way of grouping sounds in music. In a simple case, we could consider grouping sounds according to the instruments that played different notes. However, skilled composers often toy with the factors that contribute to perceptual organisation (e.g. timbre and timing), which can generate surprise within music and make the music more exciting. For example, sounds can be added together to create layers in music, in which some aspects of music are grouped together and others are segregated. Another common example is when someone plays the piano with two hands and, sometimes, each hand plays a distinct melody, whereas at other times, the notes played by the two hands combine to form a unified melody. In a similar way to how the streaming paradigm introduced in **Chapter 3** can sometimes be ambiguous and people can voluntarily switch between different percepts, many people find that they are able to do this in music too—to either perceive the piece as a whole, or pick out particular instruments within it.

6.1.5 Music and emotion

Have you ever listened to a piece of music and noticed that it sounds happy or sad? For example, imagine your friends singing 'Happy Birthday to You': often, this song sounds happy, and it would be unusual if it was sung in a sad tone. The emotions perceived in music are surprisingly consistent across people: music from North American and Western European cultures that's designed to convey happiness, sadness, or fear is usually perceived as conveying the desired emotion. Interestingly, even listeners from other cultures who have never previously heard music from North American and Western European cultures perceive it as containing the same emotions as Western European and North American listeners do (Fritz et al., 2009)—which implies that acoustical attributes of music play a major role in determining the emotions that people perceive.

> In addition to music *conveying* emotions (e.g. when a composer creates a piece of music to sound sad), the listener often *experiences* an emotional response (e.g. they may feel sad or happy) when they listen to music—which may be the same or different to the emotion that the composer intended to convey. The emotions that people experience when listening to music are surprisingly consistent across cultures. For example, people from the United States and China experience very similar emotional responses to music, both when they rate their emotion using traditionally studied categories (e.g. happy, sad) and when they use more nuanced categories (e.g. dreamy, energising) (Cowen et al., 2020).

Table 6.1 Overview of some acoustical attributes that are often related to perceived emotions in music, from Juslin and Sloboda (2013).

Emotion perceived	Tempo	Sound level	Fundamental frequency (f_0) range/variability	Rhythm	Timbre
Happy	Fast	Medium-high	High f_0, with a wide f_0 range	Smooth	Bright
Sad	Slow	Low	Low f_0, with a narrow f_0 range	Varied including pauses	Dull
Angry	Fast	High	High f_0, with moderate f_0 variability	Complex and variable	Sharp
Fearful	Fast	Low	High f_0, with a very wide f_0 range	Jarring	Soft

So, *which* acoustical attributes contribute to the perception of emotion in music? Similar to how different combinations of ingredients can make different types of cake, different combinations of acoustic attributes combine to produce a perceived emotion. For example, both happy and angry music often have fast tempos, yet people can usually distinguish between these emotions, because they differ in other acoustic attributes, such as the sound level and rhythm of the music (Table 6.1) (Juslin & Laukka, 2004). Similarly, a low sound level (corresponding to a quieter sound) has been associated with both sadness and fear in music. Yet, sadness and fear can typically be distinguished by the rhythm and tempo of music. Table 6.1 summarises how five acoustical attributes differ between pieces of music that are perceived to contain different emotions.

Interestingly, the way that acoustic attributes convey emotions within music is similar to the way they convey emotions within speech (Juslin & Laukka, 2003). For example, a fast tempo and a highly variable fundamental frequency are associated with joyful emotions in both music and speech. In both domains, a fast tempo combined with a high sound level is usually perceived as conveying happiness or anger, whereas a slow tempo combined with a low sound level is usually perceived as conveying sadness. These findings imply that people utilise similar acoustics to identify emotions in music to those that they use to identify emotions in speech.

Some people have claimed that 'You can't play a sad song on the banjo' (see Huron et al., 2014). This common phrase reflects the idea that timbre can contribute to perceived emotion in music.

See **Chapter 4** for a summary of how emotion is conveyed in speech.

6.2 Music and the brain

Researchers have studied brain responses to music to gain a greater understanding of how people process music. This section explores how the brain responds to musical structure, then compares brain responses to music and speech.

6.2.1 Brain responses to musical structure

The sentence 'Room the big in was the party' doesn't make sense, because the word order (which is known as 'syntax') doesn't follow the rules of the English language. Similarly, most music from North America and Western Europe follows rules that govern the pattern and timing of notes. These rules enable people to predict what's likely to happen next in a piece of music. Deviations from those rules are surprising—and, sometimes, musical composers deliberately violate the rules to make a piece of music more interesting, for the same reason that they might use notes from outside of the specified musical key (see Section 6.1.2).

> Most research that has examined brain responses to structure in music has focused on music from North American and Western European cultures and has tested participants from these same cultures. North American and Western European music typically uses notes with particular fundamental frequencies, which correspond to particular pitch names (e.g. 'C', 'D', 'E'; see Figure 6.1). More cross-cultural research is needed to determine if these responses are consistent across cultures (see Jacoby et al., 2020).

Consider a very simple example, in which someone is listening to the same musical note over and over again: A, A, A, A, A, A, A, B, A, A, A.

Do you notice a note that doesn't seem to fit in the sequence? You might be surprised by the 'B', given that all of the other notes were 'A's. In this example, the 'B' note has a different fundamental frequency compared to the 'A' notes. Recall the mismatch negativity response introduced in **Chapter 3**: a mismatch negativity response occurs in response to a sound that deviates from the preceding sounds in a sequence, so it would occur in response to the 'B' note, because the 'B' constitutes a deviation in fundamental frequency from the repeated 'A' notes. The mismatch negativity also occurs for other types of deviations, such as when one note is much longer or shorter than the preceding notes. Interestingly, the mismatch negativity occurs even when the listener is told in advance that they'll hear an unexpected sound within a sequence (Fitzgerald & Todd, 2020), which has been interpreted as suggesting that the mismatch negativity arises automatically and can't be eliminated with prior knowledge.

> Recall from **Section 6.1.1** that we can refer to musical notes using letters (A, B, C, D, E, F, and G) and most people perceive distinct pitches for different notes.

Brain responses also track structure in music at longer timescales. Beyond simple deviations in fundamental frequency or duration, music has a broader melodic and rhythmical structure, similar to how language follows syntax. Most people become familiar with the structure, or 'rules', of music implicitly, through listening to music frequently in everyday life. Indeed, brain responses of both musicians and non-musicians are sensitive to violations in the syntax of music. For example, recall from Section 6.1.2 that listeners usually expect the notes in a piece of music to be consistent with its musical key; a note that violates this expectation elicits a brain response called the 'early right anterior negativity' (which is often abbreviated to 'ERAN'). The ERAN is similar to the mismatch negativity, although the latter occurs when an individual note violates a simple rule (e.g. it has a different duration than expected), whereas the ERAN occurs in response to a note that violates the broader syntax of music, and is sometimes conceptualised as a music-syntactic mismatch negativity. While the ERAN is observed in musicians and non-musicians, musicians tend to have larger ERAN responses than non-musicians (Jentschke et al., 2005). Also, the ERAN response appears to be more sensitive to prior knowledge than the mismatch negativity. When listeners are told in advance that a sound will deviate from the musical structure, the ERAN occurs more rapidly after the deviant note than when listeners are not expecting a deviation (Koelsch et al., 2019). In sum, these findings show that, in general, people's brains can track the overall structure of music.

> **Further insights 6.3** Brain responses to other aspects of music
>
> Brain responses to music are widespread, extending beyond acoustic processing to areas that are involved in sensory-motor interactions, emotional processing, and reward (Zatorre et al., 2007). For example, premotor cortex and supplemental motor cortex—which are parts of the brain typically involved in movements and actions (see **Chapter 4**)—respond when people listen to music. The emotional content of music can affect the extent of motor responses: for example, happy music elicits greater activity in supplemental motor cortex compared to sad music (Bogert et al., 2016).
>
> A meta-analysis showed that the amygdala and striatum—which are thought to be involved in processing rewards (such as food and money)—respond when people listen to music (Koelsch, 2020). This evidence has been interpreted as suggesting that music is inherently rewarding. However, some people do not find music pleasurable, and show different brain responses to music to those who do (Kathios et al., 2024).
>
> Interestingly, even when people imagine hearing music (i.e. with no external stimulus), researchers have observed brain responses in areas involved in auditory and motor processing—which highlights the rich inner experience of music (Herholz et al., 2012).

6.2.2 Comparing brain responses to music and speech

If you've ever watched musical theatre, you might have noticed that speech can easily progress into song—sometimes, quite seamlessly (Further insights 6.4). While music tends to have a more regular rhythm than speech, there are several similarities between speech and song: they're both vocal, contain words that are often connected into phrases, and convey meaning. Despite these similarities, people are generally very good at determining whether an utterance has been spoken or sung, even when the utterance is from a different language or from a culture that has different musical traditions (Albouy et al., 2024). Over the years, researchers have debated whether speech and music have common neural bases, or whether they are processed differently in the brain.

> **Further insights 6.4** The speech-to-song illusion
>
> Diana Deutsch noticed that a spoken phrase seemed to transform into song after it had been repeated several times—a phenomenon that is now known as the 'speech-to-song illusion' (Deutsch et al., 2011). When the phrase is initially presented, listeners usually report that the phrase sounds spoken—but, after about 5-10 repetitions, listeners report that the phrase sounds like it's being sung.

> The speech-to-song illusion has interested researchers, because it has the potential to reveal the conditions that are required for someone to perceive a phrase as spoken or sung. Subsequent studies have revealed that, for the illusion to occur, the speech must be repeated exactly as it was initially presented: any alterations to the speech (e.g. rearranging the syllables so that they no longer make sense) prevents the illusion from occurring. Also, some phrases illicit the illusion better than others (e.g. phrases that have flatter fundamental frequency contours within each syllable are more likely to illicit the illusion when they're repeated (Tierney et al., 2018)).
>
> The speech-to-song illusion can be perceived by speakers of both tonal and non-tonal languages. However, given that different fundamental frequency contours convey different words in tonal languages and not in non-tonal languages, researchers have examined whether pitch plays a different role in the speech-to-song illusion for speakers of tonal compared to non-tonal languages. Yet the results suggest that speakers of both types of language use similar acoustic cues for interpreting a phrase as spoken or sung. Speakers of both tonal and non-tonal languages are more likely to rate phrases as sung when each syllable within the phrase has a flat fundamental frequency contour, when the fundamental frequency differences between one syllable and the next are small, and when the phrase has a steady beat (Kachlicka et al., 2024).

One approach to this debate comes from studying individuals who experience changes in music perception following brain damage. If speech and music rely on the same brain areas, brain lesions that impair music perception should also impair speech perception. However, there are several reported cases in which individuals can no longer identify tunes—suggesting they have difficulties with music perception—but they can still recognise speech. Conversely, other individuals have difficulty recognising speech after brain damage, but they can still identify tunes (Peretz & Zatorre, 2005). These cases imply that the brain areas that are critical for processing music are different to those that are critical for processing speech. However, brain lesion studies can be difficult to interpret, because the results might not reflect differences in how music and speech are usually processed in people without brain damage, but could instead reflect differences in how well music and speech processing are able to adapt to damage in particular areas of the brain (e.g. by recruiting other brain areas to compensate).

Another approach is to compare brain responses to musical and non-musical stimuli in healthy volunteers. This research has shown some similarities in brain responses to speech and music. For example, a deviant 'B' note in a series of 'A' notes produces a mismatch negativity response, and so does a deviant 'da' syllable in a series of 'ba' sounds. Also, the ERAN response (introduced in Section 6.2.1) has a similar speech counterpart: the early *left* anterior negativity (abbreviated to 'ELAN') occurs when speech violates syntax in language (see e.g. Jentschke & Koelsch, 2009).

Some research suggests music and speech may be processed in overlapping brain areas, but rely on different neuronal populations within these areas. For example, multiple studies have observed different patterns of responses to speech and music in the superior temporal gyrus, which suggests that different neurons might be involved in processing speech compared to music (Peretz et al., 2015). Consider how a gym can have different equipment that's used for different purposes: some users might use one set of equipment, whereas other users might use a different set. In a similar way, a brain area can contain distinct populations of neurons—and some neurons could be used for processing music, whereas others could be used for processing speech.

Other research has suggested that some aspects of music perception (e.g. melody perception) might involve brain areas that respond to speech, but also involve areas that respond more specifically to music (e.g. Sankaran et al., 2024). For example, parts of the anterior and posterior superior temporal gyri, in both hemispheres, have been proposed to be selective for music (Angulo-Perkins et al., 2014); this finding applies to Western and non-Western music, and regardless of whether participants have prior musical training (Boebinger et al., 2021). As an analogy, a single dance class might use both a community hall that is also used for public debate, and also a second room (e.g. a dance studio) that is used only for the dance class and not for public debate.

Direct recordings from human cortex have revealed neurons that respond strongly to sung music (comprised of singing in the presence of background instrumental music), but that hardly respond at all to instrumental music or speech (Norman-Haignere et al., 2022). These neurons are located in the middle and anterior superior temporal gyrus, near to speech-selective and music-selective areas of the brain. In other words, these parts of the brain appear to be selective for sung music. Possibly, this selective brain response could reflect responses to acoustic attributes of song, compared to speech; for example, the pattern of acoustic modulations in time and frequency might help listeners to distinguish song from speech—and seems to be common to sung music from various cultures around the world (Albouy et al., 2024). Therefore, these acoustic differences might explain why specific brain responses have been observed for sung music compared to speech. Another possibility is that song-specific brain responses reflect non-acoustic processing of song (Further insights 6.3).

> Neuronal responses can be recorded from cortex in humans using a technique called electrocorticography, which is often abbreviated to ECoG. ECoG involves placing a multi-electrode array onto the surface of the brain. Each electrode within the array records electric potentials from distinct neuronal populations, and thus ECoG has high spatial resolution. It also measures neuronal responses with high temporal precision. ECoG is commonly used to monitor seizure-related activity in epileptic patients who are undergoing invasive brain surgery. This type of surgery often involves long periods of time where the patient is waiting around and, during this time, these patients may choose to volunteer for neuroscience studies, providing researchers with a valuable opportunity to measure neuronal responses with high spatial and temporal resolutions in humans.

Ultimately, there appear to be both similarities and differences between processing (sung or instrumental) music and speech—and researchers do not yet fully understand the reasons for the differences that have been observed. Thus, whether speech and music have distinct neural bases continues to be hotly debated.

6.3 Individual differences in music perception

Have you ever wondered if you perceive music in the same way as your friends? Curiously, not all aspects of musical perception are universal. This section examines several ways in which the perception of music differs among people.

6.3.1 Effects of musical training

If you've seen musicians performing a piece of music professionally, they'll have practised a lot to reach that level of performance! When learning to play an instrument, musicians will have practised coordinating their motor movements to produce particular sounds (e.g. learning precisely where on the fingerboard of a violin to place their fingers to produce a particular note), and will have listened many times to the sounds that their instrument produces. So, does extensive musical practice influence the perception of music?

Perhaps unsurprisingly, musicians tend to perform better on musical tasks, including rhythm perception and melody discrimination, than people without musical training (Ireland et al., 2018). Yet, one question that has interested researchers is whether the effects of musical training extend beyond tasks that are obviously musical. For example, does musical training affect more basic aspects of auditory perception, such as the ability to discriminate two sounds that have different fundamental frequencies? In general, studies have shown that musicians tend to be better at discriminating small differences in fundamental frequency than non-musicians (Micheyl et al., 2006).

So, why might musicians perform better than non-musicians at fundamental frequency discrimination? One idea is that musicians might have greater frequency selectivity at the cochlea than non-musicians (Bidelman et al., 2016)—but this idea is hotly contested, because frequency selectivity can't be measured directly in humans and the same finding isn't replicated across all measures (Moore et al., 2019). Another idea is that differences in brain structure or function could explain musicians' advantages on auditory tasks. When looking at the structure of the brain, researchers examine the size of various areas of the brain (e.g. by measuring the volume of particular areas) as well as the anatomical connections that link different areas. When comparing brain structure, the volumes of auditory and motor cortices have been found to be greater in musicians than non-musicians (Gaser & Schlaug, 2003). Therefore, these differences in volume could potentially provide advantages for perception.

> Recall from **Chapter 2** that frequency selectivity at the cochlea relates to the ability to identify individual frequencies in a sound. Frequency selectivity is better for lower frequencies, but it is harder to identify separate high-frequency sounds.

> The basilar membrane varies in how 'tuned' it is along its length: it is broadly tuned at the base and gets progressively sharper towards the apex. Tuning describes how parts of the basilar membrane move in response to a sound at the characteristic frequency of another region. If a region is broadly tuned, a sound with a particular frequency will cause a wide area of the basilar membrane to vibrate: the part whose characteristic frequency matches the sound vibrates the most, but neighbouring areas vibrate too, to a lesser extent—whereas, if a region is narrowly tuned, a sound with a particular frequency will only cause a narrow area of the basilar membrane to vibrate. The idea that musicians might have greater frequency selectivity in the cochlea proposes that musical training could sharpen the tuning in the basilar membrane.

> One way to think about structural and functional brain differences is by imagining a road network. Structurally, you'll be able to see that some roads (e.g. motorways) are bigger than others (e.g. country lanes), and that they may be connected by one or more routes. Functionally, we could look at the amount of traffic on each route to gauge which are busy and which are quieter. However, just by looking at the amount of traffic, we wouldn't know how the roads are being used—for example, some routes may be used primarily for commuting to work, whereas others may be used for transporting heavy goods, yet they might be busy at similar times. Similarly, when looking at the amount of activity in a given region of the brain, it can be difficult to tell how these areas are being utilised, and whether they are part of the same 'route' or just happen to be active at the same time.

When looking at the function of the brain, researchers sometimes look at how responses in different areas of the brain are correlated over time. In other words, when one brain area shows increased responses, does another area show increased responses at the same time? Researchers have observed greater correlations between left and right planum temporale, and across temporal, frontal, and parietal areas of the brain, in musicians as compared to non-musicians, when participants are awake but not doing any specific task (Leipold et al., 2021). One reason why researchers are interested in these correlations is because they could indicate that the brain areas are 'passing' information to one another—and the extent to which information is shared among areas of the brain could differ between musicians and non-musicians. However, it is worth bearing in mind that the correlations don't actually tell us whether the information is shared: the brain areas could be working together, or they could be working separately but synchronously. Nevertheless, differences between musicians and non-musicians do imply that the brain is processing information in slightly different ways, which has the potential to affect auditory perception.

A challenge, however, in determining the effects of musical training is to isolate differences that are due to practice from pre-existing differences between musicians and non-musicians that may have been present before they began musical training. For example, some people may be more likely to pursue (and continue) musical training because they have a better aptitude for music; thus, any differences between musicians and non-musicians could be due to differences in pre-existing aptitude rather than being a consequence of musical training. To distinguish between these possibilities, we need to look at longitudinal studies that compare the same measurements before and after people received musical training. Longitudinal studies examining musical training are difficult to carry out, because many people learn music at a young age; therefore, longitudinal studies are sparse and have mostly been conducted in children, with small numbers of participants. Nevertheless, a review of longitudinal studies seems to suggest that music training changes brain structure and function, including greater brain volume in auditory cortex and greater connections between auditory and motor areas of the brain (Neves et al., 2022). Other challenges in the musical training literature are that effects of training can be small, and the results are only based on studies that have been published, whereas other studies that show no differences may have been conducted but never published due to publication bias (Schellenberg & Lima, 2024). Thus, the extent to which musical training affects perception continues to be a lively area of research.

6.3.2 Absolute pitch

If someone played a single musical note on the piano and asked you to name its musical pitch label (e.g. 'C', 'G♯', or 'B♭') without looking at their hands on the piano, do you think you'd be able to answer correctly? Most people—even many highly trained musicians—can't do this. However, some people can name the pitch label of a musical note quite easily. These people are said to use **absolute pitch**, which is very rare: only approximately 1 in 10,000 people can use it.

> In order to use absolute pitch, by definition, someone needs to be able to associate the pitch of a musical note with a label that they've previously learned (e.g. the note 'C'). If someone has never been taught the note names, they won't be able to label the pitch of a musical note.

Generally, people find it easier to name the pitch label of a musical note if they're also given the name of a reference note. For example, if someone hears two musical notes and is told that the first is G♯, they might be able to work out the name of the second note by detecting the difference between the two notes. This skill uses **relative pitch**. Many more people are able to use relative pitch than absolute pitch. So, what differentiates people who can use absolute pitch from those who can only use relative pitch?

> Absolute pitch and relative pitch are often conceptualised as two discrete categories. However, this may not be the full story—there may be a continuum between these two extremes. Consistent with this idea, some people who use absolute pitch can name a note extremely quickly and accurately as soon as they hear it, whereas, other people who use absolute pitch seem to take longer to name a note, or can be less accurate at naming some notes than others (e.g. Gao & Oxenham, 2022).

Absolute pitch is likely to arise through a combination of genetic and environmental factors. Researchers have observed that absolute pitch usually emerges at a young age and runs in families—which has led some researchers to suggest that it's hereditary, and has sparked researchers to search for genetic links that could predispose people to use absolute pitch (see e.g. Tan et al., 2014). On the other hand, individuals who are raised in highly musical families not only carry their parent's genes (if they are raised by their genetic parents), but are also usually exposed to music from a young age. Therefore, it can be difficult to tease apart genetic influences from environmental ones.

Some researchers have suggested that there's a critical period in early childhood, during which exposure to music is critical for acquiring absolute pitch. This idea is supported by studies that have examined absolute pitch among musicians who began musical training at different ages. For example, music students are more likely to use absolute pitch if they began musical training before the age of 5 than if they began after that age (Figure 6.4) (Deutsch et al., 2006). Yet, recent research has shown that, through training, some people can learn to use absolute pitch in adulthood (e.g. Wong et al., 2020). This finding argues against the idea of a strict 'critical' period in childhood, during which absolute pitch must be acquired. However, the ability to learn to use absolute pitch does seem to vary across people, possibly suggesting that only some people are able to acquire absolute pitch later in life. Researchers don't fully understand the causes of these individual differences, and it remains possible that genetics or environmental factors could explain why some people can acquire the ability to use absolute pitch in adulthood and others can't.

One environmental factor that's known to affect the likelihood that someone will use absolute pitch is language experience. In tonal languages, such as Mandarin, changes in fundamental frequency can convey differences in word meaning. Absolute pitch is more common among musicians who speak Mandarin compared to musicians who speak non-tonal languages, such as English (Figure 6.4) (Deutsch et al., 2006). Also, greater fluency in speaking a tonal language has been associated with better performance on tasks of absolute pitch (Deutsch et al., 2009). These findings highlight that, in addition to musical training, exposure to tonal languages early in life can increase the likelihood of developing absolute pitch.

For individuals who can use absolute pitch, a single tone can evoke a nameable pitch label—but does this provide advantages on tasks for which the goal isn't simply to label the pitch of a tone? People who use absolute pitch are no better at discriminating differences in frequency between two tones that are presented one after another (Fujisaki & Kashino, 2002). They are also no better at detecting which of two sequential noise bursts contains a gap, or at discriminating interaural time differences for determining spatial location. In other words, people who use absolute pitch don't perform better on frequency, temporal, or spatial hearing tests than people who can't use absolute pitch.

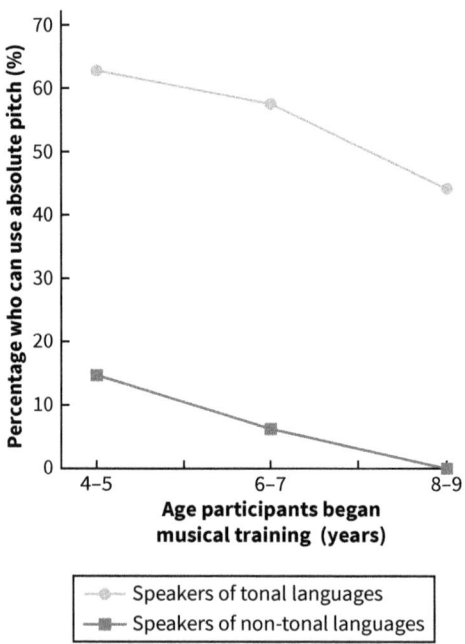

Figure 6.4 Percentage of music students who can use absolute pitch, separated by the age they began musical training (shown on the horizontal axis) and their linguistic background (shown by the two lines).
Source: data replotted from Deutsch et al. (2006).

So, can we locate differences in the auditory pathway that allow some people but not others to use absolute pitch? In general, absolute pitch doesn't seem to be associated with different processing at the inner ear (McKetton et al., 2018) and, therefore, some researchers have searched for differences in brain processing. Neuroimaging studies have revealed differences in cortical anatomy between people who can use absolute pitch and those who cannot; for example, musicians who can use absolute pitch have larger primary auditory cortices than both musicians and non-musicians who can't use absolute pitch (see e.g. McKetton et al., 2019). In contrast, studies looking at brain connectivity have found no differences between musicians with and without absolute pitch (e.g. Leipold et al., 2021), suggesting the differences may be mainly anatomical rather than functional. Another method that researchers have used to look for differences is to look more closely at the timing of brain responses to musical notes. By looking at brain responses over time, researchers have identified that musicians with and without absolute pitch show different brain responses about 200 ms after a tone starts, which could indicate differences in processing that enable some people to name the pitch label of a note (Ngan et al., 2023). Ultimately, where differences arise and the perceptual consequences of these differences are not fully understood and are still debated by researchers.

6.3.3 Amusia

Approximately 1.5–4% of the population have **amusia**, which is a long-term difficulty with musical listening that often involves difficulties perceiving pitch. Amusia can't be explained by differences in hearing ability, education, or musical exposure. Initially, amusia appeared to be specific to music: for example, people who have amusia might have difficulty identifying when a musical note is played out of tune, they might sing out of tune, and they might be able to recognise a song from its lyrics but not from its melody. Yet, whether the differences observed in people with amusia are specific to music, or whether they affect other aspects of auditory perception, has been debated. Based on decades of research, it seems likely that people with amusia have difficulties with pitch perception that are visible in music-related tasks, but that aren't specific to music. This section explains how thinking on this topic has evolved over the years.

Amusia can be present from birth or arise later in life after brain damage. There is some evidence that amusia from birth is hereditary, because people with amusia are more likely to have family members that also have amusia, compared to people without amusia (Peretz et al., 2007).

Estimating how many people have amusia is challenging, because it depends on how amusia is measured. For many years, the prevalence was assumed to be 4%, based on a test in which people detected if well-known melodies were played with the correct or incorrect notes (Kalmus & Fry, 1980). People were assumed to have amusia if they performed poorly in the test. However, this required the use of an arbitrary cut-off point to distinguish people with amusia from those without it (see Henry & McAuley, 2010). More recently, a large online study (with over 16,000 participants) defined amusia based on participants' performance on two pitch tests. Therefore, participants would only be defined as having amusia if they performed poorly in both tests. Using two tests provided a more conservative estimate of 1.5%, compared to when amusia was defined based on either test alone (Peretz & Vuvan, 2017).

> Researchers have attempted to clarify whether people with amusia have difficulties in tasks unrelated to pitch; for example, with rhythm perception. When people with amusia are asked to detect a note that's slightly delayed compared to the overall rhythm of tones, they can generally do this as well as people who don't have amusia (e.g. Hyde & Peretz, 2004). This finding implies that amusia arises from a specific difficulty with pitch perception. Nevertheless, some people with amusia do seem to have difficulty with rhythm processing, which suggests either that certain conditions are required to detect difficulties in rhythm perception, or that multiple subtypes of amusia may exist that are characterised by different patterns of skills.

People with amusia are as good at performing some non-musical tasks as people without amusia. For example, they can identify people from their voices and recognise environmental sounds. An influential study observed that people with amusia are as good at discerning intonation in speech—for example, whether someone is saying a statement or a question—as people without amusia (Ayotte et al., 2002). This finding is consistent with the idea that amusia is specific to music, because pitch is a cue for intonation, so we might expect domain-general difficulties with perceiving pitch to affect the perception of speech intonation as well as musical melody. However, fundamental frequency changes that confer intonation in speech tend to be quite large compared to those in music and, when researchers test smaller fundamental frequency changes in speech, people with amusia perform more poorly than people without amusia (Liu et al., 2010). Thus, rather than being specific to music, people with amusia may have more general difficulties discerning small fundamental frequency changes for all types of sounds.

Some researchers have attempted to quantify the smallest differences in fundamental frequency that can be discriminated by people with amusia and by people without amusia. The results demonstrate that people with amusia have higher fundamental frequency thresholds (i.e. the smallest difference in fundamental frequency they can discriminate is greater) on average than people without amusia, although thresholds differ substantially among people (e.g. Tillmann et al., 2009). However, even though the smallest fundamental frequency differences people with amusia can discriminate are smaller than those for people without amusia, those with amusia can discriminate fundamental frequency differences above their thresholds as well as those without it. This finding helps to explain why people with amusia only have difficulties with some of the pitch-related tasks that they have been tested on: when fundamental frequency changes are large—such as most changes that convey intonation in natural speech—they are above the thresholds of most people with amusia, so people with amusia generally have no problem detecting them.

> Studies have shown that the average person with amusia would find it difficult to distinguish between two adjacent notes on the piano (see Figure 6.1 for a visual representation of piano notes). However, some people with amusia may be able to detect differences between adjacent notes. For example, Tillmann et al. (2009) reported an average discrimination threshold of 1.32 semitones. Yet thresholds varied widely among the group—from 0.2 to 4 semitones. This result highlights striking individual variability among people with amusia.

One example of an everyday task that relies on pitch perception is detecting variations in speech intonation. Recall from **Chapter 4** that changes in fundamental frequency within an English sentence can distinguish questions from statements. Interestingly, these types of fundamental frequency changes within a sentence can be equivalent to roughly an octave difference in fundamental frequency (i.e. the difference between the lower and higher 'C' notes on the piano depicted in Figure 6.1). Fundamental frequency contours of the spoken sentence 'You had a party' as a statement and 'You had a party?' as a question are illustrated in Figure 6.5(a) and (b). The difference in fundamental frequency within the final word is 136–321 Hz—which is more than one octave (remember, an octave is equivalent to a doubling of frequency). Therefore, this difference should be perceptible to people who have large fundamental frequency discrimination thresholds. As a comparison, Figure 6.5(c) shows the fundamental frequency contour of the notes from the piano in Figure 6.1 played from left to right, which are much more subtle. So, what happens when people need to detect smaller changes in fundamental frequency in speech—for example

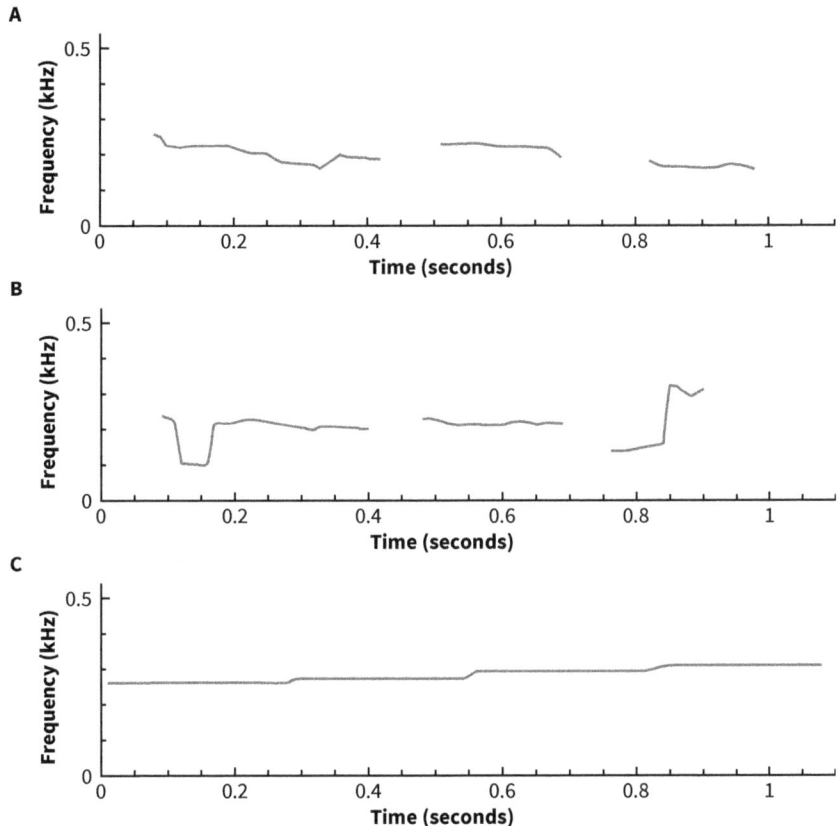

Figure 6.5 The fundamental frequency contours of the sentence, 'You had a party', is shown in panel a when it is spoken as a statement, and in panel b when it is spoken as a question. In contrast, panel c shows the fundamental frequency contour of the first four piano notes depicted in Figure 6.1, when played from left to right. Notice how the fundamental frequency changes between adjacent notes in panel c are smaller than the change in fundamental frequency within the final word of the spoken question in panel b.

when changes in fundamental frequency alter the meaning of a word? Can people with amusia detect such changes?

Recall from Section 6.3.2 that in some languages (called 'tonal languages'), such as Mandarin and Cantonese, variations in fundamental frequency convey different linguistic meanings. For example, Mandarin has four types of linguistic tones and the four tones have different fundamental frequency contours, which are depicted in Figure 6.6.

Each of the four tones depicted in Figure 6.6 has a different meaning (e.g. the 'ma' that has a constant fundamental frequency means mother, and the 'ma' that has a falling then rising fundamental frequency means horse). Crucially, some of these changes in fundamental frequency within a syllable in Mandarin are much smaller than the changes in fundamental frequency that occur at the end of a question in English (Figure 6.5(b)). Therefore, one question that has interested researchers is whether amusia affects speech perception for speakers of tonal languages. The answer isn't entirely straightforward, and many studies are limited by small sample sizes, which makes it difficult to draw strong conclusions from the results. Nevertheless, summarising results across studies, lexical tone discrimination seems to be poorer for tonal language speakers who have amusia than for those without amusia (see e.g. Liu et al., 2016). However, there are large individual differences—and some tonal language speakers with amusia don't seem to display any difficulties distinguishing lexical tones. The wide variability among people with amusia could imply that there are different subtypes of amusia, or that amusia manifests in different ways for different people.

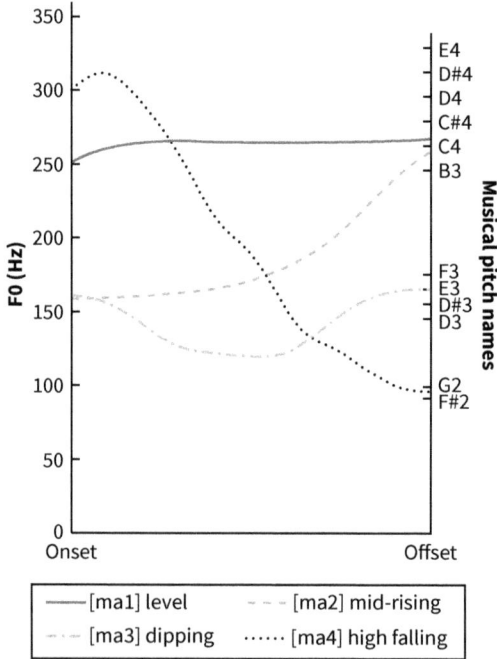

Figure 6.6 Fundamental frequency contours of the four types of linguistic tones for 'ma' in Mandarin. Notice how the fundamental frequency varies over time, which conveys linguistic meaning.

Source: adapted from Nan, Y., Sun, Y., & Peretz, I. (2010). 'Congenital amusia in speakers of a tone language: Association with lexical tone agnosia'. *Brain, 133*(9), 2635–2642.

It is currently unclear why there is such large individual variation among people with amusia, because both groups (those with and without difficulty distinguishing lexical tones) perform similarly on tests of music perception and can *produce* different lexical tones equally well when asked to speak aloud (see e.g. Nan et al., 2010). Some research suggests there might be differences in brain responses to lexical tones: Mandarin speakers with amusia who have difficulty discriminating lexical tones have a reduced mismatch negativity response to deviant lexical tones in the left hemisphere, when compared to those with amusia who can discriminate tones and when compared to people who don't have amusia (Nan et al., 2016) (for a description of the mismatch negativity response, see **Chapter 3**). The reduced mismatch negativity response could reflect weaker sensitivity to differences between lexical tones that have different fundamental frequency contours.

Researchers have also used neuroimaging to examine differences between people who have amusia and those who don't. People with amusia have thicker right auditory cortices and thicker right inferior frontal gyri than people without amusia (Hyde et al., 2007). Interestingly, the cortical thickness in these regions correlates with scores on tests of music perception: greater cortical thickness is associated with poorer performance on music perception tests (Hyde et al., 2007). As well as these structural differences, researchers have found differences in functional brain responses. Most notably, connectivity between frontal and temporal areas of the brain is lower in people with amusia than in people without amusia (Tillmann et al., 2023). Thus, differences in how frontal areas communicate with auditory cortex could contribute to difficulties with pitch perception in people who have amusia.

The Montreal Battery of Evaluation of Amusia is a test that is widely used to screen for amusia (Peretz et al., 2003). It comprises several tasks, including some that involve discriminating melodies, others that involve rhythm perception, and others that test memory for tunes.

6.3.4 Effects of language experience and culture

Recall from Section 6.3.2 that speakers of tonal languages are more likely to have absolute pitch than speakers of non-tonal languages—but does language experience have any other effects on music perception? Language experience varies across the globe, but so does culture and the types of music that people listen to.

One relevant question is whether perceptual grouping differs across cultures. If perceptual grouping principles are experienced universally, then people from different cultures should experience the same grouping of sounds. However, contrary to this assumption, the language that someone speaks and the culture they've grown up in impacts their subjective perception of music (Further insights 6.5). For example, one study found differences in sequential grouping between Japanese and American listeners. Participants were played a sequence of tones, in which the tones alternated between a longer-duration tone and a shorter-duration tone (Iversen et al., 2008). After hearing the sequence, participants were asked to indicate whether they perceived the pattern of durations as long–short or short–long. Most English listeners perceived the short–long pattern, whereas the Japanese listeners were more varied in their responses: almost half of Japanese listeners perceived the opposite long–short pattern within the sequence. These results demonstrate that grouping percepts are not universal.

> **Further insights 6.5** The tritone paradox
>
> In the 'tritone paradox', a listener hears two computer-generated tones—one after another—that are half an octave (i.e. six semitones, also called a 'tritone', hence the name of this illusion). The tones are harmonic complex tones that most people perceive as having a clear pitch, but, because of how they're constructed, their octave is ambiguous. The listener is asked to judge whether the second tone was higher or lower in pitch than the first, even though there's no correct answer because the octave is ambiguous. As a result, not everyone experiences the same percept: for a given pair of tones, some people perceive the second tone as having a higher pitch than the first, whereas others perceive it as having a lower pitch. The percept that people experience isn't determined by musical training, because even two highly trained musicians can experience different percepts. Instead, the percept seems to be affected by someone's native language and accent. For example, people who grew up in California typically hear a different pattern to people who grew up in Southern England. For a given sequence of tones that most Californian participants heard as ascending, most English participants heard them as descending. Similarly, sequences of tones that most Californian participants heard as descending, most English participants heard as ascending (Deutsch, 1991). By comparing percepts across languages, researchers have concluded that the range of fundamental frequencies in someone's native language influences how they perceive the tritone paradox.

So, what causes differences in perception across cultures? One possibility is that the syntactic structure of the language(s) someone speaks impacts their perception of rhythm, which could have consequences for how sounds are grouped together. The syntax of English produces phrases that often follow a short–long rhythm pattern; for example, consider the duration patterns in the phrases 'to read' and 'my book'. In contrast, the syntax of Japanese is different—and the content word (e.g. 'read' or 'book') is spoken before the article or pronoun (e.g. 'to' or 'my').

Research with infants is consistent with the idea that linguistic experience can impact the perception of non-linguistic sounds. Researchers can't ask infants about their experience, so they rely on other methods to understand infants' perception. One approach is to compare how long an infant looks in the direction of a loudspeaker when it plays a short–long tone pattern compared to a long–short pattern. If an infant looks for the same amount of time for both tone patterns, it suggests they have no preference for one tone pattern over the other; and if an infant looks longer when they hear one tone pattern compared to the other, it would suggest the infant prefers that tone pattern. Studies have shown that Japanese and English infants have similar looking times for short–long and long–short tone patterns when they are younger than 6 months old, but there are differences in looking times between Japanese and English infants when they are 7–8 months old. Japanese infants who are 7–8 months look for a similar amount of time when either the short–long or long–short tones are presented, like the younger infants, whereas the English infants look longer when the short–long tone is presented (Yoshida et al., 2010). These results in older infants are consistent with the differences found between Japanese- and English-speaking adults described earlier in this section. Thus, people may all start out with similar grouping percepts, but develop different percepts based on the language(s) they are exposed to early in life.

Researchers have also examined how the pleasantness of various types of music varies across cultures. For people who grew up in North America and Western Europe, the pleasantness of particular combinations of notes is usually related to **consonance** and **dissonance**. For example, when two tones that are harmonically related (i.e. that have fundamental frequencies that are integer multiples of each other, like 220 Hz and 440 Hz) are played together, they are perceived as consonant, and are typically experienced by people who grew up in North America and Western Europe as being pleasant—whereas two simultaneously presented tones that have an inharmonic combination of frequencies are dissonant, and people who grew up in North America and Western Europe typically experience these combinations of notes as being unpleasant. Some North American researchers have claimed that the relationship between consonance and pleasantness is innate, because infants as young as two months old show a preference for consonant rather than dissonant music (Trainor et al., 2002). However, other research has revealed differences across cultures. People from cultures who have never been exposed to music from North America and Western Europe experience consonant and dissonant music as being equally pleasant (McDermott et al., 2016)—suggesting that the preference for consonant music isn't innate, but could instead depend on exposure to music early in life.

Summary

Music, just like other types of sounds (e.g. speech or complex tones), can be described in terms of its acoustic attributes. Individual differences, including whether someone has received musical training and their cultural and linguistic background, mean that music is not perceived the same by everyone. Music draws on a variety of elements—including pitch perception, musical structure, and emotion—that generate rich brain responses to music. The question of whether music is represented differently in the brain compared to other sounds is still an area of active research.

Further your understanding

Deutsch, D. 'Grouping mechanisms in music.' In D. Deutsch (ed.) *The Psychology of Music* (pp. 183–248). London; Waltham, MA and San Diego, CA: Academic Press. https://doi.org/10.1016/B978-0-12-381460-9.00006-7

Sankaran, N., Carlson, T. A., & Thompson, W. F. (2020). 'The rapid emergence of musical pitch structure in human cortex.' *Journal of Neuroscience*, 40(10), 2108–2118. https://doi.org/10.1523/JNEUROSCI.1399-19.2020

References

Albouy, P., Mehr, S. A., Hoyer, R. S., Ginzburg, J., Du, Y., & Zatorre, R. J. (2024). 'Spectro-temporal acoustical markers differentiate speech from song across cultures.' *Nature Communications*, 15(1). https://doi.org/10.1038/s41467-024-49040-3

Angulo-Perkins, A., Aubé, W., Peretz, I., Barrios, F. A., Armony, J. L., & Concha, L. (2014). 'Music listening engages specific cortical regions within the temporal lobes: Differences between musicians and non-musicians.' *Cortex*, 59, 126–137. https://doi.org/10.1016/j.cortex.2014.07.013

Ayotte, J., Peretz, I., & Hyde, K. (2002). 'Congenital amusia: A group study of adults afflicted with a music-specific disorder.' *Brain*, 125(2), 238–251. https://doi.org/10.1093/brain/awf028

Bidelman, G. M., Nelms, C., & Bhagat, S. P. (2016). 'Musical experience sharpens human cochlear tuning.' *Hearing Research*, 335, 40–46. https://doi.org/10.1016/j.heares.2016.02.012

Boebinger, D., Norman-Haignere, S. V., McDermott, J. H., & Kanwisher, N. (2021). 'Music-selective neural populations arise without musical training.' *Journal of Neurophysiology*, 125(6), 2237–2263. https://doi.org/10.1152/jn.00588.2020

Bogert, B., Numminen-Kontti, T., Gold, B., Sams, M., Numminen, J., Burunat, I., Lampinen, J., & Brattico, E. (2016). 'Hidden sources of joy, fear, and sadness: Explicit versus implicit neural processing of musical emotions.' *Neuropsychologia*, 89, 393–402. https://doi.org/10.1016/j.neuropsychologia.2016.07.005

Cowen, A. S., Fang, X., Sauter, D., & Keltner, D. (2020). 'What music makes us feel: At least 13 dimensions organize subjective experiences associated with music across different cultures.' *Proceedings of the National Academy of Sciences*, 117(4), 1924–1934.

Deutsch, D. (1991). 'The tritone paradox: An influence of language on music perception.' *Music Perception*, 8(4), 335–347. https://doi.org/10.2307/40285517

Deutsch, D. (1975). 'Two-channel listening to musical scales.' *Journal of the Acoustical Society of America*, 57(5), 1156–1160. https://doi.org/10.1121/1.380573

Deutsch, D., Dooley, K., & Henthorn, T. (2008). 'Pitch circularity from tones comprising full harmonic series.' *Journal of the Acoustical Society of America*, 124(1), 589–597. https://doi.org/10.1121/1.2931957

Deutsch, D., Dooley, K., Henthorn, T., & Head, B. (2009). 'Absolute pitch among students in an American music conservatory: Association with tone language fluency.' *Journal of the Acoustical Society of America*, 125(4), 2398–2403. https://doi.org/10.1121/1.3081389

Deutsch, D., Henthorn, T., & Lapidis, R. (2011). 'Illusory transformation from speech to song.' *Journal of the Acoustical Society of America*, 129(4), 2245–2252. https://doi.org/10.1121/1.3562174

Deutsch, D., Henthorn, T., Marvin, E., & Xu, H. (2006). 'Absolute pitch among American and Chinese conservatory students: Prevalence differences, and evidence for a speech-related critical period.' *Journal of the Acoustical Society of America*, 119(2), 719. https://doi.org/10.1121/1.2151799

Elliott, T. M., Hamilton, L. S., & Theunissen, F. E. (2013). 'Acoustic structure of the five perceptual dimensions of timbre in orchestral instrument tones.' *Journal of the Acoustical Society of America*, 133(1), 389–404. https://doi.org/10.1121/1.4770244

Fischer, M., Soden, K., Thoret, E., Montrey, M., & McAdams, S. (2021). 'Instrument timbre enhances perceptual segregation in orchestral music.' *Music Perception*, 38(5), 473–498. https://doi.org/10.1525/MP.2021.38.5.473

Fitzgerald, K., & Todd, J. (2020). 'Making sense of mismatch negativity.' *Frontiers in Psychiatry*, 11(468). https://doi.org/10.3389/fpsyt.2020.00468

Fiveash, A., Dalla Bella, S., Bigand, E., Gordon, R. L., & Tillmann, B. (2022). 'You got rhythm, or more: The multidimensionality of rhythmic abilities.' *Attention, Perception & Psychophysics*, 84, 1370–1392. https://doi.org/10.3758/s13414-022-02487-2

Fritz, T., Jentschke, S., Gosselin, N., Sammler, D., Peretz, I., Turner, R., Friederici, A. D., & Koelsch, S. (2009). 'Universal recognition of three basic emotions in music.' *Current Biology*, 19(7), 573–576. https://doi.org/10.1016/j.cub.2009.02.058

Fujisaki, W., & Kashino, M. (2002). 'The basic hearing abilities of absolute pitch possessors.' *Acoustical Science & Technology*, 23(2), 77–83.

Gao, Z., & Oxenham, A. J. (2022). 'Voice disadvantage effects in absolute and relative pitch judgments.' *Journal of the Acoustical Society of America*, 151(4), 2414–2428. https://doi.org/10.1121/10.0010123

Gaser, C., & Schlaug, G. (2003). 'Brain structures differ between musicians and non-musicians.' *Journal of Neuroscience*, 23(27), 9240–9245. https://doi.org/10.1523/jneurosci.23-27-09240.2003

Henry, M. J., & McAuley, J. D. (2010). 'On the prevalence of congenital amusia.' *Music Perception*, 27(5), 413–418. https://doi.org/10.1525/mp.2010.27.5.413

Herholz, S. C., Halpern, A. R., & Zatorre, R. J. (2012). 'Neuronal correlates of perception, imagery, and memory for familiar tunes.' *Bucknell Digital Commons*, Faculty Journal Articles, 1382–1397. https://digitalcommons.bucknell.edu/fac_journ

Huron, D., Anderson, N., & Shanahan, D. (2014). '"You can't play a sad song on the banjo": acoustic factors in the judgment of instrument capacity to convey sadness.' *Empirical Musicology Review*, 9(1), 29–41. https://doi.org/10.18061/emr.v9i1.4085

Hyde, K. L., Lerch, J. P., Zatorre, R. J., Griffiths, T. D., Evans, A. C., & Peretz, I. (2007). 'Cortical thickness in congenital amusia: When less is better than more.' *Journal of Neuroscience*, 27(47), 13028–13032. https://doi.org/10.1523/JNEUROSCI.3039-07.2007

Hyde, K. L., & Peretz, I. (2004). 'Brains that are out of tune but in time.' *Psychological Science*, 15(5), 356–360. https://doi.org/10.1111/j.0956-7976.2004.00683.x

Ireland, K., Parker, A., Foster, N., & Penhune, V. (2018). 'Rhythm and melody tasks for school-aged children with and without musical training: Age-equivalent scores and reliability.' *Frontiers in Psychology*, 9(April). https://doi.org/10.3389/fpsyg.2018.00426

Iversen, J. R., Patel, A. D., & Ohgushi, K. (2008). 'Perception of rhythmic grouping depends on auditory experience.' *Journal of the Acoustical Society of America*, 124(4), 2263–2271. https://doi.org/10.1121/1.2973189

Jacoby, N., Margulis, E. H., Clayton, M., Hannon, E., Honing, H., Iversen, J., Klein, T. R., Mehr, S., Pearson, L., Peretz, I., Perlman, M., Polak, R., Ravignani, A., Savage, P. E., Steingo, G., Stevens, C., Trainor, L., Trehub, S., Veal, M., & Wald-Fuhrmann, M. (2020). 'Cross-cultural work in music cognition: Challenges, insights, and recommendations.' *Music Perception*, 37(3), 185–195.

Jentschke, S., & Koelsch, S. (2009). 'Musical training modulates the development of syntax processing in children.' *NeuroImage*, 47(2), 735–744. https://doi.org/10.1016/j.neuroimage.2009.04.090

Jentschke, S., Koelsch, S., & Friederici, A. D. (2005). 'Investigating the relationship of music and language in children: Influences of musical training and language impairment.' *Annals of the New York Academy of Sciences*, 1060, 231–242. https://doi.org/10.1196/annals.1360.016

Juslin, P. N., & Laukka, P. (2003). 'Communication of emotions in vocal expression and music performance: Different channels, same code?' *Psychological Bulletin*, 129(5), 770–814. https://doi.org/10.1037/0033-2909.129.5.770

Juslin, P. N., & Laukka, P. (2004). 'Expression, perception, and induction of musical emotions: A review and a questionnaire study of everyday listening.' *Journal of New Music Research*, 33(3), 217–238. https://doi.org/10.1080/0929821042000317813

Juslin, P. N., & Sloboda, J. A. (2013). 'Music and emotion.' In *The Psychology of Music* (third edition). London; Waltham, MA and San Diego, CA: Academic Press.

Kachlicka, M., Patel, A. D., Liu, F., & Tierney, A. (2024). 'Weighting of cues to categorization of song versus speech in tone-language and non-tone-language speakers.' *Cognition*, 246. https://doi.org/10.1016/j.cognition.2024.105757

Kalmus, H., & Fry, D. B. (1980). 'On tune deafness (dysmelodia): Frequency, development, genetics and musical background.' *Annals of Human Genetics*, 43(4), 369–382. https://doi.org/10.1111/j.1469-1809.1980.tb01571.x

Kathios, N., Patel, A. D., & Loui, P. (2024). 'Musical anhedonia, timbre, and the rewards of music listening.' *Cognition*, 243, 105672. https://doi.org/10.1016/j.cognition.2023.105672

Koelsch, S. (2020). 'A coordinate-based meta-analysis of music-evoked emotions.' *NeuroImage*, 223(January), 117350. https://doi.org/10.1016/j.neuroimage.2020.117350

Koelsch, S., Vuust, P., & Friston, K. (2019). 'Predictive processes and the peculiar case of music.' *Trends in Cognitive Sciences*, 23(1), 63–77. Elsevier. https://doi.org/10.1016/j.tics.2018.10.006

Leipold, S., Klein, C., & Jäncke, L. (2021). 'Musical expertise shapes functional and structural brain networks independent of absolute pitch ability.' *Journal of Neuroscience*, 41(11), 2496–2511. https://doi.org/10.1523/JNEUROSCI.1985-20.2020

Liu, F., Chan, A. H. D., Ciocca, V., Roquet, C., Peretz, I., & Wong, P. C. M. (2016). 'Pitch perception and production in congenital amusia: Evidence from Cantonese speakers.' *Journal of the Acoustical Society of America*, 140(1), 563–575. https://doi.org/10.1121/1.4955182

Liu, F., Patel, A. D., Fourcin, A., & Stewart, L. (2010). 'Intonation processing in congenital amusia: Discrimination, identification and imitation.' *Brain*, 133(6), 1682–1693. https://doi.org/10.1093/brain/awq089

McAdams, S. (2019). 'The perceptual representation of timbre.' In K. Siedenburg, C. Saitis, S. McAdams, A. N. Popper, & R. R. Fay, *Timbre: Acoustics, Perception, and Cognition* (pp. 23–57). Springer. https://doi.org/10.1007/978-3-030-14832-4_2

McAdams, S., Goodchild, M., & Soden, K. (2022). 'A taxonomy of orchestral grouping effects derived from principles of auditory perception.' *Music Theory Online*, 28(3).

McDermott, J. H., Schultz, A. F., Undurraga, E. A., & Godoy, R. A. (2016). 'Indifference to dissonance in native Amazonians reveals cultural variation in music perception.' *Nature*, 535(7613), 547–550. https://doi.org/10.1038/nature18635

McKetton, L., DeSimone, K., & Schneider, K. A. (2019). 'Larger auditory cortical area and broader frequency tuning underlie absolute pitch.' *Journal of Neuroscience*, 39(15), 2930–2937. https://doi.org/10.1523/JNEUROSCI.1532-18.2019

McKetton, L., Purcell, D., Stone, V., Grahn, J., & Bergevin, C. (2018). 'No otoacoustic evidence for a peripheral basis of absolute pitch.' *Hearing Research*, 370, 201–208. https://doi.org/10.1016/j.heares.2018.08.001

Micheyl, C., Delhommeau, K., Perrot, X., & Oxenham, A. J. (2006). 'Influence of musical and psychoacoustical training on pitch discrimination.' *Hearing Research*, 219(1–2), 36–47. https://doi.org/10.1016/j.heares.2006.05.004

Moore, B. C. J., Wan, J., Varathanathan, A., Naddell, S., & Baer, T. (2019). 'No effect of musical training on frequency selectivity estimated using three methods.' *Trends in Hearing*, 23, 1–9. https://doi.org/10.1177/2331216519841980

Nan, Y., Huang, W. T., Wang, W. J., Liu, C., & Dong, Q. (2016). 'Subgroup differences in the lexical tone mismatch negativity (MMN) among Mandarin speakers with congenital amusia.' *Biological Psychology*, 113, 59–67. https://doi.org/10.1016/j.biopsycho.2015.11.010

Nan, Y., Sun, Y., & Peretz, I. (2010). 'Congenital amusia in speakers of a tone language: Association with lexical tone agnosia.' *Brain*, 133(9), 2635–2642. https://doi.org/10.1093/brain/awq178

Neves, L., Correia, A. I., Castro, S. L., Martins, D., & Lima, C. F. (2022). 'Does music training enhance auditory and linguistic processing? A systematic review and meta-analysis of behavioral and brain evidence.' *Neuroscience and Biobehavioral Reviews*, 140. Elsevier. https://doi.org/10.1016/j.neubiorev.2022.104777

Ngan, V. S. H., Cheung, L. Y. T., Ng, H. T. Y., Yip, K. H. M., Wong, Y. K., & Wong, A. C. N. (2023). 'An early perceptual locus of absolute pitch.' *Psychophysiology*, 60(2). https://doi.org/10.1111/psyp.14170

Norman-Haignere, S. V., Feather, J., Boebinger, D., Brunner, P., Ritaccio, A., McDermott, J. H., Schalk, G., & Kanwisher, N. (2022). 'A neural population selective for song in human auditory cortex.' *Current Biology*, 32(7), 1470–1484.e12. https://doi.org/10.1016/j.cub.2022.01.069

Peretz, I., Champod, A. S., & Hyde, K. (2003). 'Varieties of musical disorders: The Montreal Battery of Evaluation of Amusia.' *Annals of the New York Academy of Sciences*, 999(1), 58–75. https://doi.org/10.1196/annals.1284.006

Peretz, I., Cummings, S., & Dubé, M. P. (2007). 'The genetics of congenital amusia (tone deafness): A family-aggregation study.' *The American Journal of Human Genetics*, 81(3), 582–588. https://doi.org/10.1086/521337

Peretz, I., Vuvan, D., Lagrois, M. É., & Armony, J. L. (2015). 'Neural overlap in processing music and speech.' *Philosophical Transactions of the Royal Society B: Biological Sciences*, 370(1664). https://doi.org/10.1098/rstb.2014.0090

Peretz, I., & Vuvan, D. T. (2017). 'Prevalence of congenital amusia.' *European Journal of Human Genetics*, 25(5), 625–630. https://doi.org/10.1038/ejhg.2017.15

Peretz, I., & Zatorre, R. J. (2005). 'Brain organization for music processing.' *Annual Review of Psychology*, 56(July), 89–114. https://doi.org/10.1146/annurev.psych.56.091103.070225

Sankaran, N., Leonard, M. K., Theunissen, F., & Chang, E. F. (2024). 'Encoding of melody in the human auditory cortex.' *Science Advances*, 10(7). https://www.science.org/doi/10.1126/sciadv.adk0010

Schellenberg, E. G., & Lima, C. F. (2024). 'Music training and nonmusical abilities.' *Annual Review of Psychology*, 75, 87–128. https://doi.org/10.1146/annurev-psych-032323-051354

Tan, Y. T., McPherson, G. E., Peretz, I., Berkovic, S. F., & Wilson, S. J. (2014). 'The genetic basis of music ability.' *Frontiers in Psychology*, 5(June), 1–19. https://doi.org/10.3389/fpsyg.2014.00658

Tierney, A., Aniruddh, P., & Breen, M. (2018). 'Acoustic foundations of the speech-to-song illusion.' *Journal of Experimental Psychology: General*, 147(6), 888–904.

Tillmann, B., Graves, J. E., Talamini, F., Lévêque, Y., Fornoni, L., Hoarau, C., Pralus, A., Ginzburg, J., Albouy, P., & Caclin, A. (2023). 'Auditory cortex and beyond: Deficits in congenital amusia.' *Hearing Research*, 437. Elsevier. https://doi.org/10.1016/j.heares.2023.108855

Tillmann, B., Schulz,' Ine, K., & Foxton, J. M. (2009). 'Congenital amusia: A short-term memory deficit for non-verbal, but not verbal sounds.' *Brain and Cognition*, 71(3), 259–264. https://doi.org/10.1016/j.bandc.2009.08.003

Trainor, L. J., Tsang, C. D., & Cheung, V. H. W. (2002). 'Preference for sensory consonance in 2- and 4-month-old infants.' *Music Perception*, 20(2), 187–194. https://doi.org/10.1525/mp.2002.20.2.187

Wong, Y. K., Lui, K. F. H., Yip, K. H. M., & Wong, A. C. N. (2020). 'Is it impossible to acquire absolute pitch in adulthood?' *Attention, Perception, and Psychophysics*, 82(3), 1407–1430. https://doi.org/10.3758/s13414-019-01869-3

Yoshida, K. A., Iversen, J. R., Patel, A. D., Mazuka, R., Nito, H., Gervain, J., & Werker, J. F. (2010). 'The development of perceptual grouping biases in infancy: A Japanese-English cross-linguistic study.' *Cognition*, 115(2), 356–361. https://doi.org/10.1016/j.cognition.2010.01.005

Zatorre, R. J., Chen, J. L., & Penhune, V. B. (2007). 'When the brain plays music: Auditory–motor interactions in music perception and production.' *Nature Reviews Neuroscience*, 8(7), 547–558. https://doi.org/10.1038/nrn2152

Hearing and Vision

Traditionally, hearing and vision have been studied separately. Yet, information from these two senses is often available at the same time, and each sense can exert a strong influence upon the other. For example, have you ever heard a siren and been unsure where it was coming from—but when a fire engine came into view, found that the sound appeared to be coming from where the fire engine was?

This chapter introduces the conditions under which visual and auditory information are integrated—and explores how integration can 'trick' people into seeing or hearing things that aren't really there. It then describes brain responses to visual and auditory stimuli, including if one sense isn't present or only partially functions. Finally, this chapter examines how, sometimes, visual percepts can be associated with specific auditory percepts.

> This chapter focuses on hearing and vision, because these senses are frequently studied. However, hearing also interacts with the other senses. For example, recall from **Chapter 4** that motor cortex responds when people listen to speech. In addition, somatosensory cortex connects to auditory cortex and somatosensory responses have been observed in auditory cortex (Bizley & Dai, 2020).

> If you're interested in learning more about visual perception, see Snowden et al. (2012).

7.1 Sensory dominance

Sometimes, hearing and vision provide redundant information. In other words, most people can often get similar information about the environment from either sense alone. Imagine that someone is trying to work out if fireworks are happening outside their window on New Year's Eve. They could listen for a loud bang, or they could look outside their window for light in the sky. Similarly, if someone is trying to work out whether their friend is speaking, they could either listen for their voice or look to see if their lips are moving. However, information from hearing and vision sometimes conflict with each other: in this case, which sense 'dominates' someone's perception?

7.1.1 Visual dominance

Imagine a ventriloquist performing with a puppet. The puppet's lips move, but there's no sound coming from the puppet's mouth; whereas, speech comes from the ventriloquist's mouth, but their lips don't appear to move. Given this conflicting information, where do people perceive the speech as coming from? From the puppet's mouth or from the ventriloquist's mouth?

People usually perceive the speech as coming from the puppet's mouth, even though they know that's impossible! That's probably one of the reasons why people enjoy ventriloquist performances. Yet, this phenomenon doesn't only occur for ventriloquists. Quite often in everyday life, people perceive the location of a sound as coming from the same place as a visual object. For example, if someone goes to the cinema, they're usually watching actors on a screen in front of them, yet sound is often played from loudspeakers around the sides of the room. Therefore, the location of the sound doesn't correspond with the location of the objects on screen. Interestingly, this doesn't usually spoil people's enjoyment of the movie. Instead, most people perceive the sounds to be coming from the same locations as the objects on the screen. In other words, their perception of the sound's location is fully determined by the location of visual information. Therefore, vision dominates the perception of location in these situations—and this phenomenon is sometimes referred to as the 'ventriloquist effect' (Figure 7.1(a)).

The 'ventriloquist effect' has been replicated many times in the lab using simpler stimuli. For example, in one study, a bell sound and a light were presented from different locations and people were asked to judge where the bell sound was coming from (Jackson, 1953). Even though people were told to ignore the light, their judgements about the sound's location were biased towards the direction of the light. Interestingly, visual dominance can even occur when visual information is artificially modified. When people are asked to wear glasses that compress visual space (so that everything is half the size on their retina that it would be without the glasses), judgements of sound location change too; specifically, auditory space compresses to roughly match the compression of visual space (Zwiers et al., 2003).

7.1.2 Auditory dominance

Suppose you watch a video in which a disk of light is flashed once and, at the same time, a tone is played twice. If you see two flashes, you have experienced the 'sound-induced flash illusion' (Hirst et al., 2020). Generally, the number of flashes that people report seeing is strongly influenced by the number of tones they hear: when one flash is presented with two tones, most people consistently report seeing multiple flashes. The extra flashes are entirely illusory. Therefore, in this case, auditory information dominates over visual information—demonstrating that vision doesn't always dominate over audition.

Another case of auditory dominance occurs when people are asked to judge the timing of a visual stimulus. In one study, people were shown a rotating marker, like the second hand of a clock, and they were asked to judge the position of the marker at the time that either a visual flash or a sound occurred (Fendrich & Corballis, 2001). If they were judging the position of the marker when the visual flash occurred, people reported the marker position as earlier when a sound occurred *before* the flash, and as later when a sound occurred *after* the flash—even though the flash occurred at the same time in both cases. However, if they were

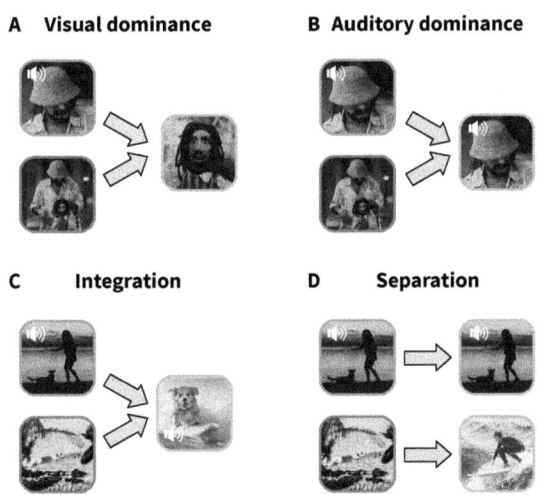

Figure 7.1 Schematics indicating various ways in which audio-visual information can be perceived. Within each panel, the upper left image indicates the acoustic stimulus, the lower left image indicates the visual stimulus, and the right image(s) indicates the audio-visual percept. Panel a illustrates visual dominance: the observer sees a puppet's mouth moving and hears speech (from the ventriloquist), so perceives the speech as coming from the puppet's mouth! Panel b illustrates auditory dominance: the observer hears and sees the same information as in panel a, but the speech is perceived as coming from the ventriloquist's mouth—which might occur if the visual information is degraded (e.g. if the observer usually wears glasses but doesn't wear them while watching the performance). Panels c and d illustrate a scenario in which an observer sees some surfboards on a beach and hears a dog barking on the same beach. If the auditory and visual stimuli are integrated (panel c), they might perceive a dog on a surf board! If the stimuli are separated (panel d), they might instead perceive two 'objects': a person on a surfboard and a dog on the beach.

judging the position of the marker when the *sound* occurred, the timing of the visual flash had less influence. In other words, the perceived timing of visual information was affected by the timing of auditory information, but the perceived timing of auditory information was less affected by the timing of visual information.

A study examining timing of rhythmic stimuli also showed auditory dominance (Attout et al., 2024). Participants were presented with either a visual or an auditory rhythm that set up an expectation for the time at which a target stimulus would appear. In the visual rhythm condition, a cross pulsated with the rhythm. In the auditory rhythm condition, a series of pure tones conveyed the rhythm. The target was either visual or auditory and the participant's task was to indicate the orientation (vertical or horizontal) of a visual target stimulus or the direction of frequency change (up or down) within an auditory target tone. Interestingly, participants were faster at responding to the target stimulus in the auditory rhythm condition than in the visual rhythm condition. In other words, regardless of whether participants judged a visual or auditory target stimulus, the auditory rhythm facilitated performance more than the visual rhythm.

> You can review rhythm in **Chapter 6**.

7.1.3 **Which sense dominates?**

From the examples described above, it's clear that vision dominates in some cases and audition dominates in other cases. Therefore, we know that one sense doesn't always dominate the other. But can we predict *which* sense will dominate in a given situation?

In the previous section, many of the examples of visual dominance occurred when people were asked to judge location, whereas the examples of auditory dominance occurred when the task involved timing. One early theory was that the most appropriate sense for a given task dominates (Welch et al., 1986). This theory assumes that different senses are most appropriate for different tasks: we might assume that vision is more 'appropriate' for location judgements, whereas audition is more 'appropriate' for timing judgements. However, exactly how this theory defines 'appropriateness' is unclear. An extension of this theory proposed that the most appropriate sense is the one that provides the most reliable information for a given task (Schwartz et al., 1998). One way of thinking about which sense is more reliable is by looking at its resolution; in other words, the smallest difference that's distinguishable. For spatial judgements, we can compare the smallest difference in spatial location that people can discriminate in either modality. People who have normal hearing and vision can discriminate much smaller differences between two objects based on visual information compared with auditory information; whereas, it's the other way around for timing information. This difference is evident from the standard rates at which auditory and visual information are presented on electronic devices: if you're playing a video on your phone, the screen display usually updates about 60 times per second, whereas the audio updates more than 40,000 times per second! Therefore, differences in resolution might explain why researchers have typically found visual dominance for spatial judgements and auditory dominance for timing judgements.

> **Chapter 8** describes how 'normal hearing' is defined from a clinical perspective.

If we assume that one sense is better suited to a particular task, then we would expect it to always dominate on that task. However, researchers have found cases that contradict this assumption. For example, when sounds are so quiet that they're close to the quietest sounds a person can hear, visual information can dominate timing judgements (Andersen et al., 2004). Conversely, auditory information can dominate spatial judgements when visual information is blurry (Alais & Burr, 2004). These findings lead us to question whether sensory dominance really occurs because one sense is more 'appropriate' for a particular task.

One influential theory, called 'maximum-likelihood estimation' theory (Ernst & Banks, 2002), postulates that the sense that dominates depends on the reliability of the stimuli in any given situation. If visual information is less reliable, auditory information is more likely to dominate; if auditory information is less reliable, visual information is more likely to dominate. This explanation seems consistent with the idea that vision tends to dominate spatial judgements and audition tends to dominate timing judgements—but it's also consistent with the two examples in the previous paragraph: if sounds are so quiet that they can barely be heard, the information they convey is less likely to be reliable, which could explain why vision dominates in this situation. Similarly, if visual information is blurry, then the information it conveys is less reliable in this situation, which could explain why audition dominates (Figure 7.1(b)).

> Studies that have manipulated the reliability of auditory and visual information have typically found results consistent with maximum-likelihood estimation theory. For example, one study trained people to judge spatial location for artificial stimuli in which the visual information wasn't informative about location. They found an increase in auditory dominance for spatial location judgements after training (Kumpik et al., 2019).

Sensory dominance isn't always all or nothing, and maximum-likelihood estimation theory predicts not only *which* sense will dominate, but also *how much* it will dominate. Imagine a situation in which the perceived position of a sound is affected by a flash of light. Rather than being perceived at the same location as the light (i.e. total visual dominance), the sound could be perceived to be in a place that's slightly closer to the light than to the real location of the sound (Figure 7.2). Maximum-likelihood estimation theory predicts that the perceived position of the sound depends on the reliability of auditory information relative to the reliability of visual information. If the information is similarly reliable, it may be perceived midway between the locations of the sound and the light; if visual information is more reliable, it may be perceived closer to the light; whereas, if auditory information is more reliable, it may be perceived closer to the real location of the sound. Maximum-likelihood estimation theory appears to account well for studies in which there's a small discrepancy between sensory information, but it has been criticised for not providing such accurate predictions when the discrepancy between the senses is very large (Heron et al., 2004).

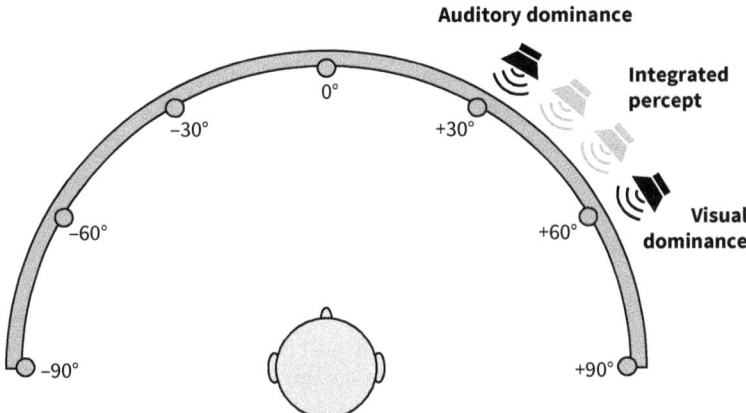

Figure 7.2 Schematic of an audio-visual setup in which a person sits facing an arc that has light-emitting diodes (LEDs) spaced at intervals of 30°. They are asked to judge the location of a sound (e.g. a bell sound) presented from a loudspeaker at +30° that's hidden behind the arc, at the same time as an LED at +60° lights up. If the visual information dominates, then they would perceive the location of the sound at +60°; but if the visual information influences the decision without entirely dominating the percept, the sound may be perceived between +30° and +60°.

> Maximum likelihood estimation theory uses a mathematical equation to predict how sensory information is combined. It assumes that people compute a weighted average of the available information, whereby more reliable information contributes more to the average. Maximum likelihood estimation theory doesn't only apply to audition and vision, but also applies to other senses. For example, many of the original experiments studied visual and haptic information.

7.2 Audio-visual integration

The previous section introduced the idea that sensory dominance isn't all or nothing. In other words, information from one sense may not be disregarded entirely. Instead, sensory information can be *integrated* in a way that matches neither the auditory nor the visual information, but instead lies somewhere between the two. This section introduces a well-known illusion—known as the McGurk effect—in which competing speech information gives rise to a percept that matches neither the auditory nor the visual information, but instead appears to generate an entirely different percept. It also considers how integrating visual information from the face and lips can help listeners to understand speech in noisy environments. Later, this section explains how auditory and visual information are integrated in neural responses, and the conditions under which they're integrated (Figure 7.1(c)), rather than being perceived as separate (Figure 7.1(d)).

7.2.1 Integration of audio-visual speech

Many people think of speech perception as relying purely on hearing—but, in everyday life, people can usually see the person who's speaking to them. In these situations, most people will look at the speaker's lips to help them understand what they're saying. Therefore, understanding speech can rely on vision as well as hearing.

McGurk and MacDonald (1976) famously observed an interesting illusion, which is now known as the McGurk effect. When a video of someone speaking the syllable 'ga' was dubbed with the audio of the person saying 'ba', most people reported hearing neither 'ga' nor 'ba'. Instead, they found that most people reported hearing an entirely different syllable: 'da'. This wasn't simply because the auditory or visual information wasn't clear: people reported seeing 'ga' when they saw the video without any audio (Figure 7.3(a)), and 'ba' when they only heard the audio with no video (Figure 7.3(b)). Instead, the percept 'da' arose only when the auditory 'ba' and visual 'ga' were presented together (Figure 7.3(c)). Arguably, 'da' is the percept that's most consistent with the two sources of information, taken together. The video is inconsistent with someone saying 'ba', because the lips are open in the video of 'ga', whereas they should be closed at the beginning of the syllable if the person is saying 'ba'. The acoustic information is inconsistent with 'ga', because the spectrogram for 'ga' is quite different to that of 'ba'. However, 'da' is more acoustically similar to the syllable 'ba' than 'ga' is, and the lips are open when speaking 'da'. Therefore, 'da' best accounts for the lip-movement information in the video and the acoustic information from the audio—and could therefore be considered a plausible compromise. In this situation, neither sense dominates, but, instead, the information is integrated and forms a new percept.

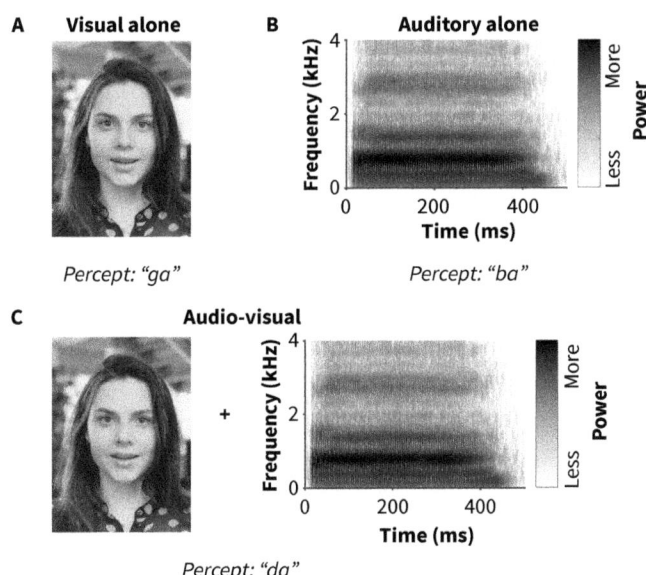

Figure 7.3 Schematic of the McGurk effect. When a video (visual only) of someone speaking 'ga' (panel a) is combined with the audio of someone speaking 'ba' (panel b), the resulting percept is usually 'da' (panel c).

More recent studies suggest there are wide individual differences in the extent to which people experience the McGurk effect. In the original study, McGurk and MacDonald (1976) found that 98% of adults reported a 'da' percept, but some subsequent studies have found that smaller percentages of people consistently experience the illusion—and the estimated percentage varies widely across studies (Alsius et al., 2018). Instead of experiencing an integrated percept ('da'), some people experience auditory dominance. In other words, they perceive 'ba' regardless of whether the visual information is present or absent. The causes of these individual differences are not fully understood, but may relate to someone's ability to perceive relevant speech information from the visual stimulus (Brown et al., 2018). People who are less susceptible to the illusion generally show weaker responses in the superior temporal sulcus to McGurk stimuli (Nath and Beauchamp, 2012).

In general, the McGurk effect demonstrates that vision can have a strong effect on speech perception—at least for some people. However, while this illusion has been useful to researchers interested in testing audio-visual integration, it's rather unusual for auditory speech information to conflict with visual speech information. Therefore, the McGurk effect might not be well suited to examining real-life audio-visual integration (Van Engen et al., 2022).

In everyday life, visual and auditory speech information are usually congruent and, when auditory information is degraded, visual information can help people to understand what someone is saying. Imagine being in a noisy restaurant: if it's difficult to hear what the person opposite you is saying, you might look at their lips in order to follow the conversation.

Using someone's lip movements to help follow a conversation is called 'lipreading'— but many people also use other information from the face to help them understand what someone is saying. Thus, using visual information for speech perception is often referred to more generally as 'speechreading'.

So, how good are people at perceiving speech from visual information? On average, people can detect one in five words correctly when visual speech information is presented alone, although there are large individual differences: some people are quite good at speechreading, others are much worse at understanding speech from visual information alone (Bernstein et al., 2022). This raises the question: Can we teach people to better speechread? Unfortunately, elucidating what makes someone a good speechreader has been difficult to determine, and attempts to improve speechreading through training have only found modest success (Bernstein et al., 2022).

Yet, when visual information is used *in combination* with auditory information, the benefits are more consistent. In other words, visual information can help people to understand speech when they're able to partially hear the speech signal. One way to quantify this advantage is to compare the lowest signal-to-noise ratio at which listeners can understand speech in noise (i.e. the threshold for understanding speech) in an auditory-only condition to that in an audio-visual condition. When listening to sentences in noise, the difference in thresholds between auditory-only and audio-visual conditions is approximately 5 dB, although the benefit varies depending on the type of background noise and the intelligibility of the target talker (Blackburn et al., 2019). In other words, to achieve the same level of speech understanding for auditory-only speech and audio-visual speech, the background noise can be more intense in the audio-visual condition than in the auditory-only condition. Thus, even though people may not be able to fully understand speech from visual speech alone, they're nevertheless able to extract some information from visual speech that helps them to work out what's being said when the auditory information isn't clear.

> Recall from **Chapter 5** that the signal-to-noise ratio is the difference between the average intensity of speech and of background noise.

So, why does visual speech information produce an audio-visual benefit to speech understanding? One reason is that seeing a talker helps people to direct their attention to auditory information at the most important times, because the opening and closing of the mouth aligns with the amplitude envelope of the speech signal. In addition, movements of the articulators—which can be seen by looking at someone's face—can distinguish between syllables that sound similar; for example, 'be' and 'he' have very different lip movements to each other. Beyond a better understanding of speech, multisensory information from the face and voice can also help people to recognise someone's identity (Further insights 7.1).

> **Further insights 7.1** Integrating hearing and vision for identity perception
>
> While the most obvious way in which people combine hearing and vision during speech perception is when trying to understand the words that someone is saying, sometimes a person's goal is to recognise the identity of the person who's speaking, particularly if they are someone they know

personally (e.g. recognising a friend at a party) or someone who is famous—(e.g. noticing that an actor from their favourite movie is sitting at a nearby table in a restaurant). In addition to integrating both auditory and visual information for speech and identity perception, people also integrate them when perceiving emotion (Kreifelts & Ethofer, 2018).

There is evidence that many people combine voice and face information when recognising the identities of people who are familiar to them. For example, studies have found that people are better at recognising someone familiar from a spoken sentence when the audio is combined with a video of that person speaking the sentence, compared to when they only hear the audio of the person speaking. Importantly, to ensure the audio-visual advantage comes from the identity information within the video, rather than a more general advantage of showing the sentence in both the visual and auditory domains, researchers have also compared voice recognition when the same person features in the visual and auditory stimuli to voice recognition when the visual stimulus shows a different person speaking the sentence; in this case, people are better at recognising the identity of the person speaking when the visual stimulus shows the same person speaking compared to a different person speaking—revealing that people combine identity information from both sources (Schweinberger et al., 2007).

People are also sensitive to face information when learning to recognise the voices of new people. Studies show that listeners are better able to recognise someone from their voice if they were exposed to a video of the person speaking at the same time as they learnt the voice than when they were only exposed to the person's voice without ever seeing their face (e.g., Zäske et al., 2015).

The process of combining voice and face information when recognising familiar people may arise from direct connections between voice-sensitive areas of cortex (e.g. mid-to-anterior parts of the superior temporal gyrus and superior temporal sulcus) and face-sensitive areas of cortex (e.g. the fusiform face area) (Blank et al., 2015).

The fusiform face area is an example of a 'category-selective' area in the brain that responds more strongly to faces than to other categories of visual stimuli (e.g. images of places) (Kanwisher, 2017). It is one of several areas that have been implicated in face perception, including the occipital face area and the posterior superior temporal sulcus. Together, these areas are thought to be involved in processing visual features of faces and recognising someone's identity from their face (see e.g. Tsantani et al., 2021).

7.2.2 Neural integration

So, how is visual speech information combined with auditory information, and at what stage of processing does this occur? For these two senses to influence each other, the information from the eyes and the ears must be combined at a neural level—so *where* and *when* is it combined?

Several theories have been proposed. On one hand, 'late integration' theories propose that auditory and visual information are processed separately to begin with, and then later combined after each sense has been processed independently. On the other hand, 'early integration' theories propose that auditory and visual information are combined during early stages of processing in each modality, such that processing one sense can influence processing of the other sense.

To look at how early auditory and visual information are integrated, some studies have measured responses of individual neurons in an area of the midbrain called the superior colliculus. Theoretically, this region seemed to be appropriate for studying audio-visual integration, because it was known to respond to both visual and auditory stimuli individually. Indeed, more than half of the neurons in this area can be classified as **multisensory** (Stein & Meredith, 1993)—that is, their responses are influenced by stimuli in more than one modality (which incorporates responses to auditory, visual, and/or somatosensory information)—and more than 35% of these neurons were shown to be influenced by both the auditory and the visual modalities. This finding implies that elements of auditory and visual information are combined at a very early stage of processing.

> Recall from **Chapter 1** that the midbrain is part of the brainstem.

Interestingly, rather than being clustered in one area, multisensory neurons appear to be mixed with unisensory neurons (i.e. neurons that only respond to one sensory modality)—and not all multisensory neurons combine information from the senses in the same way. Although it is well established that auditory and visual information affect each other, the question of how we should define multisensory neural responses—and what this means for how visual and auditory elements are integrated—remains a topic of debate (see e.g. Stevenson et al., 2014).

Even areas that were traditionally ascribed to a single sense—such as auditory cortex and visual cortex—are now known to contain at least some neurons that respond to information from multiple senses, which supports early integration (Ghazanfar & Schroeder, 2006). For example, in primary auditory cortex, approximately 15% of neurons receive input from other sensory modalities, and this percentage is even larger in secondary auditory cortex (Bizley et al., 2007). Multisensory responses in auditory cortex are thought to arise from anatomical connections between auditory and visual regions of cortex—and this finding contrasts with the traditional view of 'late integration' that information from each of the senses is first processed in isolation and later combined.

Historically, many researchers searched for an individual brain area where responses from different senses were combined—but, rather than being rare and confined to particular regions, multisensory responses are extremely prevalent throughout the brain. For example, researchers have also identified neurons in frontal cortex that respond to audio-visual speech more than to visual-only or auditory-only speech (Diehl & Romanski, 2014). A growing body of recent electrophysiological and neuroimaging research suggests that the integration of auditory and visual speech likely occurs at multiple stages (O'Sullivan et al., 2021). Under 'multi-stage integration' theories, aspects of both early and late integration are accounted for (Figure 7.4). Visual information can influence the early processing of auditory information (e.g. by informing someone about when to listen for speech), and auditory and visual information can also be combined later in processing (e.g. when speech is interpreted to determine its meaning) to help distinguish what words or syllables are being spoken (Peelle & Sommers, 2015). Ultimately, there may be no single answer

A Late integration

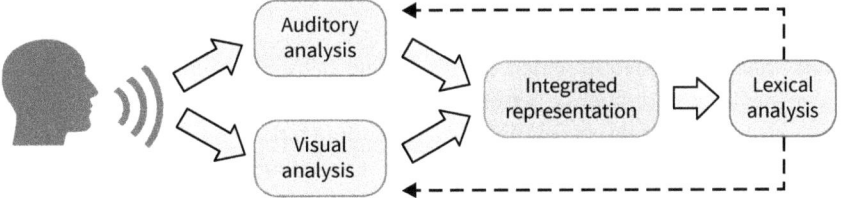

B Early integration

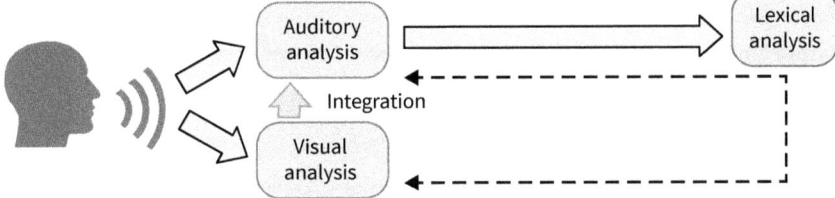

C Multi-stage integration

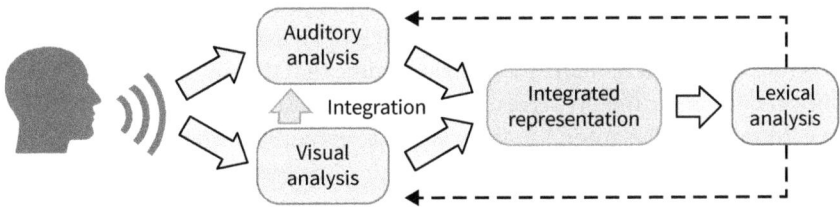

Figure 7.4 Schematics of different types of audio-visual integration theories of speech perception, based on Peelle and Sommers (2015). Under late-integration theories, an integrated representation occurs after auditory and visual information are analysed separately (panel a). Under early-integration theories, visual information is directly integrated into auditory representations (panel b). Under multi-stage-integration theories, some visual information is directly integrated into auditory representations and other visual information is integrated after auditory analysis is complete (panel c). All classes of theories allow the possibility of top-down influences from the lexicon to auditory and visual analysis (dashed lines).
Source: based on Peelle and Sommers (2015).

that applies in all settings. Instead, it's possible that the area that integrates auditory and visual information varies across listening conditions—for example, depending on whether speech is presented in quiet or in (various levels of) background noise, and also whether someone is attending to speech or not (Ahmed et al., 2023).

7.2.3 Conditions for integration

Recall from **Chapter 3** that, when multiple auditory stimuli occur, they're more likely to be grouped in some cases than others. Similarly, information sources from audition and vision are more likely to be integrated under some conditions than others. Sometimes, auditory and visual information may not be integrated at all and, instead, they may be perceived as belonging to separate objects. For example, if someone is walking down the street, they probably won't perceive the sound of a car's engine as originating from the dog they can see ahead!

When watching a video, people usually integrate the audio with the image—but have you ever watched a video in which the sound lags behind the image (Figure 7.5)? We can consider this lag as a difference between the timings of auditory and of visual information. If there's a long delay, someone might find it difficult to follow the video and, if they're watching a video of someone speaking, it might take more effort to understand what the person is saying. The extent to which auditory and visual information are consistent in time (which is called 'temporal congruence') is an important condition for audio-visual integration. In the video example, the sound and the image are less likely to be integrated when there's a greater lag—and, in this situation, it's harder to integrate them into a unified percept. The importance of consistency in time has been demonstrated across a variety of studies. For example, returning to the ventriloquist effect introduced in Section 7.1.1, the magnitude of visual dominance depends on how well the timing of visual information matches the timing of auditory information (Radeau & Bertelson, 1987).

The extent to which auditory and visual information originate from a similar spatial location (which is called 'spatial congruence') is also known to affect audio-visual integration: auditory and visual information sources are more likely to be integrated if they come from the same location. Imagine someone is walking through a forest and they hear the sound of a bird chirping. If the bird sound comes from high up in front of them, and they can also see a bird on a tree in front of them, they might assume that the sound has come from the bird that they can see in the tree. Whereas, it's less likely that they'd associate the same bird sound with a bird that's on the ground to their left side, because the sound is coming from a different direction. In experiments manipulating the directions of auditory and visual stimuli and asking people to judge spatial location, consistency in spatial location has been shown to affect the extent of visual dominance (Stein et al., 1989).

In summary, the integration of visual and auditory information isn't a given, but depends on several conditions—and, in daily life, this can prevent people from integrating auditory and visual information elements that don't belong together.

Figure 7.5 Audio-visual calls allow users to access auditory and visual speech information, but can sometimes be frustrating if the image or sound lags; for example, due to issues with the internet connection.

7.3 Cross-modal plasticity

The brain usually receives input from both vision and audition, but if one sense isn't present or only partially functions, neurons that usually respond to inputs from that sense (e.g. audition) may respond to input from another sense (e.g. vision)—which is known as **cross-modal plasticity**. Imagine a garden with light and shady areas. If the light is blocked when a new wall is built, the plants that prefer direct light won't get the inputs they need to grow, and other (e.g. shade-loving) plants might grow in that area of the garden instead. Similarly, an area of the brain that typically responds to sounds may adapt to respond to vision, and vice versa.

7.3.1 Cross-modal plasticity and neuronal responses

One way to study cross-modal plasticity is to compare brain responses to visual stimuli between people who are deaf and people who don't have any hearing loss. Individuals who are deaf show responses to visual stimuli in primary and secondary auditory cortices, and these aren't observed when the same visual stimuli are presented to people without hearing loss (Finney et al., 2001) (Figure 7.6). Researchers have also compared blind people's brain responses to sounds with those of people who don't have any vision loss. People who are blind show responses to sounds in visual cortex that aren't observed when the same sounds are presented to people who don't have any vision loss (Collignon et al., 2013) (Figure 7.6). These findings demonstrate that brain responses to fully functioning senses can be affected by other partially functioning senses.

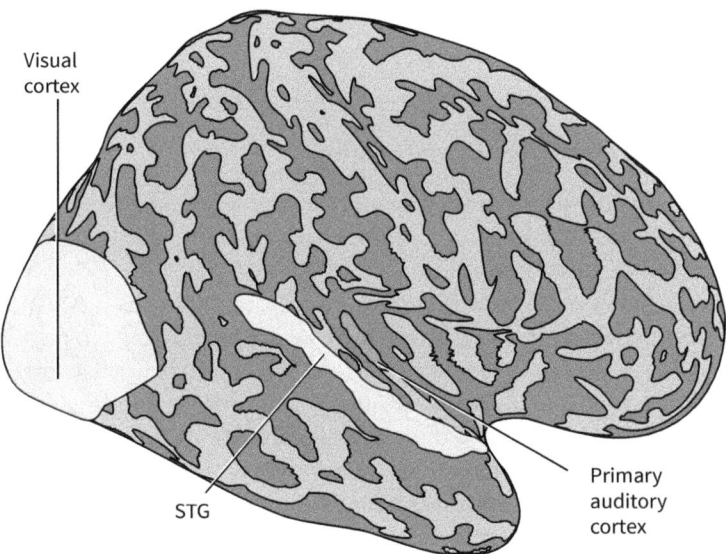

Figure 7.6 Inflated brain, highlighting the approximate locations of primary auditory cortex and the superior temporal gyrus (STG)—which are regions of auditory cortex—and visual cortex. Previous studies have found that brain responses in these areas differ between people with and without hearing loss, and between people with and without vision loss.

> See **Chapter 8** for details about how hearing loss is defined and assessed.

Interestingly, cross-modal plasticity isn't all or nothing: it's greater for individuals who have lower auditory or visual input at younger ages, implying that the brain is more adaptable when young. For example, one study compared brain responses to speech sounds between children who had almost complete hearing loss since birth and children who didn't have any hearing loss (Sharma et al., 2002). The children with hearing loss had all been using cochlear implants for about three years, which provided them with some auditory input, although the age at which the children received cochlear implants varied. The researchers focused on the timing of a brain response that typically occurs about 100 ms after the start of a sound. Interestingly, the timing of this response was similar for children without hearing loss and those who were implanted by age 3½, whereas the response differed for children who were implanted at older ages, occurring later (around 200 ms after the beginning of a sound) for children who received cochlear implants after age 7. These results suggest that there's a sensitive period for cross-modal plasticity of 3½ years, because children who are implanted by this age (and therefore receive auditory input by this age) have more similar brain responses to children without hearing loss. Likewise, studies comparing individuals who have been blind since birth with people whose blindness started in adulthood are consistent with the idea that the brain is more adaptable to changes in sensory input at younger ages (e.g. Collignon et al., 2013).

> Sharma et al. (2002) measured 'cortical auditory evoked potentials' using electrodes placed on the scalp. These brain responses occur in response to sounds and reflect how these sounds are processed by the listener.

7.3.2 Cross-modal plasticity and perception

While studies have consistently demonstrated that neural responses differ when one sense isn't present or only partially functions, whether cross-modal plasticity provides advantages to *perception* for other senses is less clear.

Some research shows perceptual advantages. Compared to people without hearing loss, people who have been deaf since early in life are better at detecting moving visual stimuli (Shiell et al., 2014). Similarly, some research has found that people who have been blind from a young age are better at locating sounds in the periphery than people who don't have any vision loss (Bell et al., 2019). Possibly, these advantages occur because cross-modal plasticity means that these individuals can recruit additional brain resources to help them perform the task. In support of this idea, when researchers temporarily interfere with neuronal activity in visual cortex (using a method called transcranial magnetic stimulation), people who are blind are worse at locating sounds as compared to their usual performance (Collignon et al., 2007). This finding implies that they're using *visual cortex* to help localise sounds.

Other studies, however, have found no behavioural advantages for the other sense, and some studies have even found worse performance (for an overview, see Singh et al., 2018). For example, people who are blind are worse at locating sounds in the vertical plane compared to people who don't have any vision loss (Voss et al., 2015).

> When discussing sound locations, the 'periphery' refers to the outer edges of perceived auditory space. For example, in the azimuth plane, this could be 90 degrees to the left or right of the listener. In contrast, 'central' locations would be those close to the midline—in other words, in front of the listener.

7.3.3 The purpose of cross-modal plasticity

Such varied results around perceptual improvements can make us question the purpose of cross-modal plasticity. A prevailing assumption is that the main purpose of cross-modal plasticity is to compensate for the lack (or partial lack) of one sense. Under this view, the brain reorganises, with the functioning sense 'taking over' the brain areas that aren't being used by the other sense. For example, in the case of vision loss, areas that typically respond to visual stimuli will be taken over and instead respond to auditory stimuli (and vice versa for hearing loss). By 'taking over' these areas, there will presumably be more resources to enhance performance for the functioning sense.

One idea is that the other sense makes use of particular brain areas that serve a specific functional purpose. Support for this view comes from neuroimaging studies that have compared brain responses to complementary visual and auditory stimuli between people who are deaf and people who don't have any hearing loss. For example, planum temporale—an area that typically responds to moving sounds in people without hearing loss—responds to visual movement in people who are deaf (Benetti et al., 2021). Similarly, areas within the superior temporal gyrus and superior temporal sulcus that usually respond to spoken voices in people without hearing loss have been shown to respond to faces in people who are deaf—potentially because perceiving voices and faces both involve recognition and identification (Benetti et al., 2017). Thus, the other sense might 'take over' brain areas that are optimised to perform similar types of processing.

It's possible, however, that the brain reorganises for a functional purpose that hasn't yet been discovered. Potentially, the purpose of cross-modal plasticity hasn't been established because the tasks that researchers use in experiments are often very specific (e.g. involving certain stimuli at specific locations)—and perhaps there's a broader functional purpose that can't be detected by these specific tests. Another possibility is that the brain doesn't reorganise and, instead, deafness and blindness simply allow researchers to observe connections that are present in everyone, but typically go undetected. Under this view, responses to auditory stimuli in the visual cortices of people who are blind are also present in people who don't have vision loss (and, similarly, responses to visual stimuli in the auditory cortices of people who are deaf are also present in people who don't have hearing loss), but they're simply harder to detect because they're masked by other brain responses that are more dominant. Returning to the garden analogy (introduced at the beginning of Section 7.3), we might only see large plants that prefer lots of light because these plants dominate the scene, whereas small plants preferring shade may be present too, but remain hidden underneath the larger plants that prefer direct light.

> Recall from **Section 7.2.2** that primary auditory cortex contains some neurons that respond to visual stimuli. This finding is consistent with the idea that cross-modal connections are typical rather than unusual—and, consequently, reduced input from one sense may make these cross-modal connections easier for researchers to detect.

Ultimately, while some features of cross-modal plasticity are well established, more research is needed to establish some nuances in the literature. For example, why do some aspects of the functioning sense improve more than others? Also, if undetected connections exist, what's their purpose?

7.4 Correspondences between the senses

We usually think of audition and vision as providing different types of information. However, people commonly associate specific auditory percepts with specific visual percepts, which implies that the two senses may in fact provide similar information. This section examines correspondences between audition and vision, first by considering correspondences that most people have in common, and second by considering cases of **synaesthesia** in which correspondences between the senses are particularly intense.

7.4.1 Common correspondences

If you were asked to decide whether a brighter or darker visual percept was more congruent with the higher-frequency tones, which would you choose? How about a higher or lower elevation?

If people just randomly guess, we would expect approximately half of the people we ask to say brighter and the other half to say darker. However, studies have shown that most people match a brighter percept with higher-frequency sounds. This finding suggests that there's a correspondence between sound frequency and visual brightness (Figure 7.7).

These types of associations are not constrained to sound frequency and visual brightness: there are, in fact, a wide variety of these natural correspondences. Higher frequencies have been associated with higher visual elevations (Evans & Treisman, 2010). For example, if people are asked whether higher-frequency tones are more congruent with a dot that's higher or lower on the screen, most people choose the dot that's higher on the screen (Figure 7.7). Higher-frequency tones have also been associated with smaller visual stimuli (Parise & Spence, 2009).

More complex correspondences also exist. When asked which of two non-words—'bouba' and 'kiki'—correspond to various images, most people match 'bouba' with the rounded shape displayed on the left and 'kiki' with the pointy shape displayed on the right (Lockwood & Dingemanse, 2015). This finding is thought to occur because, when spoken aloud, 'bouba' makes a more 'rounded' sound that can be considered more similar to the rounded shape,

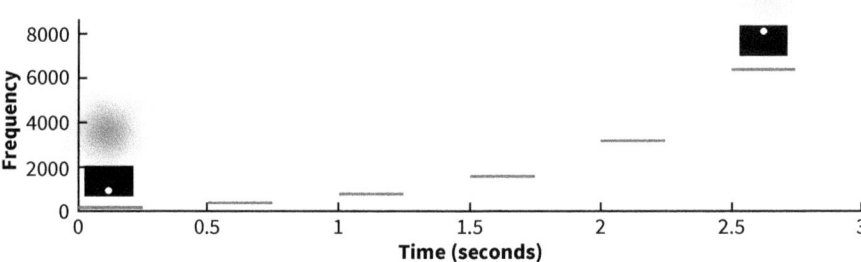

Figure 7.7 Examples of visual percepts that are associated with higher- and lower-frequency sounds. Higher-frequency sounds (towards the right of the figure) are typically associated with brighter visual stimuli and higher visual elevations.

whereas 'kiki' makes a 'sharper' sound that's more consistent with the pointy shape. The bouba/kiki effect has been demonstrated across cultures that use different writing systems, consistent with the idea that the effect arises due to natural correspondences between the senses (Ćwiek et al., 2022). In general, these types of common correspondences might have influenced the development of language because, when researchers consider how a word's meaning relates to its spoken form across many different languages, particular features of spoken words appear to be consistently associated with specific meanings (Blasi et al., 2016). Frequently used metaphors also suggest a common correspondence (see Williams, 1976); for example, it's not unusual to hear sounds described as 'bright' or 'faint', which are both visual rather than auditory attributes.

Common correspondences also affect the extent to which auditory and visual stimuli are integrated (Section 7.2.3): multisensory integration is stronger when the stimulus dimensions are congruent. For example, integration is stronger when a higher-frequency tone is presented with a smaller visual stimulus than when it's presented with a larger visual stimulus (Parise & Spence, 2009).

7.4.2 Synaesthesia

While most people have tendencies to associate some visual percepts with auditory percepts, about 1 in 2,000 people experience **synaesthesia**, whereby particular stimuli actually induce other sensory percepts (Further insights 7.2). For example, some people have a type of synaesthesia called coloured hearing synaesthesia: when these people hear sounds, they also see colours. The synaesthetic associations differ among people; Figure 7.8 shows examples from two individuals who report seeing different colours when they listen to musical notes.

> Several famous composers are thought to have had coloured hearing synaesthesia. For example, Jean Sibelius and Franz Liszt have been quoted as associating musical notes and musical keys with particular colours. People who report seeing colours when musical sounds are played have been shown to have stronger connections between visual, auditory, and frontal brain areas than people without synaesthesia (Zamm et al., 2013).

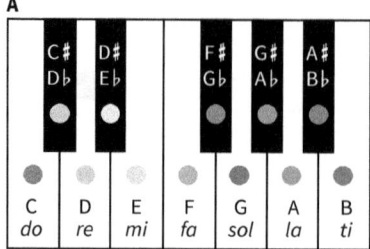 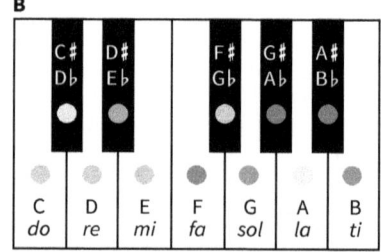

Figure 7.8 Examples of synaesthetic associations between musical notes and colours for a pair of twins with synaesthesia. Each panel shows the self-reported associations for one individual: The two individuals report different colour mappings. Colour mappings are from https://www.mileskredich.com/twinesthesia-interactive-keyboard and can be viewed at this URL. Alternatively, the colour version of this figure can be viewed in the electronic version of this book.

Source: colour mappings are from https://www.mileskredich.com/twinesthesia-interactive-keyboard.

The link between hearing a sound and seeing colours goes beyond a mere association: people who have coloured hearing synaesthesia report consciously seeing the colour as if it were physically present.

Sometimes synaesthesia can be developmental, but it can also arise after brain damage or be induced by some drugs.

Further insights 7.2 Can you 'hear' visual stimuli?

Some people claim to hear sounds when they see specific instances of moving or flashing visual stimuli. In a popular example, a short animation depicts an electricity pylon jumping up and down over power lines, similar to how someone might jump over a skipping rope. The animation is silent, but many viewers claim to hear a 'thud' when the pylon lands on the ground.

This experience is an example of a visually evoked auditory response, which is thought to be a form of synaesthesia in which moving visual stimuli elicit auditory sensations. To examine this experience in more detail, researchers have compared how people with and without this form of synaesthesia perform on other tasks. For example, when people are asked to detect whether two auditory or two visual rhythmic patterns are the same or different, people without synaesthesia are usually better at discriminating auditory rhythms than visual rhythms (see Section 7.1.2). However, people with this form of synaesthesia are better at visual rhythm discrimination than people without synaesthesia, which is consistent with the idea that they 'hear' sounds when they see the visual stimuli (Fassnidge et al., 2017). As there is limited research in this area, it's unclear how many people experience this type of sensation and what mechanisms might underlie this phenomenon.

As shown in Figure 7.8, not everyone with coloured hearing synaesthesia experiences the same mappings between particular sounds and colours. For this reason, many researchers were initially sceptical about whether synaesthetic percepts were authentic, considering it more likely that they might be made up. However, several findings suggest these percepts are in fact authentic. First, the mappings for an individual remain the same over many years (Baron-Cohen et al., 1993). Second, people who have coloured hearing synaesthesia show responses in colour-sensitive areas of the brain when they hear sounds (Nunn et al., 2002). In addition, they show a Stroop effect for their synaesthetic perceptions. In the classic Stroop

Figure 7.9 Stroop effect. In the classic Stroop effect, naming the colour of the font is easier when the font colour matches the written word (panel a) than when the font colour doesn't match the word (panel b). People who have synaesthetic associations between pitch classes and colours experience a similar effect when they are asked to name the colour of a pitch class word (e.g. 'do', which corresponds to a 'C' note: see Figure 7.8(a)) that matches the colour of their synaesthetic association (panel c, based on the colour associations displayed in Figure 7.8(a)), compared to when it doesn't match the colour of their synaesthetic association (panel d, based on the colour associations displayed in Figure 7.8(a)). People who don't have synaesthesia wouldn't be expected to show the Stroop effect for pitch class words.

effect, reading the name of a colour word (e.g. 'red') interferes with naming the font colour of the same word (e.g. green) (compare Figure 7.9(a) with Figure 7.9(b)). For people who have associations between pitch classes (e.g. 'do', 're', 'mi', which correspond to the musical notes C, D, and E; see Figure 7.8) and colours, reading a pitch class word (e.g. 'do') interferes with naming the font colour of the same word (compare Figure 7.9(c) with Figure 7.9(d)) (Itoh et al., 2019). This finding suggests that synaesthetic percepts are automatic and are evoked even when they hinder task performance. Therefore, individual differences seem to reflect real differences in perception—which could be related to particular associations that people were exposed to in childhood (Watson et al., 2014).

A question that has puzzled researchers is: Why is it that some people experience synaesthesia and others do not? While some studies have aimed to train people who don't have synaesthesia to experience synaesthetic associations, these effects are short-lived (Rothen et al., 2018). One possible explanation is based on the idea that, early in development, different areas of the brain (that respond to information from different senses) are highly interconnected and these connections are pruned away during typical development; possibly, these connections are not fully pruned for people who have synaesthesia and some of the connections remain into adulthood, causing cross-sensory associations to persist (Maurer, 1997). Another possible explanation is that dense cross-sensory connections are present in most people, but they're not normally used because of neural inhibition; whereas, if they're not inhibited in people with synaesthesia, then responses to one sensory attribute may automatically trigger responses to another attribute (Grossenbacher & Lovelace, 2001). Alternatively, some researchers have proposed that people with synaesthesia have greater neural noise in sensory cortex, which means that cross-modal pathways are simply more likely to be activated (Lalwani & Brang, 2019). Nevertheless, while these are all prevalent theories, there is currently no unanimous view on why some people experience synaesthesia but others don't. One of the most puzzling aspects of synaesthesia is that it's so varied, and it's difficult to find an explanation that is consistent with all cases. Ultimately, there may not be a single explanation that applies to all instances of synaesthesia.

Summary

This chapter highlights a variety of ways in which visual information can influence what people hear—from changing what they hear (e.g. perceiving a different syllable in the McGurk effect), to dominating what they hear (e.g. affecting spatial location judgements in the ventriloquist effect). However, this isn't a one-way street: what people hear can also influence what they see. In addition, the brain appears to be inherently multisensory. Regions of the brain that are traditionally considered to be unisensory (e.g. 'auditory cortex' and 'visual cortex') respond to stimuli from other sensory modalities. Also, when one sense doesn't fully function, the corresponding sensory cortex may respond more intensely to information from other senses. Generally speaking, there appear to be common correspondences between attributes of stimuli in different modalities (e.g. auditory frequency and visual brightness), and these correspondences are particularly striking in cases of synaesthesia. All of these observations imply that we shouldn't consider 'auditory perception' as fully separate from 'visual perception', but rather as part of a more general 'multisensory perception'.

Further your understanding

Opoku-Baah, C., Schoenhaut, A. M., Vassall, S. G., Tovar, D. A., Ramachandran, R., & Wallace, M. T. (2021). 'Visual influences on auditory behavioral, neural, and perceptual processes: A review.' *Journal of the Association for Research in Otolaryngology*, 22(4), 365–386.

Singh, A. K., Phillips, F., Merabet, L. B., & Sinha, P. (2018). 'Why does the cortex reorganize after sensory loss?' *Trends in Cognitive Sciences*, 22(7), 569–582.

References

Ahmed, F., Nidiffer, A. R., O'Sullivan, A. E., Zuk, N. J., & Lalor, E. C. (2023). 'The integration of continuous audio and visual speech in a cocktail-party environment depends on attention.' *NeuroImage*, 274(April), 120143. https://doi.org/10.1016/j.neuroimage.2023.120143

Alais, D., & Burr, D. (2004). 'The ventriloquist effect results from near-optimal bimodal integration.' *Current Biology*, 14(3), 257–262. https://doi.org/10.1016/J.CUB.2004.01.029

Alsius, A., Paré, M., & Munhall, K. (2018). 'Forty years after hearing lips and seeing voices: The McGurk effect revisited.' *Multisensory Research*, 31(1–2), 111–144. https://doi.org/10.1163/22134808-00002565

Andersen, T. S., Tiippana, K., & Sams, M. (2004). 'Factors influencing audiovisual fission and fusion illusions.' *Cognitive Brain Research*, 21(3), 301–308. https://doi.org/10.1016/j.tics.2017.03.007

Attout, L., Capizzi, M., & Charras, P. (2024). 'Enhancing rhythmic temporal expectations: The dominance of auditory modality under spatial uncertainty.' *Attention, Perception, & Psychophysics*, 86, 1681–1693. https://doi.org/10.3758/s13414-024-02898-3

Baron-Cohen, S., Harrison, J., Goldstein, L. H., & Wyke, M. (1993). 'Coloured speech perception: Is synaesthesia what happens when modularity breaks down?' *Perception*, 22(4), 419–426. https://doi.org/10.1068/P220419

Bell, L., Wagels, L., Neuschaefer-Rube, C., Fels, J., Gur, R. E., & Konrad, K. (2019). 'The cross-modal effects of sensory deprivation on spatial and temporal processes in vision and audition: A systematic review on behavioral and neuroimaging research since 2000.' *Neural Plasticity*, 2019(December), 9603469. https://doi.org/10.1155/2019/9603469

Benetti, S., Van Ackeren, M. J., Rabini, G., Zonca, J., Foa, V., Baruffaldi, F., Rezk, M., Pavani, F., Rossion, B., & Collignon, O. (2017). 'Functional selectivity for face processing in the temporal voice area of early deaf individuals.' *Proceedings of the National Academy of Sciences of the United States of America*, 114(31), E6437–E6446. https://doi.org/10.1073/pnas.1618287114

Benetti, S., Zonca, J., Ferrari, A., Rezk, M., Rabini, G., & Collignon, O. (2021). 'Visual motion processing recruits regions selective for auditory motion in early deaf individuals.' *NeuroImage*, 230. https://doi.org/10.1016/j.neuroimage.2021.117816

Bernstein, L. E., Jordan, N., Auer, E. T., & Eberhardt, S. P. (2022). 'Lipreading: A review of its continuing importance for speech recognition with an acquired hearing loss and possibilities for effective training.' *American Journal of Audiology*, 31(2), 453–469. https://doi.org/10.1044/2021_AJA-21-00112

Bizley, J. K., & Dai, Y. (2020). 'Non-auditory processing in the central auditory pathway.' *Current Opinion in Physiology*, 18, 100–105. https://doi.org/10.1016/j.cophys.2020.09.003

Bizley, J. K., Nodal, F. R., Bajo, V. M., Nelken, I., & King, A. J. (2007). 'Physiological and anatomical evidence for multisensory interactions in auditory cortex.' *Cerebral Cortex*, 17(9), 2172–2189. https://doi.org/10.1093/CERCOR/BHL128

Blackburn, C. L., Kitterick, P. T., Jones, G., Sumner, C. J., & Stacey, P. C. (2019). 'Visual speech benefit in clear and degraded speech depends on the auditory intelligibility of the talker and the number of background talkers.' *Trends in Hearing*, 23. https://doi.org/10.1177/2331216519837866

Blank, H., Kiebel, S. J., & von Kriegstein, K. (2015). 'How the human brain exchanges information across sensory modalities to recognize other people.' *Human Brain Mapping*, 36(1), 324–339. https://doi.org/10.1002/hbm.22631

Blasi, D. E., Wichmann, S., Hammarström, H., Stadler, P. F., & Christiansen, M. H. (2016). 'Sound-meaning association biases evidenced across thousands of languages.' *Proceedings of the National Academy of Sciences of the United States of America*, 113(39), 10818–10823. https://doi.org/10.1073/pnas.1605782113

Brown, V. A., Hedayati, M., Zanger, A., Mayn, S., Ray, L., Dillman-Hasso, N., & Strand, J. F. (2018) 'What accounts for individual differences in susceptibility to the McGurk effect?' *PLoS ONE*, 13(11), e0207160. https://doi.org/10.1371/journal.pone.0207160

Collignon, O., Dormal, G., Albouy, G., Vandewalle, G., Voss, P., Phillips, C., & Lepore, F. (2013). 'Impact of blindness onset on the functional organization and the connectivity of the occipital cortex.' *Brain*, 136(9), 2769–2783. https://doi.org/10.1093/brain/awt176

Collignon, O., Lassonde, M., Lepore, F., Bastien, D., & Veraart, C. (2007). 'Functional cerebral reorganization for auditory spatial processing and auditory substitution of vision in early blind subjects.' *Cerebral Cortex*, 17(2), 457–465. https://doi.org/10.1093/cercor/bhj162

Ćwiek, A., Fuchs, S., Draxler, C., Asu, E. L., Dediu, D., Hiovain, K., Kawahara, S., Koutalidis, S., Krifka, M., Lippus, P., Lupyan, G., Oh, G. E., Paul, J., Petrone, C., Ridouane, R., Reiter, S., Schümchen, N., Szalontai, Á., Ünal-Logacev, Ö., Zeller, J.,

Perlman, M., & Winter, B. (2022). 'The bouba/kiki effect is robust across cultures and writing systems.' *Philosophical Transactions of the Royal Society B*, 377(1841). https://doi.org/10.1098/RSTB.2020.0390

Diehl, M. M., & Romanski, L. M. (2014). 'Responses of prefrontal multisensory neurons to mismatching faces and vocalizations.' *Journal of Neuroscience*, 34(34), 11233–11243. https://doi.org/10.1523/JNEUROSCI.5168-13.2014

Ernst, M. O., & Banks, M. S. (2002). 'Humans integrate visual and haptic information in a statistically optimal fashion.' *Nature*, 415(6870), 429–433. https://doi.org/10.1038/415429a

Evans, K. K., & Treisman, A. (2010). 'Natural cross-modal mappings between visual and auditory features.' *Journal of Vision*, 10(1), 6. https://doi.org/10.1167/10.1.6

Fassnidge, C., Marcotti, C. C., & Freeman, E. (2017). 'A deafening flash! Visual interference of auditory signal detection.' *Consciousness and Cognition*, 49, 15–24. https://doi.org/10.1016/j.concog.2016.12.009

Fendrich, R., & Corballis, P. M. (2001). 'The temporal cross-capture of audition and vision.' *Perception & Psychophysics*, 63(4), 719–725. https://doi.org/10.3758/BF03194432

Finney, E. M., Fine, I., & Dobkins, K. R. (2001). 'Visual stimuli activate auditory cortex in the deaf.' *Nature Neuroscience*, 4(12), 1171–1173. https://doi.org/10.1038/nn763

Ghazanfar, A. A., & Schroeder, C. E. (2006). 'Is neocortex essentially multisensory?' *Trends in Cognitive Sciences*, 10(6), 278–285. https://doi.org/10.1016/J.TICS.2006.04.008

Grossenbacher, P. G., & Lovelace, C. T. (2001). 'Mechanisms of synesthesia: Cognitive and physiological constraints.' *Trends in Cognitive Sciences*, 5(1), 36–41. https://doi.org/10.1016/S1364-6613(00)01571-0

Heron, J., Whitaker, D., & McGraw, P. V. (2004). 'Sensory uncertainty governs the extent of audio-visual interaction.' *Vision Research*, 44(25), 2875–2884. https://doi.org/10.1016/J.VISRES.2004.07.001

Hirst, R. J., McGovern, D. P., Setti, A., Shams, L., & Newell, F. N. (2020). 'What you see is what you hear: Twenty years of research using the Sound-Induced Flash Illusion.' *Neuroscience & Biobehavioral Reviews*, 118, 759–774. https://doi.org/10.1016/j.neubiorev.2020.09.006

Itoh, K., Sakata, H., Igarashi, H., & Nakada, T. (2019). 'Automaticity of pitch class-color synesthesia as

Jackson, C. V. (1953). 'Visual factors in auditory localization.' *Quarterly Journal of Experimental Psychology*, 5(2), 52–65. https://doi.org/10.1080/17470215308416626

Kanwisher, N. (2017). 'The quest for the FFA and where it led.' *Journal of Neuroscience*, 37(5), 1056–1061. https://doi.org/10.1523/JNEUROSCI.1706-16.2016

Kreifelts, B., & Ethofer, T. (2018). 'Voices in the context of human faces and bodies.' In S. Frühholz & P. Belin (eds) *The Oxford Handbook of Voice Perception* (pp. 645–666). Oxford: Oxford University Press. https://doi.org/10.1093/oxfordhb/9780198743187.013.29

Kumpik, D. P., Campbell, C., Schnupp, J. W., & King, A. J. (2019). 'Re-weighting of sound localization cues by audiovisual training.' *Frontiers in Neuroscience*, 13, 1164.

Lalwani, P., & Brang, D. (2019). 'Stochastic resonance model of synaesthesia.' *Philosophical Transactions of the Royal Society B*, 374(1787). https://doi.org/10.1098/rstb.2019.0029

Lockwood, G., & Dingemanse, M. (2015). 'Iconicity in the lab: A review of behavioral, developmental, and neuroimaging research into sound-symbolism.' *Frontiers in Psychology*, 6, 1246. https://doi.org/10.3389/fpsyg.2015.01246

Maurer, D. (1997). 'Neonatal synaesthesia: Implications for the processing of speech and faces.' In S. Baron-Cohen & J. E. Harrison (eds) *Synaesthesia: Classic and Contemporary Readings* (pp. 224–242). Oxford: Blackwell.

McGurk, H., & MacDonald, J. (1976). 'Hearing lips and seeing voices.' *Nature*, 264(5588), 746–748. https://doi.org/10.1038/264746a0

Nath, A. R., & Beauchamp, M. S. (2012). 'A neural basis for interindividual differences in the McGurk effect, a multisensory speech illusion.' *NeuroImage*, 59(1), 781–787.

Nunn, J. A., Gregory, L. J., Brammer, M., Williams, S. C. R., Parslow, D. M., Morgan, M. J., Morris, R. G., Bullmore, E. T., Baron-Cohen, S., & Gray, J. A. (2002). 'Functional magnetic resonance imaging of synesthesia: Activation of V4/V8 by spoken words.' *Nature Neuroscience*, 5(4), 371–375. https://doi.org/10.1038/NN818

O'Sullivan, A. E., Crosse, M. J., Di Liberto, G. M., de Cheveigné, A., & Lalor, E. C. (2021). 'Neurophysiological indices of audiovisual speech processing reveal a hierarchy of multisensory integration effects.' *Journal of Neuroscience*, 41(23), 4991–5003. https://doi.org/10.1523/JNEUROSCI.0906-20.2021

Parise, C. V., & Spence, C. (2009). '"When birds of a feather flock together": Synesthetic correspondences modulate audiovisual integration in non-synesthetes.' *PLoS ONE*, 4(5), e5664. https://doi.org/10.1371/JOURNAL.PONE.0005664

Peelle, J. E. & Sommers, M. S. (2015). 'Prediction and constraint in audiovisual speech perception.' *Cortex*, 68, 169–181. https://doi.org/10.1016/j.cortex.2015.03.006

Radeau, M., & Bertelson, P. (1987). 'Auditory-visual interaction and the timing of inputs: Thomas (1941) revisited.' *Psychological Research*, 49(1), 17–22. https://doi.org/10.1007/BF00309198

Rothen, N., Schwartzman, D. J., Bor, D., & Seth, A. K. (2018). 'Coordinated neural, behavioral, and phenomenological changes in perceptual plasticity through overtraining of synesthetic associations.' *Neuropsychologia*, 111(July), 151–162. https://doi.org/10.1016/j.neuropsychologia.2018.01.030

Schwartz, J.-L., Robert-Ribes, J., & Escudier, P. (1998). 'Ten years after Summerfield: A taxonomy of models for audio–visual fusion in speech perception.' In R. Campbell, B. Dodd, & D. Burnham (eds) *Hearing by Eye II: Advances in the Psychology of Speechreading and Auditory-Visual Speech* (pp. 85–108). London: Psychology Press/Erlbaum (UK) Taylor & Francis.

Schweinberger, S. R., Robertson, D., & Kaufmann, J. M. (2007). 'Hearing facial identities.' *Quarterly Journal of Experimental Psychology*, 60(10), 1446–1456. https://doi.org/10.1080/17470210601063589

Sharma, A., Dorman, M. F., & Spahr, A. J. (2002). 'A sensitive period for the development of the central auditory system in children with cochlear implants: Implications for age of implantation.' *Ear & Hearing*, 23(6), 532–539. https://doi.org/10.1097/00003446-200212000-00004

Shiell, M. M., Champoux, F., & Zatorre, R. J. (2014). 'Enhancement of visual motion detection thresholds in early deaf people.' *PLoS ONE*, 9(2). https://doi.org/10.1371/journal.pone.0090498

Singh, A. K., Phillips, F., Merabet, L. B., & Sinha, P. (2018). 'Why does the cortex reorganize after sensory loss?' *Trends in Cognitive Sciences*, 22(7), 569–582. https://doi.org/10.1016/j.tics.2018.04.004

Snowden, R., Thompson, P., & Troscianko, T. (2012). *Basic Vision: An Introduction to Visual Perception* (revised edition). Oxford: Oxford University Press.

Stein, B. E., & Meredith, M. A. (1993). 'The merging of the senses.' In *Cognitive Neuroscience*. MIT Press.

Stein, B. E., Meredith, M. A., Huneycutt, W. S., & McDade, L. (1989). 'Behavioral indices of multisensory integration: Orientation to visual cues is affected by auditory stimuli.' *Journal of Cognitive Neuroscience*, 1(1), 12–24. https://doi.org/10.1162/JOCN.1989.1.1.12

Stevenson, R. A., Ghose, D., Fister, J. K., Sarko, D. K., Altieri, N. A., Nidiffer, A. R., Kurela, L. R., Siemann, J. K., James, T. W., & Wallace, M. T. (2014). 'Identifying and quantifying multisensory integration: A tutorial review.' *Brain Topography*, 26(7), 707–730. https://doi.org/10.1007/s10548-014-0365-7

Tsantani, M., Kriegeskorte, N., Storrs, K., Williams, A. L., McGettigan, C., & Garrido, L. (2021). 'FFA and OFA encode distinct types of face identity information.' *Journal of Neuroscience*, 41(9), 1952–1969. https://doi.org/10.1523/JNEUROSCI.1449-20.2020

Van Engen, K. J., Dey, A., Sommers, M. S., & Peelle, J. E. (2022). 'Audiovisual speech perception: Moving beyond McGurk.' *Journal of the Acoustical Society of America*, 152(6), 3216–3225. https://doi.org/10.1121/10.0015262

Voss, P., Tabry, V., & Zatorre, R. J. (2015). 'Trade-off in the sound localization abilities of early blind individuals between the horizontal and vertical planes.' *Journal of Neuroscience*, 35(15), 6051–6056. https://doi.org/10.1523/JNEUROSCI.4544-14.2015

Watson, M. R., Akins, K. A., Spiker, C., Crawford, L., & Enns, J. T. (2014). 'Synesthesia and learning: A critical review and novel theory.' *Frontiers in Human Neuroscience*, 8(1), 1–15. https://doi.org/10.3389/fnhum.2014.00098

Welch, R. B., DutionHurt, L. D., & Warren, D. H. (1986). 'Contributions of audition and vision to temporal rate perception.' *Perception & Psychophysics*, 39(4), 294–300. https://doi.org/10.3758/BF03204939

Williams, J. M. (1976). 'Synaesthetic adjectives: A possible law of semantic change.' *Language*, 52(2), 461. https://doi.org/10.2307/412571

Zamm, A., Schlaug, G., Eagleman, D. M., & Loui, P. (2013). 'Pathways to seeing music: Enhanced structural connectivity in colored-music synesthesia.' *NeuroImage*, 74, 359–366.

Zäske, R., Mühl, C., Schweinberger, S. R. (2015) 'Benefits for voice learning caused by concurrent faces develop over time.' *PLoS ONE*, 10(11), e0143151. https://doi.org/10.1371/journal.pone.0143151

Zwiers, M. P., Van Opstal, A. J., & Paige, G. D. (2003). 'Plasticity in human sound localization induced by compressed spatial vision.' *Nature Neuroscience*, 6(2), 175–181. https://doi.org/10.1038/nn999

Hearing Difficulties

Hearing difficulties can arise at any time in life, and for a variety of reasons. This chapter considers various methods for measuring hearing and explains how hearing loss is defined, from a clinical perspective. The chapter also outlines how hearing loss can impact auditory perception and introduces technological interventions that are available for hearing, for those who want to use them.

8.1 Measuring hearing

There are several different ways to measure a person's hearing, and the method that we choose depends on what we want to know. Imagine that you want to buy a car. You'd probably want to test how it drives before you buy it—but how might you do that? You could simply ask the salesperson to tell you about the capabilities of the car. Alternatively, you could take it for a test drive—either on a quiet road, or on a busy motorway that you regularly drive along. In each case, you're likely to compare the car against other cars that are available. Similarly, if we want to gauge someone's hearing, we can simply ask them to tell us about their hearing. We can also test their hearing in a quiet environment, or in the types of challenging, noisy environments that they would regularly encounter in their everyday lives. Typically, we use tests for which we have data from lots of people, so that we can compare someone's hearing to that of other people—which can help us to identify whether they have hearing loss. As this section explains, there are several established methods for measuring a person's hearing, and each method tells us something different.

8.1.1 Audiometry

Like taking a car out for a test drive on a quiet, smooth road, we can test someone's hearing in optimal conditions—which, for hearing, is a quiet environment. **Audiometry** assesses the quietest level of sounds that a person can hear and should ideally be conducted in a quiet place with no background noise. Audiometry is used routinely in the clinic to diagnose whether someone has hearing loss, but it's also commonly used in research studies for measuring variations in hearing ability.

The most common type of audiometry is **pure-tone audiometry** and—as you might guess from the name—involves presenting pure tones. To administer pure-tone audiometry, a pure tone is presented several times at different sound levels. The sound level of the tone is gradually lowered and raised until the person being tested can only just hear it. That level—which is called a **threshold**—is then recorded (see Further insights 8.1).

> To review sound level, see **Chapter 2**.

> **Further insights 8.1** Hearing level zero
>
> Humans aren't equally sensitive to sounds at all frequencies. If we present several sounds at the same sound pressure level, then how loud they appear will depend on the sound's frequency. Therefore, in audiometry, we compare someone's hearing at a particular frequency against the average level at which someone with normal hearing (see Section 8.2.2 for a definition of 'normal hearing') would be able to detect a sound at that frequency. These average levels (which differ across frequencies) are referred to as zero decibels *hearing level* (dB HL). This means that it's possible for someone to have thresholds lower than zero! Most audiometers can present tones as low as −10 dB HL—and a threshold of −10 dB HL simply means that someone has hearing that's better than average. For this reason, the vertical axis of the graph usually includes values below zero (see Figure 8.1).
>
>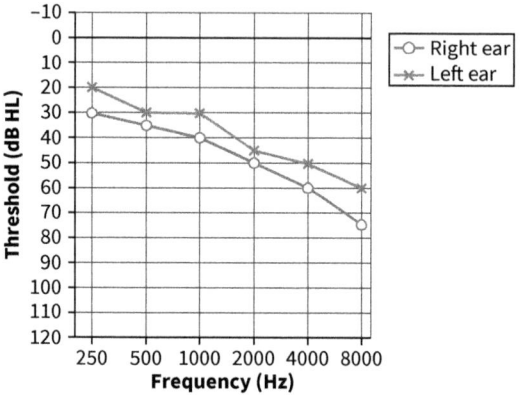
>
> **Figure 8.1** Audiogram showing example thresholds for the left (x) and right (o) ears at six different frequencies. Notice that the values on the vertical axis are lower (i.e. better) towards the top of the graph. The horizontal black line at 0 decibels hearing level (dB HL) is the threshold of average listeners who have normal hearing. In this example, thresholds for both ears get worse as frequency increases. This 'ski slope' audiogram is typical for individuals with age-related hearing loss.

> You can review how loudness perception varies by frequency in **Chapter 2**.

This process is conducted separately for each ear and, within each ear, the measurement is repeated with pure tones at several frequencies. Similar to how an athlete's ability might differ across events (e.g. a 200-metre sprint verses a marathon), we're interested in measuring thresholds at different frequencies, because a person's hearing can differ at different frequencies. We can visualise a person's thresholds at several frequencies in a type of graph called an **audiogram**, which is illustrated in Figure 8.1.

> A full audiometric examination measures thresholds at multiple frequencies (typically 250 Hz, 500 Hz, 1 kHz, 2 kHz, 4 kHz, and 8 kHz) for both ears. However, if time is limited, researchers may choose to do screening audiometry, which uses fewer frequencies (e.g. only 1 kHz). Screening audiometry simply checks that the person can hear a sound at a specific level. Rather than measuring exact thresholds, a person simply passes or fails, depending on whether or not they can hear the sound at the pre-specified level. Although less informative than full audiometry, screening audiometry can be very useful in research studies to quickly check someone's hearing ability.

Often, the results of audiometry are summarised as an average threshold, which is commonly referred to as the **pure-tone average** (**PTA**): thresholds at several different frequencies are averaged together to get a single numerical value.

> To calculate the PTA, the thresholds for some of the frequencies are averaged for each ear. The lower (i.e. better) of these two averages indicates the more sensitive ear.

Audiometry has high **reliability** (i.e. in science, the extent to which a measurement gives the same result when repeated more than once), it's easy to administer, and it can be used with a wide range of people. It's suitable for adults and children, and has also been shown to be a valid measure for people with cognitive difficulties (Bott et al., 2019). However, just as driving a car on a smooth, quiet road doesn't tell you how well it will handle an uneven country road, audiometry uses optimal listening scenarios and doesn't tell us about difficulties hearing in everyday environments (Further insights 8.2). Imagine a crowded train station, a bustling café, or a busy restaurant: these everyday environments contain background noise, and the goal often isn't to detect quiet sounds (as measured by audiometry), but to navigate the environment or understand what someone is saying. While there are currently no clinical measures that fully encompass the hearing difficulties that people can face in their everyday lives, asking people to self-report their hearing ability or measuring speech perception can be useful.

> For infants, other techniques are used to determine hearing sensitivity, which involve measuring responses from their auditory pathway directly, rather than asking them to report when they hear a sound (because they can't press a button or tell us verbally). Instead, we test their hearing by measuring responses to sounds at various places along the auditory pathway. For example, responses can be measured from the ear, the brainstem, or cortex.

> **Further insights 8.2 Hidden hearing loss**
>
> Some people have normal audiometric thresholds, but they experience difficulties hearing in everyday life. Scientists have called this type of hearing difficulty 'hidden hearing loss', because the individual's perceptual difficulties are not visible (or are 'hidden') when looking at the audiogram. Hidden hearing loss is challenging for hearing professionals (such as audiologists) to manage, because we don't fully understand the reasons that people experience these difficulties hearing.
>
> One possible explanation is that cochlear damage—specifically, damage to the connections between hair cells and auditory nerve fibres—contributes to these difficulties. Recall from **Chapter 1** that the cochlea contains approximately 3,000 inner hair cells but more than 30,000 auditory nerve fibres. Each inner hair cell connects with multiple nerve fibres; yet, each auditory nerve fibre only connects to one inner hair cell. If the connection between an auditory nerve fibre and its corresponding inner hair cell is damaged, the auditory nerve fibre won't receive any input. Consequently, the nerve fibre eventually degenerates, and this loss of auditory nerve fibres might result in difficulties hearing. Studies with animals have shown that these connections can become damaged following high levels of noise exposure, which could lead to 'hidden hearing loss' (Liberman, 2020) (Figure 8.2).
>
> Other reasons for hidden hearing loss have also been proposed. For example, poorer neural encoding of sounds in noisy environments might lead to difficulties understanding speech in noisy environments (see Valderrama et al., 2022). Yet, ultimately, as 'hidden hearing loss' is not well-defined, it may encompass a variety of different mechanisms that contribute to perceptual difficulties hearing in everyday life.
>
>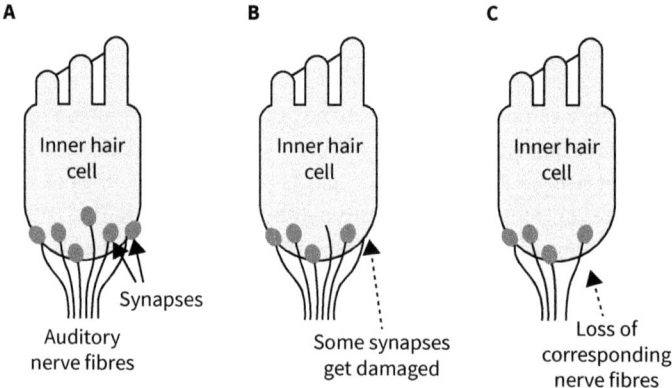
>
> **Figure 8.2** Illustration of an inner hair cell that synapses with multiple auditory nerve fibres. Panel a shows example connections between an inner hair cell and auditory nerve fibres in a healthy ear. Synapses (i.e. connections) between the inner hair cell and auditory nerve fibres can become damaged (panel b) and, over time, the corresponding auditory nerve fibres degenerate and are lost (panel c).

Hearing difficulties that aren't due to an inability to detect quiet sounds are often called 'suprathreshold' difficulties. These difficulties occur for sounds that are presented above threshold level, like many of the sounds people encounter in everyday life. For example, just because someone can detect speech, it doesn't mean that they can understand it. 'Suprathreshold' difficulties may occur due to altered temporal or frequency processing, for example.

8.1.2 Self-reported hearing

Rather than taking a new car out for a test drive, it may be quicker to simply ask the salesperson about a car's capabilities. This could also be useful if there's no test car available when you're at the car showroom. Similarly, it's much easier to ask someone about their hearing, rather than measuring their audiogram—which can be done even if there's no access to audiometry equipment or anyone who's trained to measure an audiogram.

We can ask people about their hearing in lots of different ways. To get a rough idea of whether someone might have hearing difficulties, we could ask them a simple yes or no question, like 'Do you have any difficulties with your hearing?'. If we want to know more detail about a person's hearing, we could ask questions with multiple responses (such as 'Would you describe your hearing as excellent, very good, good, or poor'), or we can ask a series of questions that require someone to assess their hearing in different scenarios. Like asking a salesperson several questions about how a car functions in different conditions, asking about a person's hearing in different scenarios allows us to get a more comprehensive understanding of their hearing ability.

Many questionnaires have been established for assessing self-reported hearing. The 'Hearing Handicap Inventory for the Elderly—Screening Version' (Lichtenstein et al., 1988) is a short, 10-item questionnaire that asks about the impact of hearing difficulties on someone's daily life. It asks whether the person has hearing difficulties that cause, for example, embarrassment when they meet new people, frustration when they talk with family members, difficulty listening to the TV, or difficulty communicating in a restaurant. Another questionnaire—the 'Speech, Spatial, and Qualities of Hearing Scale'—asks about someone's hearing in various domains: how well they can understand speech in different contexts (e.g. in quiet, when the TV is playing in the background, or when multiple conversations are happening), how well they can locate where sounds are coming from (e.g. the direction, distance, and movement of sounds), and their perceived quality of sounds (e.g. how clear and natural they appear, how effortful it is to listen, and how well different sounds can be distinguished) (Gatehouse & Noble, 2004). There are plenty of other questionnaires to choose from: a systematic review (Granberg et al., 2014) found more than 50 for assessing self-reported hearing!

One advantage of asking people about their hearing is that we can get a better understanding of how hearing loss affects their daily life—particularly if we ask questions about their hearing in a variety of everyday settings. For this reason, self-reported hearing may be a better reflection of the impact of hearing loss on someone's life than their audiogram. However, like asking a car salesperson about a car's capabilities, there are lots of potential challenges with asking someone about their hearing. For example, the way that a question is asked can lead to different answers. Also, different people have different ideas about what they consider to be 'good' hearing, and sometimes people simply don't want to acknowledge that they have difficulties hearing: for instance, it isn't uncommon for someone to say that they can't hear because the other person is mumbling. Given that self-report assesses the subjective perception of hearing, the outcomes don't always match the results of pure-tone audiometry. Sometimes, a person's audiogram indicates that they have hearing loss, but they report it has little impact on their everyday life; whereas other times, people perceive difficulties with their hearing, but their audiometric results indicate that they have normal hearing

(Goman et al., 2020). Ultimately, different people who have similar audiograms may respond differently to self-report questions, just like different salespeople might have different answers to your questions about a car.

8.1.3 Speech measures

Another way to assess someone's hearing is to test their ability to perceive speech. Many standardised speech tests are available, each using different speech stimuli and scoring approaches (Granberg et al., 2014). For example, some tests ask people to listen to single words, whereas others present sequences of words, short phrases, or longer sentences. In addition, the speech can be presented either in quiet or in the presence of background noise. When testing in quiet, the sound level of the speech can be varied from trial to trial, to find a level at which the participant can only just identify it. This threshold is known as the **speech reception threshold**. When testing in noise, the level of either the speech, the noise, or both is varied—again, until the participant can only just identify the speech—and this threshold is known as the **speech-in-noise threshold**. Alternatively, instead of measuring the person's threshold, some tests keep the sound level of speech constant and score the percentage of words that the person correctly identifies.

> In the 'digit triplets test', people are played sequences of three spoken number words (e.g. 'four, two, one') in noise and they're asked to report the numbers they heard. Their ability to report the numbers correctly, across several digit triplets, is a quick and reliable screening measure for hearing loss (Van den Borre et al., 2021). This test is available in many different languages, and online so that people can test their own hearing at home.

Like taking a car for a test drive on a busy motorway or on a bumpy country road, speech measures are often considered to be more representative of hearing ability in everyday life than pure-tone audiometry, because people often encounter speech in everyday life and less frequently hear pure tones. However, a caveat of some speech measures is that they usually require the listener to wait until after the speech has ended before responding, meaning that someone's performance also relies on their memory, and not just their hearing.

8.2 Hearing loss

It's likely that you know someone with hearing loss—there are an estimated 1.5 billion people worldwide with the condition—but did you know that there are different types of hearing loss and that it can occur at different stages of life? This section outlines the main types of hearing loss and describes how it affects auditory perception.

8.2.1 Types of hearing loss

The most common type of hearing loss is **sensorineural hearing loss**, which arises from damage in the inner ear or the auditory nerve—often because hair cells in the cochlea are damaged (Further insights 8.3).

Sensorineural hearing loss usually occurs gradually over time, although some people experience sudden sensorineural hearing loss, which happens rapidly over a few hours or days. Sudden sensorineural hearing loss is relatively uncommon and affects less than 0.03% of the population each year. In most cases, the cause is unknown, although viral infection or head injury have been debated as potential reasons (Schreiber et al., 2010).

You can learn about the function of hair cells in **Chapter 1**.

Further insights 8.3 Hair cell damage

If someone's car isn't functioning as expected, they might take it to a garage so that a mechanic can work out what's causing the issue. Similarly, if someone is having difficulty hearing, they might go to see a hearing professional, such as an audiologist, to try and work out the reasons why they're having difficulty hearing. A hearing professional will conduct a variety of tests to identify the type of hearing loss. One of the most common causes of sensorineural hearing loss is hair cell damage in the cochlea. Hair cell damage can arise from general wear and tear over time from a lifetime of noise exposure—similar to how a car might show wear and tear after many years of use. Or, it can arise from exposure to loud sounds, specific infections, or damage from certain drugs. Unlike car parts that can be replaced, human hair cells can't regenerate. Thus, once hair cells are damaged, they won't function in the way that they functioned previously (Figure 8.3). For example, the inner hair cells will be less successful in converting vibrations from the basilar membrane into electrical signals, and the outer hair cells won't be able to stretch and shorten as effectively as they used to, to amplify the vibrations of the basilar membrane. Other animals, such as birds, can regenerate their hair cells, so some researchers are trying to apply insights from these animals to regenerate hair cells in other animals that usually can't regenerate them. Some promising results have been found for regenerating hair cells in mice, although this area of research is still in its infancy (see e.g. Chen et al., 2021).

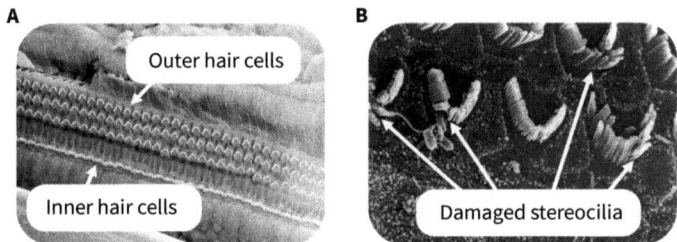

Figure 8.3 Panel a shows rows of hair cells: notice how there are three rows of outer hair cells and one row of inner hair cells. This image is from a guinea pig, but the arrangement of hair cells is similar to that in humans. Panel b shows hair cell damage arising from bacterial infection. Notice how the stereocilia on some hair cells are no longer neatly arranged.

Source: a adapted from SEM organ of corti showing rows of hair cell. Prof. Andrew Forge. Attribution 4.0 International (CC BY 4.0). Source: Wellcome Collection. *https://wellcomecollection.org/works/rruhwss6*; b adapted from SEM cochlea damaged by bacterial meningitis. Wellcome Collection. CC0 1.0 Universal. Source: Wellcome Collection. *https://wellcomecollection.org/works/uhct2473*

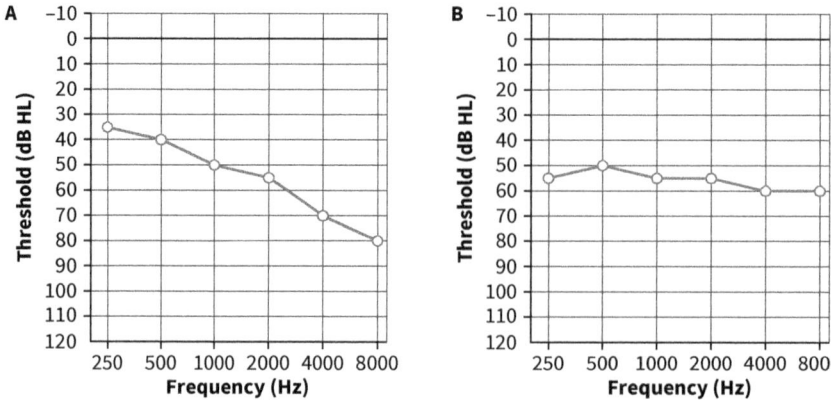

Figure 8.4 Example audiograms showing right-ear thresholds for two people. Notice how the pattern of thresholds differs between panel a and panel b. Panel a shows thresholds getting worse as frequency increases, which is typical of sensorineural hearing loss. Panel b loss shows similarly high thresholds across frequencies, which is typical of conductive hearing loss.

Typically, people with sensorineural hearing loss have less hearing sensitivity (i.e. more hearing loss) at higher frequencies. The audiogram allows us to visualise differential hearing sensitivity across frequency (Figure 8.4(a)). Notice in Figure 8.4(a) that the audiogram characteristic of sensorineural hearing loss has a sloping line; for this reason, it is sometimes informally referred to as a 'ski-slope' (or, more simply, 'sloping') audiogram.

While sensorineural hearing loss arises from damage in the inner ear or auditory nerve, other types of hearing loss are characterised by damage to different parts of the auditory pathway. **Conductive hearing loss** arises from disruption in the outer or middle ear that causes difficulties relaying sound to the inner ear. Conductive hearing loss can be temporary or permanent, and can be caused by specific infections, a blockage, or restricted movement of the ossicles (the middle-ear bones). Conductive hearing loss can also be caused by a build-up of wax in the ear canal, although this can usually be alleviated if the wax is removed by a trained professional, such as an audiologist. Unlike sensorineural hearing loss, conductive hearing loss typically affects a wide range of frequencies (Figure 8.4(b)), because sounds haven't yet reached the inner ear where they are separated into different frequencies.

> Otosclerosis is a condition that arises from abnormal middle ear bone growth that can restrict one of the ossicles—the stapes—from moving, and thus prevents the sound from passing on. You can review parts of the middle ear in **Chapter 1**.

> **WARNING!**
> You should never try and remove ear wax yourself, because anything that enters the ear canal can push the wax further in, and you could damage your ear canal and tympanic membrane. Always consult a health professional for removing ear wax.

> A combination of sensorineural and conductive hearing loss in the same ear is known as 'mixed hearing loss', which means that hearing loss occurs due to disruption with the pathway from the outer to the middle ear and with the pathway from the inner ear to the auditory nerve.

Central hearing loss refers to dysfunction further along the auditory pathway and is relatively uncommon. For example, central hearing loss can occur when someone experiences a stroke that damages auditory cortex. Even though their ears and auditory nerve function normally, some patients who experience damage to auditory cortex are entirely unable to hear sounds. Others can hear sounds, but find it difficult to comprehend speech.

8.2.2 Hearing loss severity

Hearing loss is not all or nothing, but varies on a continuous scale. For example, some people can't hear tones at 20 dB HL, but can do so at 40 dB HL, whereas others may not be able to hear tones at 40 dB HL, but can at 60 dB HL. In everyday life, this variation in hearing loss severity means that some people might be able to hear an approaching car, but aren't able to hear leaves rustling. This variability is one reason why it can be useful to plot someone's thresholds on an audiogram; higher average thresholds indicate more severe hearing loss. Another reason is that some people have different severities of hearing loss in their left and right ears.

The severity of hearing loss is based on the average threshold (i.e. the PTA). Typically, the PTA from the most sensitive ear (i.e. the ear with the least hearing loss) is used to classify hearing loss severity. The idea behind this is that people use both ears when listening in everyday situations, so their ability to detect sounds will be mostly determined by the quietest sounds they can hear in their most sensitive ear. Although, if someone has different thresholds in their left and right ears, it can also be useful to know how the severity of hearing loss differs between the two ears.

It is worth noting that different organisations use different cut-off values to categorise hearing loss, and that the exact values have changed over time. The latest criteria from the World Health Organization (2021) use 20 dB HL as the cut-off value: people with a better-ear PTA of less than 20 dB HL are classified as having normal hearing, whereas people with a better-ear PTA greater than or equal to 20 dB HL are classified as having hearing loss.

If someone has hearing loss, we can describe their hearing loss as mild, moderate, moderately severe, severe, profound, or complete based on their PTA (Figure 8.5). The WHO uses the thresholds at 500, 1,000, 2,000, and 4,000 Hz to calculate the PTA.

Although everyone's experience is different, people who have **mild hearing loss** (PTA between 20 and <35 dB HL) often can't hear sounds that have a low sound pressure level, like leaves rustling or birds singing, but they can hear other sounds that have a higher sound pressure level.

> You can learn more about loudness and the sound pressure level of everyday sounds in **Chapter 2** (**Figure 2.1**).

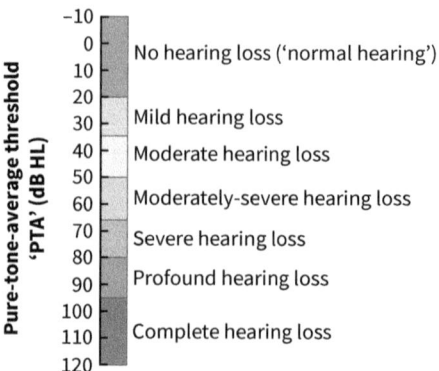

Figure 8.5 Range of pure-tone-average (PTA) thresholds for normal hearing, mild hearing loss, moderate hearing loss, moderately severe hearing loss, severe hearing loss, profound hearing loss, and complete hearing loss, categorised according to the 2021 World Health Organization criteria.

People who have **moderate hearing loss** (PTA between 35 and <50 dB HL) often have difficulty hearing sounds with a quiet or moderate sound pressure level, such as quiet conversations or the consonants in speech, but they may be able to hear ordinary conversations.

People who have **moderately severe hearing loss** (PTA between 50 and <65 dB HL) will typically find it difficult to hear ordinary conversational speech, and people with **severe hearing loss** (PTA between 65 and <80 dB HL) will find it very difficult to hear ordinary conversations.

People who have **profound hearing loss** (PTA between 80 and <95 dB HL) often experience very little auditory sensation in the affected ear(s) and therefore have extreme difficulty hearing most raised voices. A PTA at or above 95 dB HL can be described as complete hearing loss, and people with this level of hearing loss cannot hear speech and will have extreme difficulty hearing most everyday environmental sounds.

8.2.3 Hearing loss across the lifespan

Hearing loss can be present from birth or acquired later in life. Hearing loss that's present from birth is known as **congenital hearing loss**, and this occurs for approximately 1 in 1,000 children. It can be caused by genetics or a viral infection (Butcher et al., 2019) and is usually detected by neonatal hearing screening (i.e. a quick hearing test shortly after birth or in early infancy).

You might have noticed that more of your older relatives or friends have hearing loss than your younger relatives or friends. That's because hearing loss is much more common in older adults than younger adults (Figure 8.6; Further insights 8.4). With increasing age, people commonly experience a form of sensorineural hearing loss called **age-related hearing loss** (also referred to as 'presbyacusis'), in which someone's hearing thresholds gradually increase as they age (or, in other words, their sensitivity to sounds gradually decreases as they age). Age-related hearing loss is the most common type of sensorineural hearing loss (see Further insights 8.3).

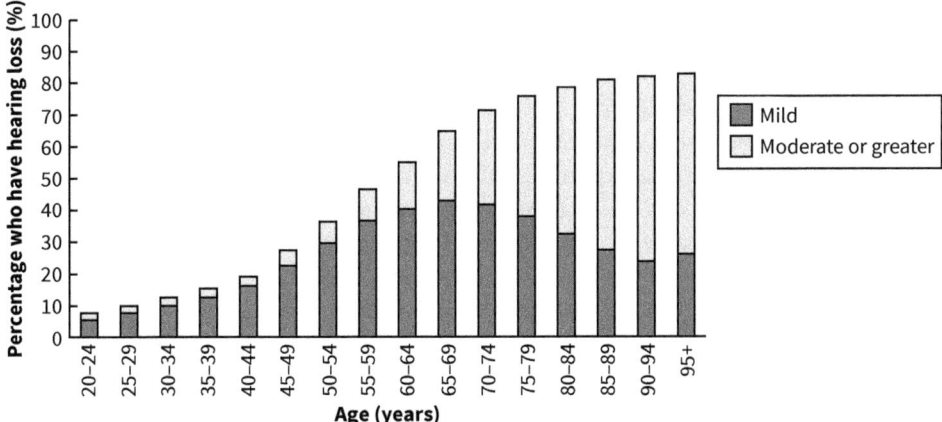

Figure 8.6 Percentage of adults with hearing loss by age and hearing loss severity. Notice how hearing loss is much more common in older adults than younger adults. Hearing loss categories (mild; moderate or greater) are based on the four-frequency (500, 1,000, 2,000, and 4,000 Hz) PTA in the better hearing ear according to the World Health Organization (2021) criteria.

Source: data from Global Burden of Disease, Institute for Health Metrics and Evaluation, University of Washington (*https://vizhub.healthdata.org/gbd-compare/*)

If someone has age-related hearing loss, their audiogram usually shows that they are less sensitive to higher frequencies than to lower frequencies, and this typically occurs in both ears (see e.g. Figure 8.1).

> **Further insights 8.4** Differences in hearing loss across age, sex, and race
>
> The most striking differences in hearing loss occur across age groups: it is much more common in older adults than in younger adults. Nevertheless, other demographic factors contribute. Hearing loss is more common among men than women, possibly because oestrogen (a hormone that's found in greater quantities in women) may help to protect against it. Racial and ethnic differences in hearing loss have also been observed: for example, Black people are less likely to have hearing loss than White people. This trend is thought to occur because the skin pigment melanin—which is found in higher quantities in the cochlea for people with darker skin than people with lighter skin—helps to protect against hearing loss (Sun et al., 2014). Why oestrogen or melanin may protect against hearing loss is currently unknown.

8.2.4 Consequences of hearing loss

Hearing loss is not 'one size fits all'. Different people with the same severity of hearing loss can find that it impacts their individual everyday lives to differing extents. Hearing loss has wide-ranging effects on how someone hears sounds: some of its consequences are obvious, others less so.

One of the most obvious and widely known consequences of hearing loss is difficulty hearing quiet sounds. Difficulty hearing quiet sounds is what's measured by audiometry (see e.g. Figure 8.1): people aren't able to hear sounds that are quieter than their thresholds. In daily life, you probably won't have an audiometer to hand, but you might notice that someone needs to raise the volume on their television, which can be a sign of difficulty hearing quiet sounds. Nevertheless, there are many other consequences of hearing loss that aren't as easy to observe.

It may surprise you to discover that people with hearing loss have a similar tolerance for loud sounds to people with normal hearing: a jumbo jet or the sound from a drill digging up a road can be unpleasantly loud, regardless of who's listening. Effectively, this means that the range of levels that a person is able to tolerate changes if they get hearing loss: the upper limit (i.e. for loud sounds) remains the same, but the lower limit (i.e. for quiet sounds) increases. We refer to this range of tolerable levels as the **dynamic range** of hearing (Figure 8.7).

As a result of a smaller dynamic range, people with hearing loss experience a faster increase in perceived loudness—a phenomenon known as loudness recruitment—than people without hearing loss. Imagine that you're driving a car on a racetrack: the car will gradually get faster as you push on the accelerator. The relationship between intensity and loudness can be considered in a similar way: loudness increases steadily as intensity increases (Figure 8.8). However, people with hearing loss experience a faster acceleration in loudness than people with normal hearing (Figure 8.8). This occurs because sounds below the hearing threshold are perceived with zero loudness (meaning that they aren't heard), and therefore people with hearing loss have a smaller difference in intensity between sounds that are perceived as quiet and sounds that are perceived as loud.

Another consequence of hearing loss is that it can be more difficult to understand speech, an effect that arises due to several combined effects of hearing loss. Difficulty hearing quiet sounds—especially at higher frequencies in the audiogram (Figure 8.4(a))—means that high-frequency consonant sounds can be difficult to hear. In addition, damage to the inner hair cells can lead to broader tuning in the cochlea, which means that the frequencies of sounds can't be as precisely determined. Someone who often asks others to repeat what they said may be experiencing these effects without realising (or acknowledging) that they have hearing loss. Often, understanding speech when there's background noise may be particularly affected.

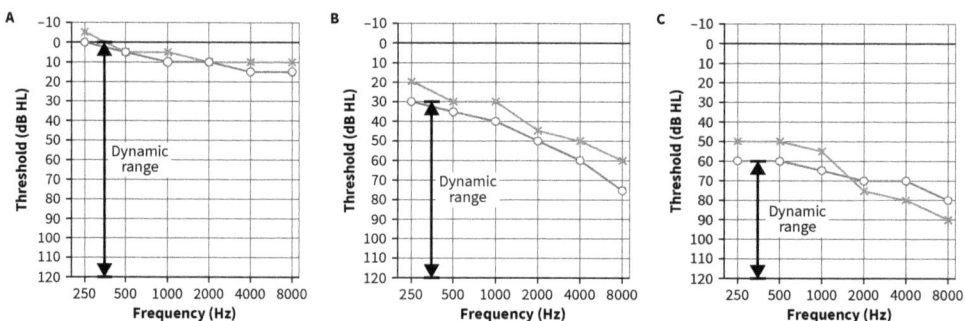

Figure 8.7 Example audiograms for left (x) and right (o) ears for three different people, the first with normal hearing (panel a), the second with moderate hearing loss (panel b), the third with severe hearing loss (panel c). The arrow on each plot indicates the dynamic range for the right ear at 250 Hz: the top of the arrow is their threshold of hearing and the bottom of the arrow is their tolerance for loud sounds. Notice that as the severity of hearing loss increases (from panel a to b to c), the dynamic range of hearing decreases. dB HL: decibels hearing level.

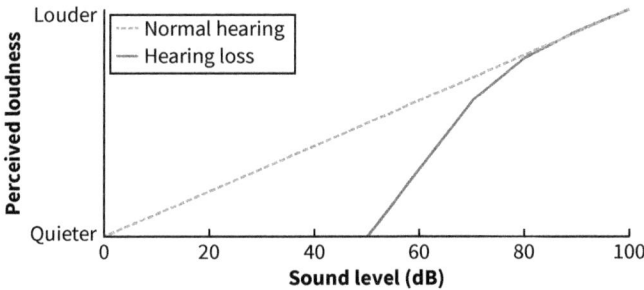

Figure 8.8 Illustration of loudness recruitment. People who have hearing loss (solid line) experience faster increases in perceived loudness as sound level increases than people who have normal hearing (dashed line). The values shown for hearing loss are an illustrative example. dB SPL: decibels sound pressure level.

Difficulties processing temporal information, such as temporal fine structure, have been seen in older adults and those with hearing loss. However, as older age and hearing loss often co-occur, it is difficult to tease apart the effects of hearing loss from ageing (e.g. Moore, 2021).

Hearing loss can have broader impacts, depending on the stage of life at which it is acquired. If hearing loss occurs in young children before or during language development, it can delay language production and cause difficulty understanding spoken speech—although there is wide variability between people (Zussino et al., 2022). Hearing loss in older adults has been associated with poorer mental wellbeing and social isolation. Also, recent research has identified associations between hearing loss and dementia (Livingston et al., 2024).

See **Chapter 6** for more detail about tuning.

Hearing loss can also impact the structure and function of the brain. Higher hearing thresholds have been associated with a smaller volume of auditory cortex (Peelle & Wingfield, 2016) and with reductions in volume across the brain more generally (Armstrong et al., 2019). These changes in structure could have implications for processing complex sounds, such as speech. The aforementioned consequences of hearing loss for the early auditory pathway also affect the signals that reach the brain, which can lead to people with hearing loss having different brain activity to those with normal hearing. In cases of profound hearing loss, in which many sounds aren't heard, the brain receives less auditory input, which can lead to reorganisation in the brain. In a 'use it or lose it' manner, underused auditory brain areas might be 'taken over' by other senses, such as vision (Glick & Sharma, 2017).

Changes in the use of brain areas from one sense to another is known as cross-modal plasticity, which you can learn more about in **Chapter 7**.

8.3 Interventions for hearing loss

There's currently no way to restore normal hearing for someone who has hearing loss. Some people choose to communicate using sign language, and there is a vibrant Deaf community (Further insights 8.5). There are, however, technological interventions available, which can help to improve hearing. This section describes two of the most common forms of technological intervention for hearing loss: hearing aids and cochlear implants.

> **Further insights 8.5   Deaf community**
>
> The Deaf community is diverse and includes people with various levels of audiometric hearing loss, as well as family members and friends. The Deaf community communicate using sign languages and—just as with spoken language—there are many different languages (which tend to be associated with different geographic regions) and dialects. Some members of the Deaf community opt to use hearing aids or cochlear implants, but many don't.

8.3.1 Hearing aids

Hearing aids contain one or more microphones. These microphones pick up sounds, which are then processed and amplified before being presented to the ear (Figure 8.9). Different frequencies are amplified to different extents, based on a person's audiogram. Given that people with hearing loss have a reduced dynamic range of hearing, hearing aids amplify some sounds more than others, to ensure that loud sounds don't become uncomfortably loud. Therefore, hearing aids need to be adjusted for each individual.

Hearing aids can't restore hearing to normal, but they can improve someone's ability to detect quiet sounds, and can improve speech intelligibility for people with mild or moderate hearing loss. People with severe hearing loss may receive some benefit from hearing aids, but the benefits of amplification could be limited if someone has a lot of inner hair cell damage.

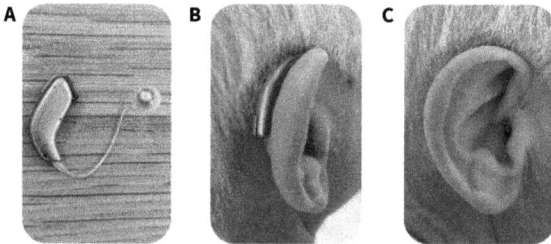

Figure 8.9 Example hearing aid. Panel a is a photo of a hearing aid. The case contains the electronic components and is designed to be worn behind the ear. A wire connects the case to the earmould, which is designed to be placed in the ear canal. Panels b and c show the hearing aid worn by an individual, viewed from the back (panel b) or side (panel c) of the head. Notice how, in panel c, the hearing aid is discrete, because it's positioned behind the pinna; however, if you look closely, you might be able to see the thin wire that enters the ear canal. This type of hearing aid is called a 'behind-the-ear' hearing aid, although other types of hearing aids are available.

When people listen in noisy places, hearing aids typically amplify the background noise as well as the sounds that someone is trying to listen to. Therefore, it can be difficult for people with hearing loss to understand speech in noisy places, even when they use hearing aids. However, most often, a listener faces the person they're trying to listen to, and many hearing aids make use of this: they use multiple microphones, and sounds are processed in a way that amplifies sounds in front of the listener and attenuates sounds behind them. This feature can be helpful for perceiving speech in noisy places when the person speaking is in front of the listener and the background noise is coming from behind. It is less helpful, however, when the speech and background noise come from similar directions.

> Using multiple microphones can help improve the signal-to-noise ratio, which can help a listener better understand speech in noise.

In addition, hearing aids don't appear to help listeners locate sounds any better than they would do without hearing aids; instead, hearing aids may lead to slightly *worse* performance locating sounds, although the reduction in spatial acuity (reported as approximately 1–2 degrees) is unlikely to be noticeable in everyday life (Akeroyd & Whitmer, 2016).

Despite these limitations, many adults find that hearing aids improve their quality of life (Ferguson et al., 2017). Yet, many people with hearing loss who could benefit from hearing aids don't have them—and even if someone chooses to get hearing aids eventually, they often could have benefited from them earlier. On average, people get hearing aids around a decade after the onset of their hearing loss (Simpson et al., 2019).

> Early use of hearing aids enables children to have better access to speech sounds, which is important for language development. Good language outcomes have been observed in children who consistently use their hearing aids from a young age (Lieu et al., 2020).

Even when someone gets a hearing aid, they may not use it all the time—and some people stop using them altogether. One reason is because sounds perceived through a hearing aid often sound different, because hearing aids don't restore all aspects of hearing that are affected by hearing loss—for example, they don't restore broader frequency tuning (see Section 8.2.4). It can take a while for people to adjust to hearing aids, and people usually need to practise using them to get the associated benefits.

8.3.2 Cochlear implants

Cochlear implants are an option for people who have severe or profound hearing loss. Under the National Health Service in the United Kingdom, cochlear implants are offered to people with severe or profound hearing loss, who have tried using hearing aids for at least three months and found that they don't get adequate benefit. However, candidacy for a cochlear implant varies across countries.

Cochlear implants get their name because an array of electrodes is implanted into the cochlea. To understand how a cochlear implant works, you first need to understand its components and how sounds travel through them (Figure 8.10). The external part contains a microphone and a coil. Sounds are picked up by the microphone, processed, then passed to the coil. The external coil then transmits the sound to an internal coil, which is connected to an array of electrodes that have been implanted in the cochlea. These electrodes stimulate the auditory nerve directly, essentially bypassing the early stages of the auditory pathway (including the basilar membrane and hair cells). You might wonder how the external coil is held in place: notice in Figure 8.11 that there's a magnet implanted under the skin, which keeps the external coil in the correct position.

Low frequencies in sounds are not conveyed well by cochlear implants. Imagine pushing a cable through a snail shell: it becomes more difficult as the cable goes further in, and you would risk damaging the shell. Put simply, positioning a cochlear implant involves pushing an electrical array into the cochlea and—to minimise the risk of damage—the electrode array doesn't extend all the way to the apex of the cochlea (see Figure 8.11). Therefore, the auditory nerve fibres that are most sensitive to low frequencies aren't stimulated by the implant. To address this limitation, lower frequencies can be conveyed to the auditory nerve by the

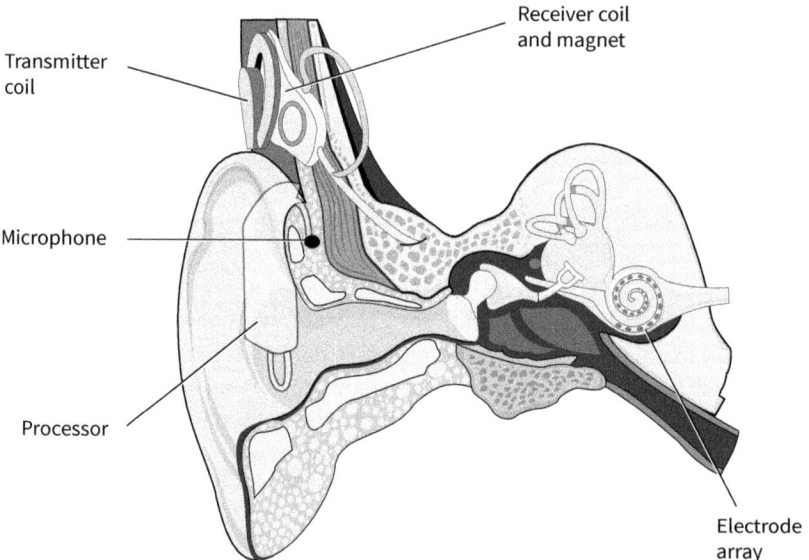

Figure 8.10 Schematic of cochlear implant external components (microphone, processor, and transmitter coil) and internal components (receiver coil, magnet, and electrode array).

Source: adapted from Lenarz, T. (2018). 'Cochlear implant—state of the art.' *GMS Current Topics in Otorhinolaryngology—Head and Neck Surgery*, 16, ISSN 1865-1011

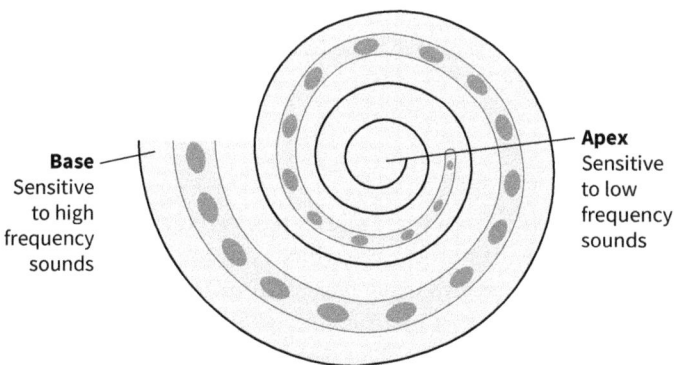

Figure 8.11 Schematic of an electrode array inserted into the cochlea. In this illustration, the rectangles are the electrodes. Notice how the electrode array doesn't extend all the way to the apex of the cochlea.

electrode that's closest to the apex. As Figure 8.11 shows, for low-frequency sounds, the electrode will stimulate a completely different set of auditory nerve fibres than those that would be stimulated by the same sound without the implant.

Cochlear implants convey the amplitude envelope of sounds, but they aren't very good at conveying the (faster) temporal fine structure of sounds, which is important for pitch perception. Given that the temporal fine structure information isn't conveyed, this can make it difficult to understand speech in noisy places.

> You can learn about speech perception in noise in **Chapter 5**.

Cochlear implants don't convey precise frequency information either. Usually, inner hair cells are connected to specific auditory nerve fibres, which provides detailed information about frequency. However, cochlear implant electrodes are quite large and there are only a handful of them (about 20–30), so they can only convey limited frequency information: each electrode stimulates a much wider range of auditory nerve fibres than an inner hair cell would (Figure 8.11).

It's important to note that cochlear implants don't restore hearing to normal. Listening to speech in noisy places, listening to music, and perceiving emotion in speech remain challenging.

Different people get different amounts of benefit from cochlear implants. Nevertheless, most recipients experience better speech perception and rate their quality of life (i.e. their health and happiness) as being better. In children who receive cochlear implants, earlier implantation is associated with better spoken language and speech recognition (Sharma et al., 2020). Also, for people who have severe or profound hearing loss in both ears, having two cochlear implants offers additional benefits over one cochlear implant alone; for example, being better able to locate where sounds are coming from, because binaural cues are available.

> To learn about binaural cues for locating sounds, see **Chapter 2**.

8.3.3 Bimodal aiding

If someone has hearing loss in both ears and has received one cochlear implant, they may decide to use a hearing aid in their other ear—which is known as **bimodal aiding**. An advantage of bimodal aiding, compared to using one cochlear implant alone, is that the hearing aid can convey low frequencies that aren't conveyed by the cochlear implant. This results in better pitch perception, which is useful for perceiving music and the emotion in speech.

Most people who use bimodal aiding report that the two devices complement each other. Bimodal aiding typically improves the ability to locate sounds and to understand speech in noisy places, compared to a single implant alone. This is because having input to both ears enables people to access binaural cues.

8.4 Other hearing differences

It is important to bear in mind that some people prefer to describe themselves as having a hearing 'difference' rather than a hearing 'loss'. There are, in fact, many sources of hearing 'difference' or 'diversity' that cause individual differences in perception (Drever & Hugill, 2022). This section covers two common differences—tinnitus and hyperacusis—for which people often seek clinical advice.

8.4.1 Tinnitus

Have you ever left a loud club and noticed ringing in your ears? **Tinnitus** has been described as a ringing, buzzing, or roaring sound that's perceived, even though there are no sounds present. Tinnitus is temporary for some people, but can be persistent for others. The perceived severity of tinnitus can also vary—from being mildly irritating to downright intrusive with a substantial impact on daily life, that affects the person's sleep, mental health, and social wellbeing (see e.g. Henry et al., 2020).

Around 14% of people experience tinnitus, but there's currently no known cure (Jarach et al., 2022). Several strategies for managing tinnitus have been proposed—for example, a variety of therapies and drugs—but evidence for their effectiveness is lacking (Hoare et al., 2011).

8.4.2 Hyperacusis

People with **hyperacusis** perceive sounds that would be considered comfortable to most people as uncomfortable. For example, particular sounds can be perceived as being uncomfortably loud and can even feel painful. Hyperacusis can have a distressing impact on daily life: people with the condition may find everyday sounds to be extremely annoying, or may fear particular sounds. The symptoms of hyperacusis vary among people and we lack effective treatments (Baguley & Hoare, 2018).

Summary

Hearing can be measured in different ways, although different methods are unlikely to give the same answer. Hearing loss is typically defined using results from audiometry. There are several different types of hearing loss, although it most commonly arises from damage to the inner ear with age. Hearing loss can also vary in severity, from mild to profound. The most widely known effect of hearing loss is difficulty hearing quiet sounds, but it also has a variety of other effects, including reduced dynamic range and poorer frequency sensitivity. There is no way to restore normal hearing, but technological interventions, such as hearing aids and cochlear implants, have the potential to improve hearing for many people with hearing loss.

Further your understanding

Hopkins, K. (2015). 'Deafness in cochlear and auditory nerve disorders.' In *Handbook of Clinical Neurology* (Vol. 129, pp. 479–494). Amsterdam: Elsevier.

Moore, B.C. (2007). *Cochlear Hearing Loss: Physiological, Psychological, and Technical Issues* (Chapter 2, pp. 39–44; and Chapter 4, pp. 93–115). Chichester: John Wiley & Sons.

References

Akeroyd, M. A., & Whitmer, W. M. (2016). 'Spatial hearing and hearing aids.' *Hearing Aids*, 56, 181–215.

Armstrong, N. M., An, Y., Doshi, J., Erus, G., Ferrucci, L., Davatzikos, C., Deal, J. A., Lin, F. R., & Resnick, S. M. (2019). 'Association of midlife hearing impairment with late-life temporal lobe volume loss.' *JAMA Otolaryngology—Head and Neck Surgery*, 145(9), 794–802. https://doi.org/10.1001/jamaoto.2019.1610

Baguley, D. M., & Hoare, D. J. (2018). 'Hyperacusis: major research questions.' *HNO*, 66(5), 358. https://doi.org/10.1007/s00106-017-0464-3

Bott, A., Meyer, C., Hickson, L., & Pachana, N. A. (2019). 'Can adults living with dementia complete pure-tone audiometry? A systematic review.' *International Journal of Audiology*, 58(4), 185–192. https://doi.org/10.1080/14992027.2018.1550687

Butcher, E., Dezateux, C., Cortina-Borja, M., & Knowles, R. L. (2019). 'Prevalence of permanent childhood hearing loss detected at the universal newborn hearing screen: Systematic review and metaanalysis.' *PLoS ONE*, 14(7), 1–21. https://doi.org/10.1371/journal.pone.0219600

Chen, Y., Gu, Y., Li, Y., Li, G. L., Chai, R., Li, W., & Li, H. (2021). 'Generation of mature and functional hair cells by co-expression of Gfi1, Pou4f3, and Atoh1 in the postnatal mouse cochlea.' *Cell Reports*, 35(3), 109016.

Drever, J. L., & Hugill, A. (2022). 'Aural diversity: General introduction.' In *Aural Diversity* (pp. 1–12). New York: Routledge.

Ferguson, M., Kitterick, P., Edmonson-Jones, M., & Hoare, D. (2017). 'Hearing aids for mild to moderate hearing loss in adults (review).' *Cochrane Database of Systematic Reviews*, (9), CD012023. https://doi.org/10.1002/14651858.CD012023

Gatehouse, S., & Noble, W. (2004). 'The speech, spatial and qualities of hearing scale (SSQ).' *International Journal of Audiology*, 43, 85–99.

Glick, H., & Sharma, A. (2017). 'Cross-modal plasticity in developmental and age-related hearing loss: Clinical implications.' *Hearing Research*, 343, 191–201. https://doi.org/10.1016/j.heares.2016.08.012

Goman, A. M., Reed, N. S., Lin, F. R., & Willink, A. (2020). 'Variations in prevalence and number of older adults with self-reported hearing trouble by audiometric hearing loss and sociodemographic characteristics.' *JAMA Otolaryngology—Head & Neck Surgery*, 146(2), 201–203.

Granberg, S., Dahlström, J., Möller, C., Kähäri, K., & Danermark, B. (2014). 'The ICF core sets for hearing loss researcher perspective. Part I:

Systematic review of outcome measures identified in audiological research.' *International Journal of Audiology*, 53(2), 65–76. https://doi.org/10.3109/14992027.2013.851799

Henry, J. A., Reavis, K. M., Griest, S. E., Thielman, E. J., Theodoroff, S. M., Grush, L. D., & Carlson, K. F. (2020). 'Tinnitus: an epidemiologic perspective.' *Otolaryngologic Clinics of North America*, 53(4), 481–499. https://doi.org/10.1016/j.otc.2020.03.002

Hoare, D. J., Kowalkowski, V. L., Kang, S., & Hall, D. A. (2011). 'Systematic review and meta-analyses of randomized controlled trials examining tinnitus management.' *Laryngoscope*, 121(7), 1555–1564. https://doi.org/10.1002/lary.21825

Jarach, C. M., Lugo, A., Scala, M., van den Brandt, P. A., Cederroth, C. R., Odone, A., Garavello, W., Schlee, W., Langguth, B., & Gallus, S. (2022). 'Global prevalence and incidence of tinnitus: A systematic review and meta-analysis.' *JAMA Neurology*, 79(9), 888–900. https://doi.org/10.1001/jamaneurol.2022.2189

Liberman, M. C. (2020). 'Hidden hearing loss: Primary neural degeneration in the noise-damaged and aging cochlea.' *Acoustical Science and Technology*, 41(1), 59–62. https://doi.org/10.1250/ast.41.59

Lichtenstein, M. J., Bess, F. H., & Logan, S. A. (1988). 'Diagnostic performance of the hearing handicap inventory for the elderly (screening version) against differing definitions of hearing loss.' *Ear and Hearing*, 9(4), 208–211.

Lieu, J. E., Kenna, M., Anne, S., & Davidson, L. (2020). 'Hearing loss in children: A review.' *JAMA*, 324(21), 2195–2205. https://doi.org/10.1001/jama.2020.17647

Livingston, G., Huntley, J., Liu, K. Y., Costafreda, S. G., Selbæk, G., Alladi, S., Ames, D., Banerjee, S., Burns, A., Brayne, C., Fox, N. C., Ferri, C. P., Gitlin, L. N., Howard, R., Kales, H. C., Kivimäki, M., Larson, E. B., Nakasujja, N., Rockwood, K., Samus, Q., Shirai, K., Singh-Manoux, A., Schneider, L. S., Walsh, S., Yao, Y., Sommerlad, A., & Mukadam, N. (2024). 'Dementia prevention, intervention, and care: 2024 report of the Lancet standing Commission.' https://doi.org/10.1016/S0140-6736(24)01296-0

Moore, B. C. (2021). 'Effects of hearing loss and age on the binaural processing of temporal envelope and temporal fine structure information.' *Hearing Research*, 402, 107991. https://doi.org/10.1016/j.heares.2020.107991

Peelle, J. E., & Wingfield, A. (2016). 'The neural consequences of age-related hearing loss.' *Trends in Neurosciences*, 39(7), 486–497. https://doi.org/10.1016/j.tins.2016.05.001

Schreiber, B. E., Agrup, C., Haskard, D. O., & Luxon, L. M. (2010). 'Sudden sensorineural hearing loss.' *The Lancet*, 375(9721), 1203–1211. https://doi.org/10.1016/S0140-6736(09)62071-7

Sharma, S. D., Cushing, S. L., Papsin, B. C., & Gordon, K. A. (2020). 'Hearing and speech benefits of cochlear implantation in children: A review of the literature.' *International Journal of Pediatric Otorhinolaryngology*, 133, 109984.

Simpson, A. N., Matthews, L. J., Cassarly, C., & Dubno, J. R. (2019). 'Time from hearing aid candidacy to hearing aid adoption: A longitudinal cohort study.' *Ear and Hearing*, 40(3), 468–476. https://doi.org/10.1097/AUD.0000000000000641

Sun, D. Q., Zhou, X., Lin, F. R., Francis, H. W., Carey, J. P., & Chien, W. W. (2014). 'Racial difference in cochlear pigmentation is associated with hearing loss risk.' *Otology & Neurotology*, 35, 1509–1514.

Valderrama, J. T., De la Torre, A., & McAlpine, D. (2022). 'The hunt for hidden hearing loss in humans: From preclinical studies to effective interventions.' *Frontiers in Neuroscience*, 16, 1000304. https://doi.org/10.3389/fnins.2022.1000304

Van den Borre, E., Denys, S., van Wieringen, A., & Wouters, J. (2021). 'The digit triplet test: A scoping review.' *International Journal of Audiology*, 60(12), 946–963. https://doi.org/10.1080/14992027.2021.1902579

World Health Organization (2021). 'World Report on Hearing.' https://doi.org/10.2307/j.ctvndv9bj

Zussino, J., Zupan, B., & Preston, R. (2022). 'Speech, language, and literacy outcomes for children with mild to moderate hearing loss: A systematic review.' *Journal of Communication Disorders*, 99, 106248.

Glossary

absolute pitch The ability to name a note without hearing a reference note

age-related hearing loss A gradual decrease in hearing sensitivity with age. Also known as presbyacusis

amplitude Describes the pressure of a sound at a specific moment in time

amplitude-modulated tone A tone whose peak amplitude changes over time

amusia A difficulty with musical perception, often involving **pitch** processing

articulators Structures above the larynx that contribute to speech production; e.g. the lips, teeth, and tongue

audiogram A visual display of hearing sensitivity as assessed by **audiometry**

audiometry An assessment of hearing sensitivity

auditory nerve Consists of auditory nerve fibres that transfer signals from the ear to the brainstem

auditory scene analysis A term used to refer to the processes involved in **perceptual organisation**

basilar membrane Stiff membrane that extends along the length of the **cochlea**

bilateral Responses that occur in both the left and right hemispheres of the brain

bimodal aiding Using a hearing aid in one ear and a cochlear implant in the other

brainstem Structure at the base of the brain that connects to the spinal cord

Broca's area A name given to part of the brain located in the posterior region of the left inferior frontal gyrus

categorical perception The phenomenon whereby people perceive discrete categories (e.g. words, phonemes) in a continuous acoustic signal

central hearing loss Hearing loss that arises from dysfunction in the brainstem or cortex

characteristic frequency The frequency that a part of the auditory pathway (e.g. part of basilar membrane or a neuron) is most sensitive to

coarticulation The influence of previous and subsequent phonemes on the speech signal for a given phoneme

cochlea Spiral-shaped structure in the inner ear

cochlear nucleus A structure in the brainstem; also referred to as the cochlear nucleus complex

cocktail party problem A term that refers to the challenge of understanding speech when competing speech is present

complex tone A sound containing more than one frequency

conductive hearing loss Hearing loss that arises from disruption in the outer or middle ear

congenital hearing loss Hearing loss present from birth

consonance Hearing multiple sounds as sounding pleasant together

cross-modal plasticity A term used to describe differences in neural responses when a sense is not fully functioning; for example, neurons that typically respond to one sense might respond to another sense

cycle One repeat of a sound wave

decibel A unit of **sound level** that describes the relative **intensity** of a sound compared to another sound

dissonance Hearing multiple sounds as sounding unpleasant together

divided attention Trying to listen and/or respond to more than one stimulus within a given time window

dynamic range The range of **sound levels** that are tolerable

ear canal The opening in the pinna through which sounds travel to the **tympanic membrane**

electro-encephalography A method for recording brain activity using electrodes placed on the scalp that measure electrical potentials (often abbreviated to EEG)

energetic masking The loss of detectable information in a sound of interest due to a masker that overlaps in time and frequency

envelope Changes in **peak amplitude** over time

equal-loudness curves A visual display of variations in **loudness** by **frequency** and **sound level**

fissure A deep groove (or **sulcus**) in the cerebral cortex

formants Peaks in the **spectrum**

frequency Number of cycles per second, usually measured in Hertz; sounds can contain multiple frequencies

frequency-modulated tone A tone whose frequency changes over time

fundamental frequency The number of times a waveform repeats in 1 second, calculated as the greatest common factor of the **harmonics** present in a sound

glimpse A portion of a target sound that is detectable due to a dip in a masker

grouping Assigning sound components to the same source

gyri Plural for **gyrus**

gyrus A ridge on the cerebral cortex (plural: gyri)

harmonic complex tone A tone comprised of multiple **pure tones** that are integer multiples of a **fundamental frequency**

hemisphere The left or right half of the brain (plural: hemispheres)

Heschl's gyrus A **gyrus** on the temporal lobe; also known as the transverse temporal gyrus

hyperacusis This lacks a universally accepted definition, but is often described as a hypersensitivity to sounds; for example, the perception of everyday sounds may be uncomfortably loud

inferior A term used to denote relative position, towards the bottom of the body

inferior colliculus A structure in the brainstem

informational masking A catch-all term referring to any difficulty from adding a masker that is not due to energetic masking

inharmonic A sound containing **frequencies** that are not integer multiples of the **fundamental frequency**

inner hair cell A type of cell found in the cochlea

intelligibility Measure of the ability to extract words or sentences from a speech signal

intensity A physical attribute of sound, describing the amount of acoustical energy that passes through a given area per second

interaural level difference (ILD) The difference in a sound's **sound level** between the left and right ears

interaural time difference (ITD) The difference in time between a sound arriving at the left and right ears

intonation Variation in fundamental frequency across a word, sentence, or longer passage of speech

ipsilateral The opposite side of the body, e.g. the left relative to the right

kilohertz A unit of frequency equivalent to 1,000 Hz

lateral A term used to denote relative position, towards the outside of the body

lateralised Responses in either the left or right hemisphere of the brain, but not both

loudness A perception of sound ranging from very quiet to very loud

medial A term used to denote relative position, towards the inside (or midline) of the body

medial geniculate body A structure in the thalamus; also referred to as the medial geniculate nucleus

medial olivocochlear reflex A circuit that connects the cochlear nucleus, superior olive, and cochlea

melody A term that describes how sounds are arranged to create a tune; specifically, it reflects the sequence of pitches that we perceive

mild hearing loss A category of hearing loss severity in which pure-tone average thresholds are between 20 and <35 dB HL

mismatch negativity A brain response measured using **electro-encephalography** that is characterised by a negative deflection, often assumed to reflect responses to deviant stimuli

moderate hearing loss A category of hearing loss severity in which pure-tone average thresholds are between 35 and <50 dB HL

moderately severe hearing loss A category of hearing loss severity in which pure-tone average thresholds are between 50 and <65 dB HL

multisensory Involving more than one sense (e.g. vision and hearing)

neuron Specialised cell found in the nervous system (plural: neurons)

noise-vocoded speech Speech that has been modified by replacing the **temporal fine structure** (in one or more frequency ranges) by noise that's modulated by the **amplitude** envelope

nuclei of the lateral lemniscus A structure in the brainstem

object-related negativity A brain response measured using **electro-encephalography** that is characterised by a negative deflection, often assumed to reflect **perceptual organisation**

octave The interval between two notes with the same label (e.g. two 'A' notes), in which the **fundamental frequency** of one note is double that of the other

organ of Corti An organ of the inner ear that is found in the cochlea

ossicles The bones in the inner ear (which are the malleus, incus, and stapes)

outer hair cell A type of cell found in the cochlea

oval window An opening between the ossicles and the cochlea, through which vibrations are transmitted from the middle to the inner ear

peak amplitude The highest **amplitude** of a sound

perceptual organisation A blanket term used to refer to **grouping** and **segregation**

phase The position within a cycle at a particular frequency and time point (often measured at the onset of the sound)

phoneme The smallest unit that distinguishes one spoken word from another in a given language (plural: phonemes)

phonemic restoration effect A phenomenon whereby speech is perceived as continuous even though parts of it have been removed and replaced by noise

phon A unit for describing the subjective percept of **loudness**

pink noise Noise with a particular spectrum, which has greater amplitude at lower than at higher frequencies

pinna The external part of the ear that protrudes from the head

pitch A perception of sound ranging from low to high

precedence effect The phenomenon by which people typically perceive multiple repeated instances of a sound (e.g. due to reflections) as a single sound coming from the location of the first sound

primary auditory cortex An area of cortex found in the temporal lobes that is sensitive to basic properties of sounds

profound hearing loss A category of hearing loss severity in which pure-tone average thresholds are between 80 and <95 dB HL

prosody A term that encompasses changes in pitch, level, and duration in speech; in other words, how something is said

pure tone A sound containing only one frequency; also referred to as a sine tone

pure-tone audiometry An assessment of hearing sensitivity involving the presentation of **pure tones** at different **sound levels**

pure-tone average (PTA) The mean **threshold** across frequencies from **pure-tone audiometry**. The pure-tone average (PTA) is often calculated from four frequencies (0.5, 1, 2, and 4 kHz), but sometimes other combinations of frequencies are used

relative pitch The ability to name a note after hearing a reference note

reliability The consistency of a measure. In other words, the extent to which a measure gives the same result when repeated

resonant frequency The natural vibrating frequency of an object

rhythm The pattern of sounds over time, determined by the relative timing between the onsets of successive notes

secondary auditory cortex An area of cortex surrounding **primary auditory cortex**, that is thought to be sensitive to more complex sound features; also referred to as association cortex

segregating Assigning sound components to different sources

selective attention Directing attention to one sound in a mixture

semantically related Words, sentences, and and/or longer passages of speech that have similar meanings

semitone The smallest separation between notes in Western music

sensorineural hearing loss Hearing loss that arises from disruption in the inner ear or **auditory nerve**

sequential grouping Grouping of sounds that are separated in time

severe hearing loss A category of hearing loss severity in which pure-tone average thresholds are between 65 and <80 dB HL

signal-to-noise ratio The (average) intensity of a target sound relative to the intensity of a masker (often abbreviated to SNR)

simultaneous grouping Grouping of sounds that overlap in time

sine-wave speech A stimulus containing only the formant information from speech; it contains frequency-modulated tones at the frequencies of the formants from a speech signal

sound level A measure of relative **intensity**

spectrogram A three-dimensional graph, often plotting power at combinations of time windows and frequencies

spectrum Magnitude of various frequencies in a sound, often plotted on a graph of amplitude by frequency (plural: spectra)

speech reception threshold **Sound level** at which a listener can only just report speech. The speech reception threshold is often defined based on the **sound level** at which 50% of words can be correctly identified, but sometimes other cut-offs are used

speech-in-noise threshold **Sound level** at which a listener can only just report speech in the presence of noise. The speech-in-noise threshold is often defined based on the **sound level** at which 50% of words can be correctly identified in noise, but sometimes other cut-offs are used

stapes footplate Part of the stapes (one of the **ossicles**) that pushes on the oval window

steady-state noise Noise that has a constant amplitude

stereocilia Found at the top of hair cells, stereocilia convert mechanical vibrations to electrical signals

sulcus A groove in the cerebral cortex (plural: sulci)

superficial A term used to denote relative position, towards the surface of the cortex

superior A term used to denote relative position, towards the top of the body

superior olive A structure in the brainstem; also referred to as the superior olivary complex

synaesthesia Sensory perception that is elicited from a different sensory input. A common example is coloured hearing synaesthesia in which people see colours when they hear sounds

tempo A term that refers to speed—for example, the speed at which speech is spoken or the speed of music (plural: tempos)

temporal fine structure Rapid changes in **amplitude** over time

temporal lobe One of the four main lobes of the cerebral cortex, closest to the ears

threshold Refers to the smallest value (or smallest difference in values) that a person can detect. For example, the lowest **sound level** a person can hear or the smallest difference in **frequency** that a person can discriminate

timbre A perception of the quality of sound, which is affected by spectral and temporal factors

time series A graph with time on the horizontal axis and amplitude on the vertical axis

tinnitus The perception of a ringing, buzzing, or roaring sound without an external source

tip links These connect adjacent **stereocilia**

tone-vocoded speech Speech that has been modified by replacing the **temporal fine structure** (in one or more frequency ranges) by **amplitude-modulated tone**(s)

tonotopic Spatial arrangement by frequency; for example, different areas within primary auditory cortex respond to different frequencies, resulting in an organised 'map' by frequency

tympanic membrane Thin membrane that vibrates when sounds reach it; more commonly known as the eardrum

vocal folds Two pieces of elastic tissue in the larynx that are the source of vocal sounds, sometimes called vocal cords

vocal tract The cavity above the **vocal folds** that filters vocal sounds

wavelength The duration of one cycle, typically measured in seconds or milliseconds

Wernicke's area A name given to part of the brain located in the posterior portion of the left superior temporal gyrus

white noise Noise that has a uniform distribution across frequency

The manufacturer's authorised representative in the EU for product safety is Oxford University Press España S.A. of el Parque Empresarial San Fernando de Henares, Avenida de Castilla, 2 – 28830 Madrid (www.oup.es/en or product.safety@oup.com). OUP España S.A. also acts as importer into Spain of products made by the manufacturer.

www.ingramcontent.com/pod-product-compliance
Ingram Content Group UK Ltd.
Pitfield, Milton Keynes, MK11 3LW, UK
UKHW052348180426
470105UK00021B/166